P9-DVY-529

ALSO BY EDWARD MARRIOTT

The Lost Tribe

SAVAGE SHORE

SAVAGE SHORE

*Life and Death
with Nicaragua's
Last Shark Hunters*

EDWARD MARRIOTT

Metropolitan Books
Henry Holt and Company | New York

Metropolitan Books
Henry Holt and Company, LLC
Publishers since 1866
115 West 18th Street
New York, New York 10011

Metropolitan Books™ is an imprint of
Henry Holt and Company, LLC.

Published in Canada by Fitzhenry & Whiteside Ltd.,
195 Allstate Parkway, Markham, Ontario L3R 4T8.

Library of Congress Cataloging-in-Publication Data
Marriott, Edward, 1966–
Savage shore : life and death with Nicaragua's last shark hunters / Edward Marriott.
p.   cm.
ISBN 0-8050-5555-X (hc. : alk. paper)
1. Shark fishing—Nicaragua. 2. Bull shark—Nicaragua.
3. Fishers—Nicaragua.
4. Marriott, Edward, 1966–   I. Title.
SH691.S4 M37   2000
799.1'734—dc21   99-043262

First American Edition 2000

Designed by Kelly S. Too
Map design by Stephen Raw

Printed in the United States of America
1   3   5   7   9   10   8   6   4   2

SAVAGE SHORE

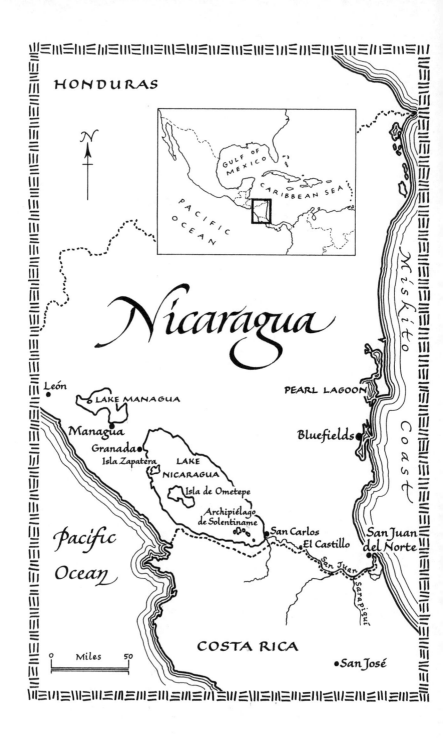

HONDURAS

N

GULF OF MEXICO

CARIBBEAN SEA

PACIFIC OCEAN

Nicaragua

Mískito Coast

León

PEARL LAGOON

LAKE MANAGUA

Managua

Bluefields

Granada

Isla Zapatera

LAKE NICARAGUA

Isla de Ometepe

Archipiélago de Solentiname

San Carlos

San Juan del Norte

El Castillo

Pacific Ocean

San Juan

Sarapiquí

COSTA RICA

•San José

0   Miles   50

1

The shark-fin dealer, sweating heavily, coughed wetly into his handkerchief.

"Go on," he said to his assistant, an old man who stood silently before us. "Open the bag."

The old man lowered his eyes and began to untwist the plastic. He smoothed it, shook it down, and then, very slowly, started to roll back the top. The plastic sighed and crackled; the dealer's mongrels—scabby, balding—growled, dozily.

"Bull-shark fins," announced the dealer, his hands clasping and unclasping in his lap. "Dorsal, pectoral, tail fin. Go on, you can look."

I sat forward; the old man nodded encouragingly. From the bag I lifted a small handful, laid them in my open palms, surprised by how little they weighed. They cannot have come from large sharks—the longest fin was no more than eight inches across, the smallest less than five. They were a pure, dull gray, with a skein of palest blue: a painter's stormy sky. The knife cut had exposed a tidy wound, already sun-dried hard as wood: a slice of ivory ligament and, between the edges of skin, a wafer of caramel-colored flesh.

"And the rest?" To judge by the number of boards I'd seen around Bluefields with the dealer's name and address and his trademark grinning shark, he was surely the biggest buyer on the coast. It was to this man, Obregón, that my friend Arturo, the shark fisherman, sold his catch, and I half expected to see a freezer truck unloading fins—at the very least, a fridgeful in the house.

"The rest?" He tried to smile, but it came out all lopsided, a post-dentist smile. "This is all I have. Maximo—the other dealer, that crook—he and my wife, they smashed in, took my dollars and my shark fins. I built this"—he waved a hefty arm about his yard, indicating the steel mesh that enclosed us, overhead and above each perimeter wall—"because next time they come for me."

Obregón was near-cylindrical, a vast, neckless mestizo with a pale, waxy face and hair that, through either neglect or some quirky Atlantic Coast fashion, was pasted flat to his scalp. Beside him he'd laid a jailer's hoop of keys, and he would pick these up and stroke each in turn, feeling across the ridges, then lift the whole bunch to his chest, pressing them close. The night of the robbery—just two weeks earlier—he'd been here, in the house.

"Did you see what happened? Try and stop them?" Even stumbling and bleary, a naked Obregón would have cut a pretty intimidating figure.

He shook his head. "Asleep." He rattled his keys, snapped out an order. The old man shuffled away toward the house.

"And no one else heard?" It was hard to believe there was much privacy in this street; the houses were of wood or corrugated zinc, their backyards separated only by wire fence.

Obregón stared at his knees, chewed the inside of his cheek, blinked repeatedly.

"It just seems odd," I went on, when it was clear he wasn't planning to answer. "I mean, they can't have been particularly quiet."

"Yes, well." He threw his keys onto the seat beside him and mumbled, "*Mi mujer.* My woman."

"Your wife?"

"My woman, my girlfriend. She was here."

"With you?"

He blushed at this, wiping a hand hard across his face. He made as if to stand up, then, overbalancing, fell back heavily in the swing seat. "*No sé.* I don't know what happened."

"Your girlfriend. Where's she now?" Far better to hear her testimony: taken alone, Obregón's accusations amounted to little more than hearsay.

"Not here."

"She'll be back?"

"No, she left. The day after they took my fins."

Obregón's fins—a month's haul, almost a hundred pounds in weight—had been stored in a triple-padlocked chest in one corner of his living room. The chest was nailed to the floor and to two walls. His house, which stood on stilts, was small but secure, or so he believed: Barred doors secured front and back, and every night at seven, Obregón would bolt and lock up, transfer six Victorias from fridge to portable cooler, sit down to three hours of subtitled American movies on satellite, then sleep the sleep of a dead man, content in the knowledge that both he and his booty were untouchable.

Then, two weeks ago while he slept, they sawed through his floor. Obregón, frothing a little at the mouth now, led me inside the house and lifted the lid of the chest. "What do you see?" he said, but I'd stepped too close to his raised arm and, before realizing, sucked in a lungful of sour sweat. I backed off, dizzy, and approached again more slowly, keeping my distance this time. In the bottom of the chest was a jagged hole: a triangle, perhaps eight inches across. And, three feet below that, the littered earth. I reached down, amazed that Obregón could have slept through: his bed was only in the next room, separated from here by a plywood partition. One of his dogs, hearing us, had sloped under the house and was looking up through the hole, head on one side. It sniffed the wood, pressed its nose through, sawdust on its whiskers.

"Useless dog," Obregón spat, and slammed the lid.

A hundred pounds of bull-shark fins were worth four thousand dollars; Obregón bought from fishermen at thirty-six dollars a pound, which, on a haul this size, spelled a dealer's cut of four hundred dollars, handsome earnings in a country where the monthly salary hovered around fifty dollars. Until he'd set up shop two years ago, his rival Maximo had enjoyed a monopoly in Bluefields—dictating the prices, buying from the fishermen at ten dollars a pound and shipping to El Salvador and Miami at forty dollars. He'd become a very rich man, according to Obregón, and must have guessed that, sooner or later in the new, free-market Nicaragua, competition would arrive.

Yet, compared with thirty years before, Maximo and Obregón were really just squabbling over the leftovers. In the 1960s, by contrast, there had been fifteen or twenty shark-fin dealers on the coast. This figure accelerated exponentially until, in 1969—so shark fishermen would ruefully remind me—the dictator Anastasio Debayle Somoza built a processing plant on Lake Nicaragua. From then until 1979, when the Sandinistas overthrew his regime and closed the plant, many thousands of bull sharks were slaughtered each year for their fins, their oil, and their skins.

They were hunted here, in Bluefields; at the mouth and up the length of the Río San Juan; and throughout Lake Nicaragua itself. It was hard to believe there wasn't some measure of revenge in the very scale of the slaughter: a desperate assertion of man's supremacy, coupled with a horror of the deep, of everything unseen.

Nicaragua's jungle coast. Not the "Caribbean"—despite cartographers' insistences—but, deliberately, the "Atlantic." No one here spoke of this ocean, with its broken, unlovely shoreline, as the Caribbean: that would have been too misleading, too obvious a misrepresentation. No, this was the Atlantic Coast, with its mangrove swamps and alligators, hurricanes and stiff westers that washed up bales of high-grade cocaine, shrink-wrapped for export. Three hundred years ago, pirates sheltered here, at constant war with the Spanish; now, the people still

viewed themselves as being apart. They had lost their king and
they had lost their power, were poorer than they had ever been,
but soon, they warned, they would rise up again.

The Atlantic coast and, sixty miles to the south, the mouth
of the San Juan River marked the beginning of all these jour-
neys: here, in these unquiet, shifting waters, bred the bull shark,
Carcharhinus leucas, the most willful and aggressive of all tropical
sharks. Like no other shark, it possessed the ability to cross from
salt water to freshwater, hunting far upriver to the lake beyond,
cruising the coast, the bar mouth, and the San Juan's brackish
lower stretches. The coastal and the river people hunted the
shark for its fins and for its oil, feared it and revered it; every village had had family taken in its jaws. It was shark where shark
should not be—in fresh water, on human territory.

I come from a small island, never overrun. Water—its very
coastline—has kept Britain safe. She has, for her size, exerted
an extraordinary influence, and her people still feel themselves touched by this. Still, though we are now stripped of
Empire, struggling to keep pace even with the rest of Europe,
we somehow imagine ourselves inviolate. Even the most casual
barroom conversation reflects this persistent jingoism. We feel
ourselves enclosed, elevated above the vulgar hordes, secure in
our history.

Nicaragua, though, was a land where nothing was safe, where
the native people had been crushed and near-extinguished by the
conquistadores; where successive generations of pirates and
bounty hunters, American marines and British traders, had
exploited what and who remained; where a despised dictatorship
had been overthrown by socialist revolutionaries who'd fought

a decade-long civil war against—again—American righteousness, and lost. And, more than all this, water, which in Britain was a comforting presence and a symbol of precious independence, was, in Nicaragua, the conduit for all invaders, of which the freshwater bull shark remained the most persistent symbol. The shark was the image that had triggered my journey. For me, nothing could have been farther from home.

As I began to learn about the bull shark's habits and its hunting grounds, to understand a little more about the Atlantic coast, the San Juan River, and the lake it made its home, I came to see that the shark was indivisible from the region's difficult history. It had hunted alongside pirates, colonists, and traders, had been here long before 1522 and the first Spaniard, Gil González Dávila.

So many stories: of the giant shark that stalked the lake; of the last dictator, who'd done his best to exploit the bull shark to extinction; of Indians on remote islands in the lake who were said to still worship its image; of the ruthless last remaining shark hunters who worked the coast at Bluefields. And it was at Bluefields that, one humid, rain-swept winter morning, I had begun my journey. Only by starting here, and following the shark all the way inland, could the whole story be told.

Since the break-in, Obregón had imprisoned himself in his own house, adding padlocks to the doors, screwing bars across the windows. In the caged backyard was a stack of corrugated zinc sheets, and with these he planned to caulk the underside of the house. "Even I," he said, managing a half-smile, "will hear them if they cut through that."

Such was his paranoia that he'd reneged three times on our

appointment before finally meeting me. Each time, I'd arrive punctually, rap on the doorjamb, then, when no one came, rattle the bars. Finally, blinking like he'd just awoken, the old man would come to the door, standing some way back as if afraid I'd lunge at him. No, he'd say, Obregón wasn't there. And, with the big man snoring audibly in the other room, he'd fix another time. And then another, and another.

All of which, as I would discover, was fairly typical Bluefields behavior. The town, squatting among mangroves at the edge of a poisoned lagoon, was a bastard brew of Creole, Miskito, Sumu, Rama, black Carib, and, finally, mestizo, the hated "Spaniards." Each distrusted the other, and the streets, on even the breeziest off-duty afternoon, wore an air of imminent menace. Limping through the dirt lanes in front of sputtering Lada taxis came hawkers, con artists posing as lottery salesmen, money changers, whores, drug peddlers. There was no work—80 percent unemployment, by common estimate—and no shortage of cocaine, fenced through here on its way north from South America. The people lived warily, aware that, with their history, only the simpleton or the newcomer could remain optimistic.

Since its settlement in the 1630s by British pirates, Bluefields had been the focus for competing imperial ambitions: American, Spanish, British. Till the nineteenth century, it was the British who held sway, the British and their Indian allies the Miskito kings, a monarchy set up and sustained by the Empire, which saw the kings educated in England and Jamaica and installed in Bluefields, with supreme eccentricity, with the Canterbury Cathedral coronation service.

Then, in 1894, Bluefields was stormed and the Atlantic

Coast forcibly "reincorporated" into Nicaragua; a hundred years
on, this date was spoken with as much anger and bitterness as
ever. It was graffiti'd on every street corner. It had become short-
hand for violent revolution; the threat of an uprising, fueled by
poverty and resentment and sheer nothing-to-lose, could be
smelled on the air.

Obregón, like most of Bluefields, was a man under siege,
though the extent of his fearfulness came as a surprise and
dawned only slowly. Despite an initial reluctance, he now jabbered incessantly at me, standing outside in the backyard under
white-neon striplights, with darkness falling. He talked com-
pulsively, as if I was the first to have shown an interest; as if I,
more important, might be able to help.

"Coffee?" he said suddenly, breaking off midsentence. Before
I could answer, he had turned, a jangle of noise: the keys, loose
in his big fingers; the slap of rubber thongs against his duck-flat
feet. He swayed up the steps of the house and was gone inside. I
heard him muttering, then the knock of crockery, raised voices,
and the old man, flustered, hurried down the steps into the backyard. He eyed me, nodded briskly, and looked away; yet whenever I made even the smallest move, his eyes were on me again.

Eventually, Obregón reappeared at the back door, his skin
visibly looser round his eyes and mouth. It surprised me that he
could talk at all: he looked stricken, paralyzed.

"No coffee," he said, banging down the steps, shaking
his head. He approached the old man, muttered something I
couldn't hear, then, as the old man turned again toward the
house, Obregón pushed him heavily between the shoulder
blades. The old man lost his footing, stumbled forward, flailed
for the handrail. He made it up the steps at a crouch, almost on
his knees.

Obregón fell back heavily onto the swing seat. "That man he see what happen," he said, speaking for the first time in English.

"Him?"

"He was in the house on the night. He is not deaf." He spoke with his eyes closed, head back against the cushion. "I can trust no one."

I would have liked to feel able to refute this, but it seemed exactly right: he was clearly friendless. His girlfriend, his one remaining employee: both had turned against him.

"My lady, though," he muttered, as if reading my thoughts. "She is a good woman. She will be back."

I coughed weak agreement, adding that I should go: Bluefields was never a safe town, much less so at night. But Obregón was not finished. His neighbors, he insisted, used to call him "uncle." "They were my friends," he said. "They used to eat here with me." He puckered his mouth, as if recalling the very dish. Now, he said, he was afraid even to leave his house, even to buy rice from the stall across the road. "I don't let anyone come round here now. They want to eliminate me."

He stared at my chest; I could hear him snuffling slightly. I reached out for his hand, intending to make my good-byes, but he took mine and held on and would not let go.

"And all this," I said, meaning the cage that ran overhead and along both neighbors' boundaries, "all this is since the robbery?"

"The garden, too," he said, pumping my hand still harder. "This was grass, pretty flowers." Now where we stood was pale, fresh-smoothed concrete, cambered to a gutter about the perimeter. Near the swing seat was a dog turd, dark as chocolate under the striplight. The only green was a neighbor's banana tree, leaves flat against Obregón's bars.

"Why?"

"This way," he said, "they can't dig a tunnel. Every way they try, their heads hit concrete."

Interrupting us, saving me from some trite reply, came a hammering at the front door. Obregón dropped my hand, shaking it violently from him, and strode toward the house. Standing behind him, I could see a small man at the front bars, squinting through the gloaming toward us. He called out Obregón's name.

"All right, all right," Obregón shouted, and in that moment all around us—all down the street, the whole town, it seemed— there was complete silence, as if all the prattlers and gloaters who'd observed Obregón's earlier downfall were now listening, eager for the next installment. No dogs barked; even Obregón's two stopped sniffling and drooling and sat, watching; no trucks or motorbikes or corroded taxi-jeeps passed; a street away, there was a weighty, percussive splat, a mango tree letting fall its ripest. And Obregón, halfway up the steps, oblivious, screaming, "*Que quiere, hombre?* Uh? What you want?"

"Fins," the man stuttered. "You're the shark man, right? *Verdad?*" He was Chinese, I now saw, one of only a handful who had remained after the flight of so many hundreds when the Sandinistas seized power in 1979; under white neon his face looked brittle as rice paper. He creased his eyes, trying to smile.

Obregón stamped through the house, faced the man through the bars, gripped the steel with both fists. "You make fun of me?"

The man backed off, almost falling as he stepped off the pavement into the road. "They say you have best prices." He waved his hands about in the air, as if that might make things clearer. "But perhaps," he added, about to break into a run, "I will come back. Tomorrow?"

"Forget it," Obregón yelled at his receding back. "It's finished."

He was sweating copiously now, droplets bulbing at the end of his nose; he had to blink his eyes continually to see at all. He glistened like an oiled vegetable just out of the fryer. I motioned toward the road, said that I too should go, afraid he might, in this state, turn on me as well. His eyes rolled back in his head and he held up the bunch of keys, shook them in front of my face. "You can thank Maximo for this."

The door was bolted and secured with six padlocks, which he sprang open in turn, fumbling interminably for the key to the next. I offered to help but he waved me away. A scabrous German shepherd, thin as a whippet, hobbled up and began to lick Obregón's knuckles as he worked to release the last, bottommost padlock. He didn't punch the dog away, as I expected, but let it be, wiping its gummy eyes with his fingertips.

"You go talk to Maximo," Obregón said finally, holding the door open for me. "Then you tell the world what happens here in Bluefields." He seemed calmer now; the dog nuzzled the back of his knee.

"Maximo?" I wondered, in truth, whether I dared; he'd hardly been painted as the image of reasonableness.

"Yes, you must do it." He put his hand on my shoulder, shoved me onto the pavement. "That way," he said, pointing down the broken road to the corner, where the bend climbed steeply out of sight. "The big house. See?"

At the corner, commanding a view down both angles of the street, was a house markedly more ostentatious than the wood-and-zinc shacks that filled every last foot of space along the roadside, and that had, since the hurricane, spawned unchecked across wasteland all the way to the airstrip. It was broad-fronted, finished in concrete white as stucco; at two stories, it was the tallest building this side of the police station. It was ringed with a razor-wire security fence; inside the front yard, where in other houses grandmothers would sit on rocking chairs and watch the days pass by, was a Toyota pickup, gleaming under the security spotlight. I turned to Obregón, wanting, now I'd seen something of what he was up against, to express at least my sympathy, but he was already back inside, closing the first of the padlocks.

"Yes," he nodded. "That's Maximo." He paused, shook the bars as if worried for their strength, and clapped his hands at me. "Now you go."

The noise of Maximo's place first hit me fifty yards down the street. Two pickups were pulled up, engines running, coughing out clods of unfiltered diesel exhaust that spilled along the gutters. Two men in overalls were rolling out gasoline barrels from a shed. A motorbike skidded past me and was flagged down by a shorter man with a stubble-shaven head and cowboy boots. The two men shook hands; the biker palmed something into the back pocket of his jeans, kicked the machine to life, and hammered off uphill.

This was my second attempt: I'd tried the night before, after Obregón had shut his door on me, but had had no luck. Then, there had been people inside the house, but no one had answered. So I'd waited the night and the morning and now was here late afternoon, a good time, I hoped, to find Maximo at home, the businessman counting his day's haul: flush and benevolent enough to grant me an audience.

I stood in front of the house, as I'd done before; now, as then, and even though this was daylight, the building was shuttered; the steel gates on to the front yard barred and padlocked. I stepped up to the buzzer, hoping this time I'd not be ignored, and at that moment two blood-eyed mastiffs sprang at me. They hit the end of their chains at speed and barked still louder, straining at their leashes till their eyes bulged and oozed and their tongues slapped about their fangs, saliva white as wallpaper paste. I leapt backward, arms flailing, tumbling into the road.

From the look of the chains, hammered to steel wall-brackets, it was as if the dogs were on permanent guard. I wondered how I'd missed them the night before. Perhaps the music had confused them—that and the pickup parked across the doorway.

"Shhh," I tried, but they only drooled and snapped more viciously, up on their hindquarters, clawing the air.

A man came out of the shed, glared at me, shouted something I didn't catch, then vanished. The dogs retreated, snarling. I waited. I'd been spotted: if I stood here long enough, then someone would surely come. Slowly, the dogs lost interest, folded themselves to the ground, jaws to the concrete. I could hear someone moving about inside, and men's voices from the back of the shed, to the side of the house. A tiny jailer's window in the front door slid open and, through close-knit steel mesh, an old face, tufted with stubble, squinted out at me.

I smiled, hopefully. "Maximo?"

The face retreated, window banged shut. Again, from inside, the scrape of furniture.

I looked around, wondering whether to try the buzzer again, or, bolder, call out at the open shed. Maximo's buffed-brass business plaque, and a sign advertising his rates, stared down at me. Under them was a larger, wooden board. JUST ASK FOR MAXIMO—BEST PRICES IN TOWN, it read, underneath a fearsome, gape-jawed shark. Where Obregón's billboard shark grinned oafishly, almost kittenish, this representation was altogether darker: drastically foreshortened, its jaw as big as the rest of its body, it looked starved and wolfish; along each glistening white tooth the hunting-knife serrations had been detailed lovingly in scarlet.

Sí?" One of the men in overalls had sneaked round the side of the house and now stood facing me: legs astride, engine oil smeared up his arms, a half smile playing on his lips.

"I'm here to see Maximo. I came last night."

"And you are?"

I explained, as briefly as I could: my interest was the sharks, which I planned to track all the way inland. Bluefields was my starting point; I wanted Maximo to tell me about his business, and about the bull shark. I said nothing about Obregón, nor the break-in that had ruined him, nor the sense I had that these two enemies were very probably the last of their kind, hurrying not only the shark's demise but also, as swiftly, their own.

He took this in, ran a hand over his chin, nodded once, twice, then walked past me and unlocked the gate to the front yard, slipping each padlock with an easy, practiced hand.

"Sit there," he said, indicating a bench that stood against the house, well within reach of the dogs. I lowered myself gingerly and the dogs, drooling loops of saliva, followed me with their eyes. "I'll find Maximo," he added. "Don't you move."

▼ ▼ ▼

Across the road two bread sellers watched me, elbows on the box of sugary buns between them, swatting bluebottles against their aprons. When I stared back, hoping they'd find someone else to trouble, they only eyed me more intensely, pointing, covering their mouths to giggle. Behind me, inside, a child was pressing, insistent—"What does he want?" "Who is he?" "What's he doing outside?"—followed by a woman's snapped rebuke. Down the road, trailing parachutes of dust, cranked a decrepit taxi, driver leaning from his window, yodeling for custom. As it passed, I noticed its exhaust system, most of its undercarriage, dragging on the rocks, triggering showers of sparks. Two copulating dogs, locked to each other, struggled out of the way. As if encouraged by this display, the bigger of Maximo's hounds stretched to its feet, sniffed my ankles, ran its nose up the inside of my thigh to my crotch, began snorting and snuffling; I felt a sudden wet patch, warm dribble against my scrotum.

"Hey!" I pushed down at the flat of its skull.

"Yes?" The front door had opened an inch; I saw the cowboy boots first, then the nipple-tasseled Texan shirt, then the eyes, dark as bullets. "You want to see me?"

"Maximo!" I sprang to my feet, tipping the dog onto its back, but the man had already shut the door.

"Stay there," he ordered, his voice now muffled and underwater-sounding. "I'm coming round."

Moments later he was shouting from the shed, warning me he was busy, that I'd better get it over with quickly. I ran out through the gate, round the side of the house, stopped at the shed mouth. Inside was dark, no electric light, just a wedge of daylight falling across the floor from a far-end doorway.

"Come on," he shouted, from somewhere in the shadows. "*No tengo todo el día.* I haven't got all day."

The ground was sticky underfoot, and engine-oily; a gangway led between oil drums. Maximo, I now saw, was standing at the end of the shed, half in the light, one boot up on a packing case, gesticulating at the man in overalls. He grabbed the man's hand, shook it, then peeled off a wad of dollars from a leather clip. "Tomorrow, early," he finished, as I approached.

"So, *Inglés* . . ." He turned to me, unlit cigarette in his mouth, thumb on his lighter wheel, seemingly oblivious to the ripe gasoline fumes all around us. "So, you want to know about the sharks?" And before I could reply he was out the back exit, into the backyard, the first three drags billowing out behind, like a steam engine.

I followed, each tread sticky in the hot-oil tar, almost tripping over a coiled gasoline hose. Wicker chairs, tagged as if for export, were stacked near the door, in the daylight. There was a desk here, scarred and propped level with a brick under one leg. On it was an old calculator, along with illegible notes, and an empty Victoria beer bottle with a dead poinsettia in the neck. And, smooth to the wall, a tear-off garage calendar picturing a smiling blonde in microscopic denim shorts, bending to select a spanner from her toolbox.

"Look at this," Maximo called, cigarette twitching in his lips. He was standing in the middle of a dusty yard, beside a long strip of galvanized roofing trestled on two packing cases. He waved me over. He was a small man, even in Cuban heels, laughing aggressively at nothing in particular, baring yellowed teeth and streaky-bacon gums.

Scattered across the zinc, like rare fungi laid out to dry, were shark fins, the skin a little wrinkled, curling at the edges. "Just one day, this lot," he said, still snickering, as he swept them into a large cardboard box; they clattered like balsa, sun-baked to weightlessness. Twenty or thirty fins, which he passed to a boy at his side. A gecko stopped at our feet, clicked its head back, watching. Maximo, tutting, lifted his boot and crushed it in the dirt, wiped greeny innards from his heel onto the corner of the packing case.

"Yes?" he snapped, no longer smiling, suddenly belligerent. "*Eso es todo.* That's all? Because I'm a busy man."

He was hurrying me now, and I'd not been here five minutes, much less asked about Obregón. I was unsure how to broach this, nervous of Maximo's fury, sure, now I'd witnessed his respect for the animal kingdom, that the very mention of Obregón's name would flip him psychotic. No: if I brought it up, it would have to seem relevant.

"Is this your only business, the shark fins?" I began. "Because I noticed the gasoline, all those drums in the shed."

"I am a businessman. I sell anything." He seemed flattered by this question, narrowing his eyes, refolding his arms. "Those chairs you see, those go to Costa Rica. I sell shark fins to Salvador and Miami. The gasoline"—he winked—"is more complicated."

"And the fins? How long have you been a dealer?"

"Seven years. I was the first." He bought from whoever had fins to sell: from trawlermen who gillnetted sharks by mistake while dragging for shrimp and lobster, from specialist shark fishermen. The best waters were round the offshore cays, ten miles to the south. Trade, he conceded, was not so bad, though nothing compared to before.

"Before?"

"Before that fat prick Obregón came. Back then, I made

money, real money . . . oh yes." A monkey's grin: lips peeled
back; old-cabbage breath.

"So, you've got some competition." This didn't seem unrea-
sonable: the fishermen, at least, were now more fairly paid.

He snorted, flashing gold bridgework, back to his larynx.
"Better for the fishermen? Yes, yes, better for them. Not so good
for me."

He waved me back inside the shed, the boy with the box of
fins still close behind him. Maximo was ushering me along now,
and it was clear my time was running short, that pretty soon
he'd be closing the door on me, as likely as not midquestion, and
I'd have lost my chance. And now he was in the darkest corner,
bending over a low chest.

Without looking up, he called out, "Have a look at this.
This'll show you." And he slid back the cold-steel top, and I
heard the hum of the fridge motor and, as I stood beside him,
felt the wash of coolness against my chest, spilling over the edge
of the fridge. Maximo rolled up his sleeve and plunged in his
arm. "Come on," he urged, and when I did the same I found
myself shoving down through two feet of shark fins, and still
not reaching the bottom. They were light as wood shavings,
odorless.

The boy passed him the box and Maximo clattered the fins—
today's takings—across the rest, stirring with his forearm.

"How many sharks is this?" I said, still astonished by the
sheer volume of it.

"Hundreds. *No sé exactamente.*" This one-month haul—five
hundred pounds in weight—would earn him twenty thousand
dollars, delivering a straight profit of two thousand dollars. He
was paid in cash, always greenbacks. He was shipping out
tomorrow, by boat up the Escondido to Rama, then by pickup

overland to El Salvador. He personally escorted each load as far as Rama, and there switched fins for cash with his Salvadoran partner. He returned to Bluefields the same day, briefcase handcuffed to his wrist.

He slid the cooler shut and began to scurry me out the door, hand against the small of my back. I tried to slow up, twisting back to catch his eye, but he muttered, "Enough, enough, it's getting late."

"*Una cosa más,*" I managed to say. "Just one more thing. About Obregón—"

"That ratfart—why him again?" We were on the curb now, and he was checking round, looking both ways down the street, proprietorial and substantial, not-to-be-crossed.

"People say he was robbed—that's why you've got all the business now."

He coughed into his fist. "Yes, he was robbed. What do you want me to do about it?" He turned to close the shed doors, kicking away the bricks that blocked them wide. He was cursing audibly, Mother-of-God and worse.

"They say . . ." I took a deep breath, my throat dry as the road, tasting diesel dust on my tongue. "They say it was you."

"Clear off, *Inglés,*" he hissed. He shook his head, as if I'd somehow let him down, disappointed good expectation. He kicked his boot heel in the dirt. "So this is why you come, shitdigger."

"That's just what I've heard, Maximo," I went on, knowing this to sound worse than feeble. I wiped my palms, clammy as that squashed gecko, down the back of my shorts.

He stared at me, fists clenching and unclenching, stretching his fingers as if about to try on gloves. He said nothing. I stuttered, stepping backward into the road, "I mean, it's of course unlikely, a man of your—"

He held up his hand. "Enough. I have heard enough. Obregón sent you. Well, you can squirm back home to him, crawl back in that cage with him. But don't try to come back here again. No one plays with me—no one." He whistled through his teeth and the dogs, just beyond the railings, snapped their heads toward us, began their wolfhound moan. "No one messes with Maximo."

2

Tracking down a shark fisherman prepared to take me to sea with him had not been easy. After a week of false leads, of hunting down men who turned out to be drunkards, another who'd been dead a whole six months, I finally discovered Arturo, a mixed-blood Miskito, who promised to show me how it was done. The stories I'd heard—how men fought four-hundred-pound bull sharks on hand lines from wooden dugouts—had sounded so unlikely that, I figured, the only way to find the truth was to set out myself. And Arturo, whose name was muttered low—the oldest, most experienced shark man in town—seemed clearly the right companion.

It had been hard enough finding his house in daylight. Now, in the absolute dark between three and four, with only sporadic moonlight, I was struggling just to keep on the road; twice already I'd blundered into potholes, once into an overhanging tree. This was the north end of town, just in from the water, and somewhere along here, though so far I'd recognized no land-mark, was a lane that wound through dirt yards, down to Arturo's shack at the shore.

I'd been warned of the dangers of Bluefields at night, but, this once, had had no choice: to reach the sharking grounds before daybreak, Arturo liked to cast off at four; only by leaving so early could he work the wind, rather than fight against it, since by midmorning, when he was done fishing, it would turn toward land again. For today, he'd predicted just a whisper at dawn, the perfect conditions. Which made me wonder: even from here I could tell the wind was gusting off the sea, the trees ashiver.

The lack of streetlights did not come as much of a surprise, since the electricity supply was at best erratic, sometimes cut-ting in only long after the bars had closed, in a roar of sound and sodium brilliance that had people flung upright in their beds, wide awake and cursing. Rumor had it that the blackouts were less the result of shortage, or faulty equipment, than of some willful trickery on the part of the "Spaniards"—as the coastal people still, four hundred years after the first invasion, referred to those in central government—who'd pull the power just to remind the black man who was boss. Either way, the result was the same: candles for the rich; for the rest, early bed.

With the moon briefly out I glimpsed its milky skin on water and guessed, seeing the shape of the land, that I must be coming to the lane. Much further, and I'd have overshot. So somewhere along here—the shiny leaves and pebbles picked out white in the moonlight—was the cut-through to Arturo's shack. I slowed up, ran my fingers along the fence. It had rained earlier and in the moonlight the wet mud seemed to glitter, gave off that doughy smell of wetted dust. Perhaps the wind, like the rain, would die away. Arturo had promised a flat-calm dawn; perhaps he'd still be right.

I was about to call out, hoping he might be up and listening out for me, when the fence ended and my hand, groping for clues, fell into space, then, a moment later, hit another wall. In the space between, facing the shore, ran the downward path. I jogged the first, flat section, imagining Arturo already waiting impatiently. There were steps; two dogs that snuffled in their sleep; a well whose deep hollow echoed my hustling breath; and then the moon disappeared and I fumbled the last stretch in soupy darkness, warm as velvet. Only at the shore, coming into Arturo's yard, did the first cockerel wake.

"Arturo?" I whispered, as a second chorused its good-morning; it was scratching at its tether, somewhere round the back of Arturo's shack. Fearing that any moment the dogs would join in too, I spoke through the crack in his doorframe, soft as I could. There was a grunt from inside; then a torch winked on and off. I drew back, felt around for a place to sit.

At the water's edge, six feet off, there was a noisy lapping: driftwood and debris, knocked by the wash. This was nothing like the stillness Arturo had promised, where one could hear the heron's wings, or cormorants taking off across the sound. I'd never sailed in a dugout before, much less gone shark fishing in one, and would have preferred an absolute calm.

I sat on an upturned bucket, near the heap of lines and hooks Arturo had been preparing when I'd met him yesterday. The wind had been high for a while, he'd said then, but the signs all pointed to change: earlier that day he'd spotted a pair of butter-flies passing low over the water—a sure promise of calm. The bad omens—"pig jumping up happy," or cockroaches spiraling crazily, both of which presaged "plenty breeze"—he'd not seen in a long while now.

While he worked, he talked. Shark fishing was his living, but in recent years, with the polluting of Bluefields lagoon and the sheer volume that had been taken through the 1960s and 1970s, he'd been forced farther and farther offshore. There were fewer shark fishermen now, but those that survived were tougher and more resourceful. Arturo made a modest living—perhaps eighty dollars a month when there was calm and luck was with him— but this month he'd been out only twice and was clearly growing desperate, hard though he tried to act nonchalant. His house showed this: intended only as a temporary shelter, thrown up in a day after the hurricane tore down his childhood home, it was still standing nine years later—patched with oil-drum plastic, the splintered planks that stood as walls plugged and pasted with mud, and inside, just one picture, of the last Miskito king, in all his sepia finery.

Now, with no warning, Arturo pushed the door open and strode out into the yard, sniffing the air, his head up. From his pocket he took a pinch of what looked like sawdust and threw it into the air. The wind, gusting, peppered his shirt and trousers.

"Plenty wind," he murmured, moving to sit beside me. "More than I thought." He was thickly unshaven, rubbing his eyes.

"You thought there'd be less?" He'd spoken with such authority yesterday that I almost believed he could foretell the weather, that he had access to the files. It was his manner, as much as his words: the long-distance gaze, the regal way he had with his neighbors, the near-biblical simplicity of his life. Then I noticed the detritus in the yard—a ditch of stamped-in beer cans, over by the neighbor's fence—and was reminded, not for the first time, of my own romantic weaknesses.

He rolled a cigarette, held a wetted finger to the wind. "It is possible it will get less." He yawned, then yawned again. "But perhaps you are right—too much wind. I'm not sure."

"And the other fishermen? Will they be out this morning?" Having struggled up at three, I was not keen to let this chance slip: if others were going, then we should too.

"*Quién sabe?* Who knows?" All the fishermen, it seemed, were determinedly secretive; only at the end of a good day, with a big shark to brag about, might you discover who'd been where.

"But the shark is always there," Arturo added, taking his first drag on the cigarette. "Whether it's rough or it's still. It's just that the dory"—he cackled rottenly, smoke spouting from his nostrils—"might not be so happy."

Already the light was changing: I could see the outlines of the roofs along the shore. There was nothing stopping us from going. Yesterday I'd bought the gas and Arturo had assembled the lines and hooks. When I'd looked through them all, wondering what exactly out of all this old nylon rope and corroded hooks would be strong enough to land a three- or four-hundred-pounder, he'd dug deep in the bucket and pulled out a red woolen glove.

"So it don't burn my hand." He'd held it up between two fingers. It had looked like a lady's winter mitten, half the size of his palm. "But you're going to help me too. When he go look for deep water, then we *all* have to pull."

And now he stood, as if he could smell the dawn. It was well past five, and the wind seemed as high as ever. He was going to walk to the end of the spit, he said, where there was a view to the entrance of the lagoon, and to the sea beyond. If the waves were breaking on the bar, we'd have to wait another day. "This is the best way," he said, grinning, tipping an imaginary cap. "You want to go, don't you?"

With Arturo gone I stretched, paced around his yard. Dawn was stirring, my eyes were growing accustomed to the almost-dark; I could move without tripping. I sat on the edge of the dory, which yesterday I'd helped Arturo heave onto the mud. Looking at it again, I wondered how wise this whole trip was: the "dory" was only a one-trunk dugout, bigger than many but a dugout nonetheless, and would rock and slop like one in even moderate seas.

Arturo's outboard, however, which he'd borrowed from a neighbor, marked him as different from most fishermen, who drifted under huge, hand-stitched plastic sails. Early morning, looking out across the lagoon, or in the evening as the fishermen returned, it was as if the twentieth century had never been—as if this ancient landscape had somehow escaped the yoke of empire.

In truth, of course, there had been a colonial presence since 1670, when Spain ceded Mosquitia, this coastal slice of Nicaragua, to "Great Britain for ever." But the white men, even the buccaneers of the next sixty years, never settled in any numbers. They took local mistresses, left their names and their sandy-haired children, and quit as soon as they'd made enough. Bluefields itself was poor one decade and prosperous the next, depending on who was buying what and how bad the fighting was.

By the mid-nineteenth century, Britain having been forced to renounce its hold on the coast a half century earlier, the town numbered six hundred blacks and mulattoes and only three whites. "The blacks," wrote one former resident, in language perfectly of his time, "though somewhat kept up to the mark by

Europeans trading and living among them, yet were slowly relapsing into the superstitious, gloomy, half-savage state into which the blacks, left to themselves, always sink back."

The Miskito king himself, according to another account, was "shy, but not without the benefits of an ordinary English education, which he received in England. He is nothing more or less than a negro, with hardly a perceptible trace of Indian blood, and would pass at the south for a likely young fellow, with twelve hundred dollars as a body servant."

The first blacks, so the unlikely history has it, clambered from a wrecked slaver that foundered on the coastal reef in the 1640s. Over the generations, they mixed with the indigenous Miskito, were joined by other slaves, were taught English by Moravian pastors from Germany, and lived off the lagoons and ocean and ever-humid jungles. At Bluefields, in water now opaque and oily-edged, there were, once, abundant manatees— bovine, lumpen seals with tender, fat-streaked flesh—jewfish, best hunted by torchlight; tapir ("exceedingly laxative," according to one unfortunate); stingrays, alligators, teal, duck, coot, shag, pelicans—and shark. Even in Arturo's childhood, Bluefields lagoon had been so thick with shark that no one dared swim there. Men capsizing—those that lived to tell of it— would say they smelled the shark as they hit the water: a rotten fish-head stench, caused by the shark's vomiting up of bones and scales, of everything spiny and indigestible.

And all over the ground now, clear as scattered toothpicks, I could see these fishbones, trodden into the mud. I bent to examine a bigger piece, a disk of cartilage as perfectly round as a checkers counter, when Arturo came bounding back into the yard. He stood in front of me, his trousers rolled up over his calves. He was panting heavily, his shirt open to the waist.

"What's that?"

I handed it to him.

He turned it over, picked at it with his nail. "We ate this two weeks ago. Hammerhead—this was its spine." He paused, bounced it in his palm, then, gravely, looked away. "We can't go today."

"No?" Though I'd seen this coming, and guessed it was the right move, disappointment fluttered in my gut.

"The sea's big, and getting bigger." He looked me in the eye, shrugged. "So I get it wrong. Sometimes even I make mistakes."

Inside, with Arturo still muttering about the sea, his wife began to brew coffee. She pulled a bench out from the wall, motioned me to sit. A baby girl was sleeping on a beer crate by the stove, a torn rag of sheet pulled up to her chin. The floor was dirt, the windows polyethylene; water was ladled from a bucket. Arturo's wife—he never introduced us and, when I asked her name, she mumbled too low to hear—was in her early twenties, a good thirty years his junior. We drank coffee from chipped enamel mugs and Arturo, restless, paced the room.

"Here, Arturo." I moved along the bench. "Have a seat. It's okay."

He put down his coffee, looked out of the window. "Everyone is hungry. It's been a long time that the wind's been high." He passed his wife his empty mug, sat down on the bench, hands heavy on his knees. He wanted to know how long I'd be staying, keen as anything, I guessed, not to lose the gas I'd paid for. I reassured him: I was in no hurry; this was my beginning.

"And after this?" he said. "Where do you go?"

"South to San Juan del Norte, then up the river, across the lake."

He smiled. "With the shark." He nudged me with his elbow,

playfully. "Why else would you come here at three in the morning?"

Arturo knew the river and lake as well as the coast; he'd spent the early 1970s working the rich sharking waters at San Carlos, where Lake Nicaragua begins its run down the San Juan River, toward the ocean. Arturo didn't know how many sharks he'd landed and split open, how much he'd made from their oil and fins and hide in those five or six boom years, but guessed at many thousands. Only one man, he said, had been more successful—a "Spaniard," a non-Indian mestizo—but he'd been a good ten years older, was now perhaps already dead. "We were rich men, for a time," Arturo said. "But it's better here. Up there, after a time, there was blood in the water. Too much money, and men got greedy."

Arturo's wife made us breakfast—rice and beans, fried in a slug of pork fat—and watched us eat. This was, I couldn't help thinking, some way short of the traditional Miskito feast, with its turtle, white-lipped peccary, boiled baby cassava, coconut milk, and banana porridge. I ate mine quickly, nonetheless, fork clacking against the enamel; when I looked up, she was smiling at me, eyebrows raised. Arturo was offering nothing, so I thanked her, even though this *gallo pinto* was heavier than most, congealing on my fork before I even raised it to my mouth. When we finished she held her hands out for the plates, stacked them unwashed inside the pan.

Arturo lifted his hand. "Fatima, will you feed the pig? And check the cockerel?" He gave her his brightest, most worked-on smile. "Thank you, my dear."

As she let the door fall shut behind her, Arturo turned to face me. "What she doesn't know," he said, "is that I've got another family. We lived in San Carlos during the shark days."

"The 1970s?"

He nodded. "My first wife was a Spaniard too."

"Children?"

"Two sons. It's been a long time."

They lived now, or so he'd heard, in San Juan del Norte, the settlement at the mouth of the San Juan, sixty miles down the coast. His sons would now be in their early twenties, his first wife about forty-five. He had no answer for why he'd let ten years slip by so fast. When he spoke of them his breath quickened; he gripped my arm.

It was the civil war that had split them: she'd backed the Sandinista revolution; he, unhappily neutral for six years until 1985, finally sided with the men he'd grown up with on the Atlantic Coast, and joined the Contras. Though the war had long since ended, he'd not dared trace his family.

"Come with me," I offered. This might also work for me: travel on the coast was hard and unpredictable; Arturo knew the waterways, could sense danger, understood the wary etiquette of men who'd been so long at war.

"To San Juan?" He stood abruptly, walked to the door. He inched it ajar, stole a glance outside, then cushioned it shut again. "I don't know," he said, his back still to me. "This is my life now. My family is here."

"That's okay, I just thought—"

He snorted derisively. "How much do you know? How much do I have to teach you? Tell me, for instance: You have heard about the San Carlos shark? The monster? It is perhaps ten or fifteen meters long. And where does it live?" He paused theatrically. "It lives close by San Carlos, perhaps ten minutes' paddling in a dory. Where you see the dark water, that is where it lives."

He'd picked up his empty mug and was tapping his fingers against the rim; his wife's face appeared at the window, then, as quickly, dropped from sight. Arturo spoke again more softly, as if embarrassed at his outburst. "The shark guards the emerald mine that is at the bottom of the lake. It is much deeper; that is why the water is a different color at that point." In the 1930s a boatload of Indian divers had tried to reach the mine. All failed: the mine was too deep, a black absence that remained out of reach to even the strongest swimmers. Within a month of their expedition, all were dead. "What do you think of that?"

I shrugged, unsure what was required, whether to be intimidated or awed.

"And still today," he added, "the Indians worship the shark."

He pushed the door open, scanned the yard. He put the bucket against the open door and morning flooded the shack. He nodded at me, schoolmasterly. "That is why it is not so simple."

I wondered what I'd said, to what I owed this lecture. I'd come to him to go shark fishing, but, three hours on, was still sitting here in his house while he paced and reminisced. I stood, explaining I'd return when the wind had dropped. "How long do you think that will be?"

"Tomorrow, more likely the next day, or the one after. I'm going out there as soon as I can, I tell you." He rubbed his big hands together. "And if we're going to San Juan," he said, grinning at the surprise on my face, "we'll have to catch a few: we'll be gone a while, and my family needs to eat."

So not tomorrow, but Sunday, three days away: enough time,

he felt confident, for the wind to slacken. He'd been watching the skies, and was surprised only that it had not happened sooner. In order to rise early enough, he suggested, I should spend Saturday night in his house. "You can have the chair," he said, indicating an armless rocking chair beside the stove, stacked with yam and cassava roots. For now, he defied me to hurry away. "Sleep later," he said. "To fishermen, the night and the day are one."

He disappeared into the other room and there was a heavy scraping, then the chink of bottles, and he reappeared in the doorway with a bottle of Victoria in each fist. "Sit down," he said. "Tomorrow we work."

3

When darkness came, those next few waiting days, it was squally, almost wintry; down the streets the crack of falling coconuts was heard. I'd not seen Arturo since that abortive dawn start, but doubted we'd get out on Sunday, as he'd promised. The wind was higher, if anything, and was bringing with it rain, great banks of storm clouds from across the ocean that swept the town, scattering flocks of birds and throwing mud against the storefronts, strewing the streets with branches and palm fronds.

The wind reminded people of the hurricane, and that evening—before fleeing to a bar to try to forget the violence of my meetings with Obregón and Maximo—I'd seen old men standing on their porches, watching the sky and scanning for twisters, sniffing for the certain stillness that presaged destruction. The hurricane was nine years ago now, but was recalled by all with absolute clarity: at nine in the evening it shook the roofs; by ten most houses had been peeled apart, the dockside flooded, boats turned turtle. A priest told me how he'd sheltered the homeless in his church, easily the strongest building that side of town, but its roof went too, tearing away with a rusty screeching like some prototype flying machine. He'd tried to protect his people, pushing tables into one corner, cajoling women and children underneath, but the door became jammed by a fallen coconut palm and the church began filling with water. The electricity was down; lightning split the sky above them. "You could taste the salt in the air," he remembered. "The sea was upon us." A child's head was cracked open; the water turned to blood. All night it went on. Seventeen were killed, their town smashed to rubble.

The Miskito lexicon reflected this meteorological heritage, with up to thirty expressions for different wind conditions. Times of year, too, were often referred to in purely atmospheric terms: July was "*pastara kati*," strong wind month; October was "*sant kari*," hurricane month. Recent history focused on hurricane years, and the memories of the elderly were judged on their ability to recall the details. Some storms, like that of 1865, no longer had living witnesses, but the stories of ravenous jaguars, driven from the desolate jungle into town in search of food, of the leveling of crops and whole groves of coconut palms, the destruction of oyster beds, were as clear as if it had been just last year. "The lagoon was covered with trees, branches and leaves for a long time," one eyewitness wrote of 1865. "The water turned quite black, and the fish died by the hundreds, no doubt poisoned. They floated on the surface of the lagoon until the exhalations arising from their dead bodies became almost unbearable. . . . The beach all round was lined with hundreds of

dead fish, alligators, sharks. A few days later the parrots came to
the settlement in thousands, and great numbers dropped dead
from sheer starvation. Then, the tigers [jaguars] made their
appearance, lean, gaunt, and savage, eating up everything that
came their way." The scars of such holocausts took many decades
to heal—and when they had, residents could be sure, the next
would not be far away.

The men in the bar—a baseball team from up the coast, drinking to obliterate the whipping they'd just endured from the
Bluefields squad—would have been boys at the time of the 1988
hurricane, and they drank and bantered as if they'd already forgotten. They were Creole, each one, and though the game had
ended hours before, they still wore their pajama-strip, knees and
elbows grazed with dirt. We toasted Bob Marley, shouting above
an old, stretched cassette cranked to distortion; when the music
ended they called for more. "A prophet, man!" shouted the backstop, too close to my ear. "Our Jamaican brother!"

Most of what they said, their patois thickened with alcohol,
was as foreign to me as pure Miskito: they spoke so fast, drumming their hands on the bar, jamming in unison, big mouths
open, yelping with laughter. Their language—Miskito Coast
Creole, in linguistic longhand—was older, even, than Jamaican
Creole, since the English began trading with the Nicaraguan
Atlantic Coast in the 1630s, a good twenty years before they
wrested Jamaica from the Spanish. It took a hundred years, with
blacks shipped in as pirates' slaves and plantation workers for
the early colonists, for Miskito Coast Creole to emerge as a distinct language. And it has survived, this compromise lexicon
of English, Miskito, African tongues, New World Spanish—

survived the imposition of English as the coast's first language in 1740; survived the steady influx of Spanish-speaking mestizos since the 1870s. Slowly, though, it is receding: blacks may speak it when they're alone together, but the younger ones can rap in Spanish too—an equally curried brew.

With these men, on this night, as with so many other speakers of undiluted Creole, I found myself listening, staring, pausing while I rewound to deconstruct the sentence, and only then, cautious, attempting a reply. *"Bot a wa tu do?" "Yu mi dringkin, das way yu no mi wahn kom ya."* Snatched phrases, the logic in the rhythm. And, offered as reassurance, the old favorites: *"lang taym,"* to describe almost any passage of time; *"plenty,"* meaning "much" or "a lot"; *"Who'ppen?"*—the most everyday greeting— "What's happening?"

Many of the older blacks, educated in the Moravian mission schools by Jamaican teachers, also possessed a textbook spoken English. These people—lost in a jasmine-scented nostalgia for the old Bluefields, before the hurricane smashed to splinters their clapboard villas, before crack dealers stood on every street corner—were ashamed of Creole, of its slipshod "wrongness," and to a white man like myself would claim they never spoke it, that it was "bad," another corruption of the young.

No one in all Bluefields, though, was harder to understand than the Chinese, of whom, since their 1920s heyday when they'd all but controlled the town's commerce, only five families now remained. One such—an electrical-store owner, so elfin he had to stand on tiptoe on a box behind the counter—had, earlier that day, shouted his replies at me, each time corrected by his wife, who stood behind him, jabbing a finger in his ribs. "No like politics!" he barked, when I mentioned the civil war that had seen him and every other Bluefields capitalist dispossessed and exiled. "Life simple Chinaman!" he said with a grin when I asked him how he lived. "How much you earn?" he demanded, shoving a pen and paper across the counter. But when I suggested a figure, hoping he'd return the confidence, he pressed a finger to his lips. "No talk! Money is politics!"

He'd obtained his wife by mail, I learned later, by advertising in a Canton newspaper. He was illogical, paranoid, exhausting; an average sentence would steamroller together English, Spanish, Cantonese. He gave me a headache and I ran for the door.

And now, six hours on, well into the turbulent night, the barman was shouting: he'd just got a phone call, something about the dock, the police. The baseball team turned to stare, listened hard, then began yelling too. This was drunken Creole at speed, and I struggled to keep pace. There was anger and excitement; the barman, with no warning, swept empties off the counter, shut off the music, began to cut the lights. He led the way out, not once turning, not waiting to lock up.

On the street, where normally at this hour there would have been unholy quiet, just the late-night yelping of nameless, hungry dogs, there was a swell of people, coursing downhill toward the harbor. A little boy was tumbling after a ruck of men, trawlermen I recognized from earlier. He pulled at their hands, called up to them, but they clipped him away, ordering him home.

I tailed the barman and the baseball team, under streetlights knocked sickly by the wind, that flickered weak orange through torn branches, over rain-shiny roofs. Women watched from first-floor rooms; a block further on, the power died. Two men switched on flashlights, but a fullish moon was enough to guide the rest of us—that and the gathering din as we neared the dockside, that and the hammer of the municipal generator, the smell of refuse near the edge.

The security gates were closed across the jetty and the crowd was pressing up against the bars, already two or three thick. On the other side a police launch was pulled up to the dock; fifteen or twenty officers stood on the deck of a rusted trawler. There was movement on the launch, its outboards still spluttering water, twin spotlights narrowing out across the lagoon, knocked low, then skyward, by the swell. An officer with a bullhorn was snapping orders in Spanish, but he'd got too close and was shouting too loud and all that reached us was distortion: high-pitched, electrical welter.

"Eduardo!" Arturo—beery, excitable—had crept up on me. He seemed boyish, high on spectacle. "Where you been, *hombre?*"

"Around," I said, my eyes still on the dock; two policemen were clambering out of the launch, pulling themselves up the jetty steps, straightening their epaulets. "I met Maximo."

Arturo shook his head. "That pirate. What did I tell you?"

"Nothing about Maximo, as I recall. You mentioned Obregón. I saw him too. Not a happy story."

I'd arrived too late. Minutes earlier, Arturo said, a police jeep had passed through. The crowd that surrounded us now, that was just starting to quiet and disperse, had, only moments before, been howling for the prisoner's blood. At one point, Arturo added, he'd thought there would be a full-scale riot.

"What happened?" I said, wishing I'd been there. "Who was he?"

"Drugs." Arturo was picking at his teeth with a fishhook. "Drugs. Cocaine."

"You knew him?"

He passed a hand over his chin. "His family, yes." They were peasant farmers, he said, occasional fishermen, from Punta Gorda, down the coast. A bale of cocaine had knocked up in the surf and this man, out one day for driftwood, had found himself hefting home twenty kilos of class A narcotic instead, and with it the possibility of undreamed-of riches.

It was not unknown, I'd heard, for families in these remoter reaches to bless their luck, tear open the polyethylene cladding, and set to work over the stove, pummeling "dough" from this fine-grained, floury powder, baking it into loaves, and then, just as surely, enjoying swift, hallucinatory deaths. But this man, like most others along the coast by now, knew exactly what he'd stumbled upon; he had, moreover, said Arturo, been waiting a decade or more for just this chance, and the next day began paddling his dory north, heading for Bluefields, the surest market he knew of. And now, five days later, he'd been arrested at El Bluff, just across the lagoon, teasing the trawlermen to buy, cocaine dust under his fingernails, in his hair, his eyes electric-wide.

"And now?" I said. "What happens next?"

"Prison. They take him to the cells. Then perhaps he sees the judge."

"Perhaps?"

He looked at me, shook his head. "They don't always last too long, you know, in our prison in Bluefields. It's a bit crowded, too many men. Hot, too. You know, things happen." He paused. "Everyone does this. Anyone who finds drugs sells them."

"You?"

"Not me, no." He shrugged. "I don't like drugs. But this boy," he gestured up the main street, toward the police station. "Who cares about him? He's a *machaca*." He pinched the air between thumb and forefinger. "Small fish. There are *tiburones* out there, real big sharks, the South Americans in their speedboats and helicopters. The cops should be chasing them, not this little *chacalín*, this prawn."

"Speaking of sharks," I said, as the last of the crowd drifted off and the stall keepers pulled their shutters down again, "what about this wind?" How come his weather forecasting had gone so awry? When *would* we get out to sea?

Rain was scurrying off the quay, bringing with it the smell of oil and fish heads. Arturo buttoned his shirt to his neck. "Next week, I should think." He tasted the tip of his finger. "Sometimes the wind just turns—like this—but next week, it will get smooth again." And now, casting about one last time, he was off home, telling me to look him up when the sea had stilled. He ignored my impatience—the frustration I felt that must have been obvious—and his final words, spoken as he turned to go, for a second made no sense.

"The *jefe*," he said, waving an arm in the direction of the jetty. "The police chief, he's here. That fat Spaniard, see him? Talk to him now. Ask him about the drugs business. Could be your only chance." And he left, straight-backed, flat-footed, starting a tune.

The *jefe*. Arturo knew, because I'd complained at length, that every time I'd arranged a meeting with this man, he'd somehow,

mysteriously, have just left, or be running late, time of return
unknown. The police headquarters—a three-story, terraced villa
on the south side of town, with a view clear across the prison
exercise yard and the slaughterhouse gut slide—always seemed
empty when I arrived, perhaps just a face high up, watching
from a top window, pulling back inside the moment I stepped
into the front yard. And, in the *jefe*'s office on the second floor,
the same uniformed secretary resting her elbows on the same
Corona manual, with never any clue as to where the boss man
was, or when he might come back. I only needed five minutes,
I'd stress each time, just enough to hear his explanation of the
burgeoning beachcomber culture, how and why so much cocaine
came to litter these shores. I'd begun to wonder whether he was
avoiding me, or whether, perhaps, he treated all outsiders, all
inquiring foreigners, the same.

Now, even in the guttering moonlight, out ahead on the
jetty, it seemed clear enough which was he: the smallest of them
all, slope-shouldered, brandishing a revolver, men scattering
around him. He struggled into the jeep, craned his neck around,
clapped his hands above his head. A much larger man climbed in
behind the steering wheel, kicked the engine to life. As they
drew nearer, I could see the *jefe*'s face in the upthrown dash light:
a waxen dewlap, eyes screwed to slits.

As they slowed at the gate, I ran round to the passenger door,
called out. The *jefe* looked up, punched an arm across the dash-
board; the jeep bounced to a halt.

"*Sí?*" They'd pulled up right next to me, so close I could
smell his breath: like roses, unexpectedly sweet. He was breathing shallowly, like a newborn, his body soft under the sweated
cotton.

I congratulated him, hearing my own transparent toadying.

The war on drugs was a hard one, I said, against powerful odds; every victory, however small, should be celebrated.

"*Sí?*" He turned the barrel of the revolver slowly in his fingers. "What do you want?"

"Drugs," I stuttered. "They a big problem here?"

"Eighty percent of Bluefields has no job," he said. He cowboy-spun the revolver on his index finger, bounced it snug into his palm. He smoothed wind-roughed hair flat to his scalp, and I smelled something else: hair tonic, synthetic pine forests.

"The Colombians use this region to traffic cocaine." He spoke in a monotone, as if he'd repeated the same many times before. The eighty-second parallel, cutting north-south, fifty miles offshore, between the Nicaraguan Islas del Maíz and the Colombian island of San Andrés, marked the international boundary, but this was open ocean, and proved near-impossible to police. "The drug dealers are rich; we, in Nicaragua, are poor. They have planes and five-hundred-horsepower boats. The best we have is a hundred-and-seventy-five-horsepower dory."

"That one?" I pointed down the jetty.

He nodded, sighed. "Drugs have become a way of life in Bluefields. It is the easiest way to make money." Before the lagoon was poisoned, and the shoreline overfished by American lobstermen, when the bull shark was still abundant and scores of Chinese merchants haggled up the price of fins, there had been no need of such tainted income. "Fifteen years ago, people smoked grass. Now it is cocaine and crack and heroin. What can I do?"

"But the drugs on the beach? Why does so much get washed up?"

"We chase the drug dealers, they throw the drugs overboard." He covered his eyes with his hand, massaged his temples.

"Simple." He stared at me, as if I were partly to blame. The remaining policemen had gathered round the jeep; when he spoke, they nodded in unison.

"And you know what this means? What all this free cocaine means for our town?" He banged his fist on the dash, ordered his driver on. "It means that nowhere in the world can you buy cheaper drugs."

4

For days the wind raged, and I was forced, despite my impatience, to wait. Normally, the fishermen all agreed, it should have been calm this early in the year, and they should all have been out at sea. But the sea was high, and so, resigned, they were marking time until the weather cleared.

Further up the coast—Pearl Lagoon, Sandy Bay, Puerto Cabezas—villagers would have been turtling, had the conditions been better, though turtles, like so much else, were growing scarce. Off the entire Atlantic coast of Nicaragua extended a shallow marine shelf, seldom deeper than ten or twenty fathoms, the perfect coral-and-cay environment for the sea grasses that nourished the hawksbill and green turtles. In calm weather, turtlemen used to stay out a week or more, tracking these ocean wanderers, whose powers of navigation were greater even than

those of birds, and who wept "tears" of lubricating fluid when
they were netted and hauled aboard.

The best time to head shark fishing, the fishermen agreed,
was under a new moon, though this, too, had its drawbacks. "In
de new moon, de fish mouth soft," one large Creole, waking
from a long siesta, told me. "You hook many, but dey slip off all
too easy." Another, sidling up, threw me a theory I thought
highly unlikely—that the sharks frequented these shallow reefs
through centuries-old habit, having first been drawn here by the
wrecks of slaving ships, and by the slave traders' habit of throwing captives overboard—until I heard it repeated, much later, by
shark fishermen on the San Juan River.

Waiting for the wind to drop I traveled north, up inland
waterways to Pearl Lagoon and beyond, and here the faces
became more Indian, the shoulders broader and more Miskito—
Arturo's people. Few pure-blooded Miskito remained, however.
Smallpox and yellow fever in the eighteenth and nineteenth centuries had accounted for the lives of many thousands, and when
their monarchy died at the beginning of this century, so did
much of the Miskito belief in their ability to govern themselves.

The last Miskito king, languishing in Bluefields as the nineteenth century drew to a close, cut a pathetic figure; dressed in
white cotton suits, claiming to feel the very Englishman with
his bookshelves full of Walter Scott, Byron, and Shakespeare, he
knew, even as he spoke, that the end was upon him. He was
developing a taste for strong liquor and would be, as he must
have realized, the last of the line.

His sole surviving descendant, as far as I could establish,
was a peasant woman who lived in a concrete shed in Pearl
Lagoon and helped out in the Centro de Salud for five hundred
córdobas a month. "Sure, I'm proud," she'd admitted when

finally convinced I had not come to mock her. "But I keep it pretty quiet. Take a look around you—do we look like royalty to you?"

And now, a week later and with the onshore wind finally beginning to drop a little, I was tramping the streets of Bluefields again, searching for Arturo. His wife, up to her elbows in a bowl of scarlet tripe, said he'd left at dawn, with no word of where he was headed or when he might return. His dugout was there, though, dragged up high on the mud below his shack, so he'd clearly not gone sharking. His hooks and lines were heaped in the bow, awash in two weeks' rainwater; bluish prawns, bait gone bad, whiskered the surface. As I left, I noticed his red woolen glove, pegged by a finger to the washing line, as startling in this monochrome shantyscape as an ink splash on an ancient daguerreotype.

Stallkeepers offered conflicting information. One claimed he'd seen Arturo off upcountry, hitching a ride in a logger's jeep; another, that he'd been down at the police station all morning; three—almost a consensus—suggested I try the dockside.

At the dockside, men in undershirts were rolling gasoline drums along the jetty, up a gangplank, bouncing them into the hold of a rusting trawler. On the deck of a larger, yet more decrepit fishing boat, its cranes and haulage gear corroded solid, was a chaotic stack of fresh-varnished rocking chairs, half-covered with tarpaulin. Cash was changing hands: wads of old córdobas, smelling of underpants.

"Arturo?" said a man pushing a gasoline drum, pausing for a cigarette, looking me over, sweat running in his eyes. "Try Bluff."

"Bluff?" This was the island at the mouth of the lagoon, a lobster-fishing settlement.

"Yes, that's right," said another, drawing alongside, cadging himself a cigarette, lighting up from the other's tip. "There's a riot going on. That's where he'll be."

It wasn't hard catching a ride: El Bluff was just two miles distant, and fiberglass *panga* speedboats—loaded with lobstermen, their wives, their whores—worked the route throughout the day. With the weather calming, we rode high on the plane, the stern rattling hard over the chop, outboard screaming, the helmsman standing, face stretched to rubber by the wind. Bluff rose from the heat haze: a thicket of trawler masts, twin giant gas silos, another for diesel. The island itself, as we banked and slowed toward the pier, was slight, beaten down: just hurricane-blown scrub, hot sand, the water a churny olive-dun, with swollen plastic bags, like body parts, nodding just below the surface.

With the engine off it was clear which way to go: from the direction of the moored trawlers came the howl of a crowd. The men in the *panga* leapt ashore when we were still pulling in, stamping through the shallows to the beach and the path. I ran after them, dizzied by the heat, already thirsty.

Along the shore path, through blizzards of insects. As I neared the trawlers—each one numbered, all a uniform red-striped white—I saw the crowd for the first time, veering from silence to uproar, pressing up against a security fence that separated the boats, the dockside, a factory complex, from the rest of the island. One man stood higher than the rest, a bullhorn jammed to his mouth.

"This is slavery!" he was shouting. "The Americans are treating us like slaves!" And at each staccato delivery, fist punched in the air, the crowd howled agreement, dust rising like horse sweat, the police on the other side of the fence looking increasingly edgy, behind their sunglasses their eyes tiny and restless, hands twitching above their holsters.

There were no women, just broad-set, heavy-jawed men, in work boots and denim, each with a "Gulf King" baseball cap. It was against Gulf King, their American employer, that they'd rioted the day before. Gulf King, they claimed, had shrunk their pay to a mere four dollars for each hundred pounds of shrimp they landed; during this, the low season, it might take a week to trap that many.

The strike had been running a week; every day, with the company refusing to talk, the fishermen trod one step closer to anarchy; yesterday, in the melee, two machinists had had their faces broken; now, with the men hungry and flagging through heat exhaustion, a stampede—notwithstanding the waiting cops—seemed imminent. It was a question of respect, the man with the bullhorn was yelling. "The Americans don't respect people from Nicaragua. Never have. They may not call us slaves, but we are their slaves. They pay us so little we are bound to them."

"Fuck that, chief," came a scream from the crowd, so naked in its fury that the rest, momentarily, stilled. "No more words. Let's fucken blow de boats up. See what they do then."

I knew that voice, though never so taut, so near-explosive. It was Arturo, I was sure, but in the surge of the crowd and the pall of dust I couldn't pick him out. More policemen had moved in along the security fence, automatic rifles crooked and ready, and this slowed the crowd a little, gave the feeling of a little more time, a little less headlong chaos.

When the crowd moved again I saw him: smaller than the trawlermen, and older, his bald spot like high-buffed shoe leather, being elbowed to the edge. He noticed me, held up his fist.

"What are you doing here?" I shouted. He'd escaped the throng, was breathing hard, eyes dark and brilliant.

"This is our lives," he said. "This fishinin"—that extra Bluefields syllable—"this is all we have."

"What's going to happen?"

"There's a lawyer." He looked around, stretched to tiptoe. "A woman. She's here somewhere."

"A woman?"

"Well," he pursed his lips. "She's good, as good as a man." He paused, scanned the faces again. "There . . . see her?" He pointed toward the back of the crowd, where a large woman in a billowing floral dress was in vigorous debate with a knot of trawlermen. Her earrings flashed in the sunlight. She looked up when she saw us, began to move our way.

"And you," Arturo went on, "you've come at the right time. See the wind? What did I say? We'll be shark fishing soon. Tomorrow perhaps."

"You think so?" I squinted hard at him, trying to work out whether, this time, he meant it. I wanted so badly to go, was growing stale from the waiting, but over the last ten days there'd been so many tomorrows. It was hard to believe this one would be any different.

▼ ▼ ▼

The lawyer stood in front of us, hand stretched out. She filleted a business card from her wallet, laid her briefcase on the ground between us. We shook hands, both slippery with sweat.

"You're representing the fishermen?" I said.

"That's me." She rolled her eyes. "We've been waiting a week just to talk to the bosses. Two hours ago there was supposed to be a meeting. And what do you see?" I looked toward the compound, at the line of policemen, the company trucks, the masts and rigging of the waiting trawlers, the stillness of the afternoon. She nodded. "Exactly. No change."

The longer the strike went on, she said, the more damage it would do the fishermen: the company, bolstered by the dollar, could hold out indefinitely. Already three crews had been bribed back to sea and now, since they had broken the picket line, their lives were at risk. The problem, she said, was not just the derisory pay offer, but the progressive whittling-away, over the past three years, of every basic workers' right. Now there was no health insurance, no paid holiday, both of which were, in theory, required under law. "And the work is dangerous," she said. "This is no peanut harvest."

The government, so far, had sided with the company: everywhere I turned, it seemed, were compelling arguments for Atlantic independence, for the coast to shuck off the yoke of central government and operate according to its own best interests, rather than because of some imposed, historically dubious idea of nationhood. Along the Miskito Bank, once the world's richest shrimping grounds, now thronged fleets of all nationalities, all year round, despite pleas from Nicaraguan crews for a three-month downtime during the breeding season. Not, of course, that it had been any better before the revolution: then, two hundred shrimp and lobster boats fed six Bluefields processing plants, four of which were part-owned by the Somoza family.

Now, these men said, they'd soon have no fishing left: no fishing, no food, no life. "It shouldn't be a matter of discussion, all this," the lawyer finished. "Only in such a poor area could you get away for so long paying the people so little."

"Slavery" was the word the strikers were yelling out, slavery to a government they despised not for any particular set of policies, but because it was not theirs and did not care. When the Frente had seized power in 1979, it imagined, in its first rush of passionate naivety, that every Nicaraguan would want a part in its shiny new socialist revolution, somehow forgetting that, for five hundred years, the Costeños, the coastal people, had wished only to be left alone and that, to them, there was little difference between Somoza, the dictator, and Daniel Ortega, the new president: both were "Spaniards," both were meddlers. To many Costeños, every Nicaraguan leader back to José Santos Zelaya, the 1894 president and architect of the *reincorporación* of the Atlantic Coast under the Nicaraguan flag, was of equal malignity.

The only foreign influence on which they looked kindly was that of England, coastal colonial power until Zelaya's seizure. The English, claimed many of the older people further up the coast, even one forty-year-old mayor, had been a benign, supportive presence, and should be lobbied hard to return.

In Pearl Lagoon, an old logger had pressed a letter into my hand. "The Queen of England," the envelope read, in shaky script.

"Be careful," he whispered. "If the Spanish see it, then big trouble." All I had to do, once back in London, was find a post-box. "She'll come and help us, I know she will."

Every ten minutes the lawyer stood at the gates and demanded to be heard, shouted for the meeting that had been promised, and, at three in the afternoon, four hours late, two policemen began unlocking the gate. The fishermen, who'd fallen back under the trees, unable, in such heat, to sustain their earlier volume of fury, rolled to their feet, suddenly alert again. They pressed up behind the lawyer, all at once demanding to be let through. Arturo pulled my arm.

"Come on. This is the moment."

We fought through, me tailing him closely, so hot in the press of the crowd, the acid smell of anger and too much fervid proximity, that I felt my vision blurring. Hands pushed me from behind; Arturo, in front, shouted to keep up; we reached the gate to find the way barred by police, their guns raised. The lawyer was pleading, sounding close to desperate.

"We have names," the policeman was saying. "There is a list—only those will be able to come to the meeting."

"List?" the lawyer spluttered. "I've seen no list. We've got a meeting. Let us in." And she elbowed through the gap, lowering her head under the razor wire, followed by two, then three, fishermen and Arturo, gesturing me after him. A policeman stepped in front of us. "No more!" he shouted, retreating, sweat darkening his shirt even as I watched, his mouth opening and closing, as if underwater.

"The lawyer? Who's the lawyer?" A man stood in the doorway to the nearest warehouse, clearly an official in his pleated white shirt and pressed slacks. The lawyer stepped forward, held up her briefcase.

"How many of you are there?" the official shouted, shading the sun from his eyes.

"Just these," the lawyer said, turning to us, waving the rest back, pleading with them to stay where they were.

"Come on then," the official said, turning back inside. "What are you waiting for?"

It was cooler inside. Cardboard boxes containing oil filters, air filters, and machine screws were stacked to the roof, each one stamped "Made in America." We were led down a long corridor, past a glassed-in office where a white man in cowboy boots was talking on a portable, flagging wildly with his hands. A policeman tailed us, close on my heels, muzzle nudging the back of my legs. The lawyer, seeing this, turned, held up a finger.

"Back off." She pointed at his face, though all she could see in his sunglasses, I guessed, was her reflection, darkly gesturing. "Do your job."

The policeman waited a step, then followed again. In an upper room, as the fishermen unstacked chairs to sit on, he stood sentinel at the door, rifle at his side.

"Right, let's begin," said the official, forcing a smile. "I wonder what all the trouble is." To me, in English, he murmured lightly, "Beautiful country, Nicaragua, don't you think?" As if he were a holiday guide.

"You can tell me what the policeman's doing here, number one," said the lawyer. "Who's he working for? The company or the government?" She opened her briefcase, took out a notepad, wrote something down: a long sentence, twice underscored.

The fishermen grunted approval; two, short of chairs, remained standing, shifting their weight from foot to foot, looking round hopefully, as if suddenly they'd be made at home.

The official jabbed his pen in the direction of the wooden planking, strewn with wood shavings and ticker-tape wadding. "The floor will do just fine." And turning away, shaking his head so forcefully I heard his cheeks slap against his gums, he took down our names, letter by letter, going over the spelling, letting the fishermen wait as the room grew hotter and more airless, sun raw against the roof above our heads.

The discussion, when he allowed it to open, came in furious bursts: fishermen interrupting each other, the lawyer struggling, amenable as she could be, to have each heard in turn, the official looking up seldom, and then only to glance at the policeman or myself, never the one addressing him. A fisherman, his lips pale, blood rising in his neck, said quietly, "You don't know what will happen here if this goes on. The boats are old and dangerous. We spend too long at sea. We get hungry. When we come back we get no money. What do you expect, hey? Everybody to be happy?"

The official sat very still, nodded slowly, hardly seeming to breathe, his face unreadable; by now he'd stopped writing; had begun, it appeared, to listen just a little. One of the fishermen— a Creole with hands as big as his feet—had a book open on his knees and was peeling through the pages: *Código del Trabajo,* code of working practice.

The policeman, clearing his throat, leaned over. "What's that?" Just the hint of a smile, an attempt, it seemed, to demonstrate a little humanity.

"Back off!" the lawyer shouted. "Your job is to keep quiet, say nothing!" She stared him back to his place, then stood up, stepped outside the chairs, strode round the circle. She ran through the issues—pay agreements reneged on, workers' rights torn up, the disrespect and carelessness that could almost be smelled in the air, like so much rotting meat—and then, crossing back to the center, turning to address everyone, flourished her trump. Tomorrow, she said, she'd be on the dawn flight to Managua for a meeting with the minister. He'd decide what was legal and what was not. "And then," she said, lowering herself back into her chair, "we'll talk about the future."

From outside, from nothing, came a great roar: an exploding zeppelin of sound, thrown upward, rattling the warehouse we stood in, shocking the fishermen and the lawyer upright, chairs knocked over. Up here there were no windows, just a long letterbox of daylight where the roof met the wall, and in front of this the fishermen knelt, eyes straining against the heat shimmer. But then, as suddenly as it came, it died away and I, looking too, could see nothing that had not been there before: the strikers up against the fence, the policemen in shirts as blue as the sky, rifles at their shoulders, facing down the protest. The voices fell to a rumble; from behind us, near the dockside, I heard the rumble of heavy machinery, heard a marine engine cough to life. The official clapped his hands, waited for the fishermen to turn and meet his eye.

"I as much as you," he said, "want to see the end of this." He waited; they made no reply; the lawyer, head down, silent, began to make for the staircase. The official, with a sudden, confused cry, cut in front of her and swung into the stairwell, jumped the stairs in threes.

We found him outside, flanked by policemen, showing us the gate. He shook hands with the lawyer, checked his watch, and, wiping his mouth, ferreted back inside, double-speed toward the warehouse, leaving dust devils spinning in his wake. Before we were out, engulfed by heat and hands and frantic questioning—"What did they say?" "What about the money?" "What now?"—he was gone, not once looking back.

I rode back to Bluefields at dusk with Arturo in a *panga* full of fishermen; weary, still talking, they'd be drinking on the quay that night with money borrowed and pooled, their last few cordobas, before starting out tomorrow, for Bluff again, at first light. The sea now was the calmest I'd seen it, and Arturo made much of scanning the sky, trailing a hand in the black-glass wake, tasting the water on his fingertips. The sky was red and gold; the lights of Bluefields, in a rare moment without blackouts or power surges, hovered like fireflies over the water. Both ways from the center the town stretched to blackness, out to the shanty desert of plywood and zinc roofing and gutters stuck with refuse and offal.

"Tomorrow, then," Arturo said as we climbed out onto the jetty. "You come at four in the morning. Tomorrow will be perfect, you'll see I'm right." He smelled the air, made me do the same, though all I could pick up was the sweet scent of gasoline, still wet on the concrete from earlier.

"Catch that?" he said, pinching his fingers together like some roving gourmet. "That's shark. I feel it already."

5

At Arturo's request, I'd brought bananas—fat, ripe claws, still on the stalk—and carried them through the tropical night, down tracks I now knew well, almost able to gauge the distance by the incline, the exact crunch and give of the rubble underfoot. Down the tight alleyway to Arturo's yard, I smelled the gutterswill again, less rich now than during the day, and felt my way along the walls of houses, testing each step before moving on, doubling the length of the journey so that by the time I arrived it was past four and Arturo, to my surprise, was already up, brushing his teeth with lagoon water, not five yards from the outflow from the open sewer.

He greeted me silently, mouth afroth. Together we bailed the dugout, heaping nets and hooks high in the prow, scraping at the swollen wood with coconut halves. We worked until the boat was dry and people in nearby shacks were coughing in their sleep. In Arturo's shack, through a square of grease-smoked glass, I glimpsed his wife moving about slowly, a slight shake to her movements: too many dawn starts, I guessed, too much broken sleep. And there was, as Arturo had predicted, just the faintest breeze tickling onshore, barely strong enough to ruffle the water, detectable only in a sweet cooling of the skin.

As yet, though, we had no engine. Arturo wanted to fish further out, ten miles south, and to do that he needed an outboard. His neighbor Elias had one, and had promised to come if they split the catch, but he was nowhere to be seen. Arturo made me wait and cut round the back of his shack, muttering to himself. It was ten minutes before he returned, and in those minutes came the first intimation of dawn: a lifting of the absoluteness of night, the first edges of things rising into focus. I carried the gasoline over to the dugout, found the paddles, laid out the bananas and the bread Arturo's wife had baked, and waited.

Ten minutes later, they both emerged, Elias running apologizing after Arturo, yawning continually, dressed only in his underpants, one hand on the sagging elastic. He'd overslept, but promised we'd be out there soon. He hurried to the water's edge and began lifting away palm branches from what I'd thought was a heap of refuse, and soon was heaving the outboard clear, setting it on its back beside the tank of gasoline. He maneuvered it one-handed, with seeming ease: hard to believe an outboard that weighed so little was as quick as he boasted. I watched, feeling the first flurry of concern, uncomfortably close to my bowels. Elias looked up, grinned, hoisted his underpants. "Five minutes," he said, and was gone again.

"We'll be going soon," Arturo said, nodding, looking east across the lagoon to the bar mouth and the slowly opening sky. Dawn was edging in, nudging a slip of palest gray along the horizon, letting me stagger about less blindly. Arturo had always impressed on me the importance of a pre-dawn start, and I detected under his current resolute optimism a fear that time was running by too fast; that Elias would be a half hour, not five minutes; that the other shark fishermen were already out there working the best reaches; that we'd miss our chance and, within hours, the weather would turn again. He began to sharpen his knives, blade to blade—long, determined strokes, ending in a conjuror's flourish. The first of the cockerels awoke, bleating red-throated, tremulous.

"Where's Elias?" Arturo muttered finally, sheathing the knives. He looked at his watch, shook it, held it to his ear. "Time to go."

We did what we could—dragged the dugout to the water's edge, sat the gasoline flat in the stern, wedged blocks in the hull to serve as seats, one behind the other—and were struggling with the outboard, our feet sliding in the mud, when Elias appeared, breathless but dressed, carrying a throw net and a clutch of hooks.

"I thought we'd need some more," he said, seeming even younger than earlier, his hair now slicked back; he was chewing a clod of white bread. He walked over and took the engine from me without explanation, and he and Arturo lowered it onto the flat-backed stern, spinning tight the butterfly screws. From there to the water it took all three of us, leaning full weight, to get the dugout to move at all; it inched heavily through the mud, leaving a shallow grave into which dark water rose uncertainly.

Elias was the last, pushing off from the stern while Arturo and I weighted the prow, leaning over each other in our efforts to cast off. When we were afloat, Elias heaved himself in, mud drooling from his knees and calves, the dugout shipping gouts of water till I scrambled to midships and, finally, we lay flat in the water, with barely an inch of clearance. Behind us, the edge-dwellers were waking: an old man took to his porch and peed noisily; Arturo's wife stood in her open doorway, blank-faced. Coconut palms were stenciled against the lightening sky. Elias wound a length of twine round the starting mechanism and knelt in the hull and pulled hard. The engine sputtered soggily. I leaned back toward Arturo.

"We're not too late?" I said. Though it was a relief, at last, to be off, I was troubled by other matters—this rickety transport, for one, and whether it would withstand a larger sea—but it was clear no good would come of airing them. This question, at least, was answerable.

Arturo laughed, pounded me on the back. "You worry too much."

The engine kicked in, a single-cylinder sneeze that spat oily smoke clear to the bank. Arturo congratulated Elias, settled on his bench seat, laid the red glove flat beside him. "You'll see," he grinned, as we juddered forward, in gear at last. "The shark—he waits for us."

To a shark hunter from the West—from North America, or Australia—equipped with 300hp cruiser and air-con cabin and satellite navigator and submarine radar and high-velocity harpoon, the approach of Arturo and his kind would have seemed laughably amateur. In Nicaragua, any man with a dugout and a hand line could turn shark hunter; it was not so much a romantic calling as a means of survival, a way to feed the family, since fins commanded high prices. The attendant danger was accepted

because that was the way things had always been. In richer coun-
tries, where economic hardship seldom forced men to sea to hunt
sharks, shark fishermen had become heroic figures, emblematic
of a braver, simpler age.

This century's best-known shark hunter was William
Young, a sturdy Californian adventurer, later naval captain, who
spent his life fishing shark in Australia, Florida, and French
Somaliland, but who settled in Honolulu. Known to the locals
as "Kane Mano," Shark Hunter, Captain Young died aged
eighty-seven, having killed, by his own estimate, a hundred
thousand sharks: an average day's haul was twenty or thirty. In
his dotage, reminiscing over the carnage that had been his life,
his callused feet cradled in sharkskin pumps, he recalled how
he'd first learned the trade: he'd kill a horse, drag it to sea, slit
open its belly, then harpoon the circling sharks. To him, sharks
were "arrogant," "cold," "rapacious."

From photographs, Young himself appears little more,
though something else is evident, too: behind those Bakelite
spectacles is a hard face, with dark, animal eyes. As he stands,
clad in blood-smeared overalls, behind that strung-up fifteen-
foot hammerhead, the impression is of a man who has never once
questioned himself, nor anything he's done.

He died in 1962, his conscience untroubled. At that point,
marine biologists had not yet isolated the shark as a threatened
species; then, talk was still of the "war" with sharks, and what
research there was focused on the protection of man, not fish.
Shark deterrents, of variable efficacy, proliferated. The "bubble
fence," invented by the owner of an eastern seaboard hotel in
1960, in response to a particularly vicious attack off the New
Jersey coast, carried the boast that "sharks will not even cross it
to get to a juicy steak." Which would have been excellent, if

true, since the bubble fence—a perforated pipe, laid on the seabed, through which compressed air was pumped, creating a rising curtain of bubbles—was certainly cheap to produce. Unfortunately, as later tests showed, sharks parted this curtain as if it were so much gossamer.

Depth-charging, attempted first in 1958 off Margate, South Africa, was equally unsuccessful: sharks possess no swim bladder, and are thus impervious to anything other than a virtually direct hit. Indeed, the vibrations from a depth charge draw sharks almost as quickly as does the scent of blood: survivors from the U.S. destroyer *Frederick C. Davis*, torpedoed in the Atlantic on 25 April 1945, told of fellow seamen torn apart by sharks attracted to the scene by the detonation of depth charges on the sunken ship.

During the first years of World War II, the lack of an efficient, portable deterrent badly undermined the fighting spirit of U.S. forces. "Reports of shark attacks on members of our combat forces have created a wartime sea survival problem that can no longer be neglected," counseled an Army Air Corps bulletin. "The possibility of attack is a growing hazard to morale."

Triggered by President Roosevelt's personal intervention, urgent research began into the possibility of chemical deterrents. In the early 1940s, at Woods Hole Oceanographic Institute in Massachusetts, no less than seventy-nine different substances were tried out. Only one—copper acetate—proved effective, and this, blended with an inky dye, became Shark Chaser, issued to all servicemen and strapped to every life raft. It was indescribably malodorous, dead-rat funky; was, in fact, the closest chemical approximation of decomposed shark ever manufactured—which, to any half-canny fisherman, made perfect sense: no shark, however ravenous, will touch another that has been left to rot.

When all deterrents failed, and sharks broke through beach
nets to kill sun-pinkened bathers and puppy dogs, men exacted
disproportionate revenge. Two days after the fatal mauling of a
fifteen-year-old Hawaiian surfer just before Christmas 1958,
government officials and community leaders on Oahu called for
nothing less than extermination of every shark that menaced
their shores. Twenty-seven thousand dollars was raised to man
and fuel a shark boat. Within the year, 697 sharks—snared on
overnight half-mile lines—were captured and destroyed. They
weren't even given the dignity of being mashed for fertilizer, the
lowliest possible by-product: just incinerated, in great mounds,
like the corpses of diseased cattle.

Yet now, four decades later, there was no figure more reviled
by the marine biology establishment than the shark hunter. One
in particular—a Queenslander, Vic Hislop, self-styled "Shark
Man," with his shark-tooth pendant and deep-pile chest hair,
his quick line in self-justification, his highly lucrative and for-
midably gory "Shark Show"—has become almost an outlaw in
Australia. The "authorities," he believes, are engaged in a full-
scale cover-up, obscuring from the public, to protect the tourist
industry, the true extent of shark-related deaths off Australian
coasts. In south Australia, where the great white is a protected
fish, Hislop claims to have suffered police harassment, has regularly had his boat impounded. The authorities, in turn, accuse
him of misleading journalists, of talking up the shark threat to
keep himself and his bloodthirsty sideshow in the limelight.

In conversation Hislop comes across as garrulous, obsessed,
paranoid. When I asked to meet him, he declined; when I persisted, he agreed only on condition that I pay him. I hedged; we
ended up talking on the telephone. He'd grown to distrust jour-

nalists, he said: so many times he'd allowed them access to his life, had permitted camera crews to film him on the hunt, and every time he'd ended up being portrayed as a simple-minded, single-issue propagandist.

He sent me his "book," a self-published glossy brochure, in which he marshaled his arguments in full and lingered over past heroics. It was hard not to smile as the eye passed over yet another photograph of Hislop—scrawny and diminutive, despite the Popeye posturing—leg up on yet another carcass, but there was something, some grain of the possible, in what he said. All those autopsies that read, "missing, presumed drowned"; all those swimmers and surfers whose friends had seen them sucked clean under, leaving no clue, no trace. What *had* happened to them? And what of Hislop? Had he, as he claimed, been cast out simply because his message was too unpalatable? It was not impossible.

By the time we'd reached the middle of the lagoon, still some way from the open sea, there was a slight chop on the water, the surface splintered into tiny corrugations, no longer oily-smooth. Arturo sat in the bow, I in the middle, Elias at the stern, with one hand on the tiller. We were kicking up a fine spray, which soaked us like drizzle; leaves of water spilled over the side and I bailed hard, nervous we'd founder, since we'd started with an inch in the hull and neither Elias nor Arturo seemed especially concerned.

In this spectral light I could just make out the shapes of other dories, their sails like origami triangles, inching toward the sea in the windless pre-dawn. There were twenty, perhaps more, but they made no noise, and glimmered in and out of sight, moving separately and then in convoy, floating in the pale haze as if through smoke, after a battle. When our engine died—just the fuel line coming loose, though the diagnosis took Elias a while—the voices of the other fishermen carried clear across the water, all their early-morning rumblings about cloud formations and the day's prospects, along with the hard crackle of the plastic sheeting as they roped their sails tight, the kiss of their paddles on the water, their labored breathing.

We stopped, engine off, in the lee of the mangroves at the far side of the lagoon. We needed prawns, Arturo explained, untangling the throw net: prawns would serve as bait for snapper and whitejack, which, in turn, gaffed bloody and alive, would lure the sharks. He stood in the prow, gathering the skirts of the net, taking the first corner in his teeth, laying the net in folds across his arm, then, with his breath held in, he cast it spinning over the bow. It landed a perfect circle, the lead-weighted circumference pulling the filaments down through the murk. When he pulled it up, guiding it back to the edge of the dory, it came effortlessly, shedding water from its topknot, the weights gathering the bottom shut. Only when he held it up, clear of the water, did I see that there were scores of tiny prawns in the netting, blue-gray and wriggly, snared by their whiskers.

"Ha!" Arturo said, triumphant, shaking out the net into the bottom of the boat. "A good day is coming."

The prawns spun free, bouncing off the sides of the hull; each time he repeated the maneuver they clustered more thickly round my feet, swilling about in the oily floodwater in the bottom of the hull. Arturo became ever more jubilant, convinced that their abundance was a sign—proof of the harvest to come.

▼ ▼ ▼

As we crossed from the lagoon to the ocean, emerging from the lee of Bluff Island, the hull began to fill alarmingly. Out in this swell, the dugout, even at low revs, was shipping water over the bow and gunwales. I shouted back to Elias, pointing at my feet, which were awash to the ankles; he grinned, indicated the bailer. "A little bit of water," he said. *"Es normal."*

Here, where the lagoon met the sea, the currents boiled and surged. It took a while to breach this section, the propeller biting air in a frantic whine as we nosed off the back of each swell, but rhythm came easier once we were clear. While I bailed, just about keeping pace with the in-fill, Arturo stretched his back and massaged his knees, using the spare bailer to ladle up the prawns, sieving them through his fingers.

"Just here," he announced abruptly.

Elias, sleepy from the start, jolted upright. "Already?"

I stopped bailing. Arturo twisted round, waved a finger at both of us. "The sea horse. This is where I see the sea horse." He eyed us eagerly, as if expecting some clamorous response. I waited. Finally, when it was clear Elias wasn't planning to speak up, I said, "Sea horse?"

"Big storm day," Arturo said, nodding. He turned back to face the sea, gesturing toward the wide horizon, toward the first nudgings upward of a huge dawn sun. He threw his voice like an orator, waving wildly with a shark hook. "I see a big reeling of water and a great animal stuck out his head and was gone."

"You were out here? In a storm?"

He held the hook in front of my face, as a teacher might, growing short-tempered. "So I get up near to where it come out and when I'm there it come right out again and it's braying as a horse, same as a horse bray—'neeigh!'—and then it was gone again. It really was a sea horse—same mane as a horse, same head, same big ears." And his eyes were wide as a horse's after all this, wholly earnest, defying disbelief. Eventually, during a lull in the engine and before the next swell hit, Elias spoke.

"Arturo, *hombre,* enough. The light is coming. Can't you see?" And he heaved the boat toward the sea again and, still grinning, opened the throttle into the waves.

Further to sea, with the pelicans banking for shore, Elias leveled our course; we were running parallel to the coastline, at least two miles distant from the dark sand and wind-beaten coconut palms that formed the beachhead. Elias would watch four, five waves ahead, turning windward or away, gunning the engine or easing off, to minimize the pitch and yaw, but still we took on water, regularly, evenly, never less than inches-deep about our feet. I bailed, but less anxiously: we were out here now; the sky, now dawn had fully come, seemed to threaten nothing more than flat, absolute heat; nothing was looming; the far rim of cumulus seemed easeful, unhurried. But whenever I dropped my shoulders and, forgetting, emptied less determinedly, water filled steadily. "Eduardo!" Arturo would shout, looking round. "Your job!"

He was crouched forward in the prow, knees to his chest, backside uncomfortably on our anchor of rude-welded rods. With a scrubber of steel wool he was working through the six-inch shark hooks, concentrating on the point and barb, buffing till the steel showed through again. His equipment was aging and eclectic: the link sections, the "trace" between hook and line, which in the collection of a better-off shark fisherman would have comprised three-foot strips of tempered steel wire, were, in his case, corroded sections of chain, scavenged from other machinery.

From here, far offshore, the coast stretched to infinity: south to Costa Rica, Panama, Colombia; north to Pearl Lagoon, Cape Gracias, Honduras, the United States. It was at Pearl Lagoon, some days earlier, that the mayor, like the old logger who'd entrusted me with his letter for the Queen, had pleaded with me, as an Englishman, to mobilize my government to rid his people of "the Spaniards." If I did not, he warned, revolution was inevitable. "If these Spaniards don't stop thieving all our natural resources—all our timbers and fish—then we will have no choice but to fight. Every man here will fight."

Up those inland waterways, north from Bluefields, where once Dutch and English buccaneers hid their schooners from the Spanish overlords, where spreading mangroves and shifting sandbars constantly kept fishermen and campesinos on their guard, the bull shark lurked. Pearl Lagoon had a narrow, silted bar, dividing ocean from freshwater lagoon, and its fishermen spoke of it with dread.

Hard to imagine, traveling this coast and hearing such stories, that any shark could have ever been dismissed as "wretched" or "cowardly," but a U.S. Army manual, published before World War II, attempted just such vapid reassurance. "The shark is a cowardly fish which moves about slowly, and is easily frightened by surprises in the water, noise, movement and unusual shapes. This last point alone would be enough for a shark not to attack man." And, should one confound expectation and do just that, then all the alert marine had to do was pull a knife and "open up its stomach . . . you cause water to enter—that will kill it almost instantaneously."

Misunderstood creatures, feared and worshiped in equal measure. In the Solomon Islands, before the missionaries came, sharks were kept as captive gods, corralled in sacred caverns, appeased by regular human sacrifice. William Ellis, an early-nineteenth-century missionary, observed similar practices in the Archipel de la Société: "Temples were erected in which priests officiated, and offerings were presented to the deified sharks, while fishermen and others, who were much at sea, sought their favour."

Ancient Hawaiians, too, valued the shark, but more for its potential as entertainment: at Pearl Harbor, Hawaiian kings ordered underwater jousts between ravenous, penned-in sharks and gladiators armed only with shark-teeth swords. In the 1920s, Fijians were observed "shark-charming," a skill unheard of anywhere else. A French missionary, who'd witnessed islanders kissing sharks into submission, reported, more than a little stunned: "It's some occult power they have which I can't define, but once the native kisses it, that shark never moves again."

There were no such eccentricities with the bull shark. All the Costeños comprehended was that most basic rule, that a dorsal fin above the surface meant a hungry shark, though undisturbed calm was, conversely, no guarantee of safety. Like the great white, the bull shark as often foraged underwater, breaking the surface only at the last moment, jaws stretched to a perfect, serrated oval.

It was as stealthy as it was unpredictable, taking squid, sea urchin, crab, stingray, porpoise, whale, other shark, and each other: if one bull shark was injured in a food fight, the others would tear it to pieces in seconds. Its memory for blood was unerring, and it was impossible to read, "always inclined," according to a 1962 paper in the *Journal of the Royal Naval Medical Service*, "to be offensive . . . a particularly ferocious species which will attack large fish without apparent provocation and not for food."

Only gradually, and with the accumulation of years of data from marine biologists, coast guards, and fishermen, was a full portrait of the bull shark beginning to emerge. Off the shores of Natal, in South Africa, where once it was assumed that the near-mythical great white was responsible for most deaths, it now appeared that the pig-eyed bull shark, a good deal more compact, with its disproportionately large incisors, accounted for something like four times the number of victims. It was the hardiest of all tropical sharks, the most resilient to change, and it was able to survive many years in captivity with less stress than any other. Its depredations on the Ganges, preying on the half-burned bodies thrown from sacred ghats, were most often blamed on the Ganges shark, *Glyphis gangeticus,* but this in truth was a needle-toothed softie, a mere plankton-sifter by comparison.

As to why all this should be, there was little agreement. Certainly the bull shark's taste for both fresh and brackish water had brought it into close and regular contact with animals and men, and where the pickings are easy, so sharks make their home. A hundred years ago, Charles Napier Bell, a longtime Bluefields resident, recorded in his memoirs that "there is no harbour in the world more dangerous for sharks than

Greytown"—modern-day San Juan del Norte, the settlement at
the mouth of the San Juan, for which I was headed—and so it
remained.

In these waters the bull shark scavenged ceaselessly, swallowing whole anything that tumbled from the bank: orange peel,
empty rum bottles, stones, twigs. Along the turbid coast, and in
the heavily silted rivers and mangrove waterways, with visibility
often down to zero, it had developed a preternatural olfactory
sense: at a hundred meters, a single drop of blood was lure
enough.

And now we were heading south, to a lone cay so small it was
still invisible, ancestral property of the Rama Indians, who,
whenever the ocean was calm enough, would paddle across from
the mainland to tend their microplantation and fish for shark.
The lee of the island, Arturo said, was rich with fish, though he
had discovered this only by accident, stranded late one afternoon
when the wind had turned on him: the next dawn, casting from
the rocks, waiting for better weather, he'd landed three big
sharks. He wasn't sure why the cay had proved so abundant,
what aquatic alchemy had produced such a swarming, but had
made sure of one thing: he'd told no other shark fishermen, and
though they had grown suspicious, and often quizzed him
and Elias, none of them had an outboard and so never managed
to follow the two men much further than the bar.

Ideally, he said, we should have made it there at dawn, but
things had taken longer than anticipated. But he remained confident, yelling out at first glimpse of the cay—a distant thumb-
smudge splintered by the heat haze—breaking off to point out
flying fish, which flitted weightless across the water, flashing
like chain mail. We drank lukewarm coffee from Arturo's flask,

and above the noise of the engine threw out theories about what best attracted shark.

Blood, we all knew, was the surest lure, even in minute quantity; so too, Arturo held, were vomit, offal, garbage, and carrion—all rank-smelling, signaling easy pickings. Elias, who'd seen a friend taken on Bluefields bar, believed there was something in the flailings of panicked or inexperienced swimmers that triggered a shark's aggression: perhaps because the vibrations felt like those of a wounded fish.

From what I'd learned, it seemed that almost anything could provoke attack, anything unusual, particularly any large impact: more sailors, according to one breathtaking statistic, were taken by sharks in the worst World War II shipwrecks than had been killed in attacks close to shore in all of recorded history.

Sharks, so the thinking goes, have hearing acute as a trip wire, and the commotion of a ship going down or a plane scything into the sea draws them from hundreds of miles away. The torpedoing off Natal on 18 November 1942 of the English troopship *Nova Scotia*, for example, left 850 dead, from a total of 1,042; according to survivors' estimates, more than half—young men, able swimmers all, adrift in bath-warm seas—were taken by sharks.

The sinking of the Philippine ferry *Doña Paz* on 20 December 1987 was more sanguinary still: the ship, though authorized to carry only 608 passengers, was that night wedged with between 3,000 and 4,000 villagers returning home for New Year fiestas. At ten that evening the ferry was rammed portside by an oil tanker. Both vessels exploded. Those who weren't burned alive jumped into the raging sea, aslick with flame. Only twenty-five survived; over the next few days, three hundred shark-mutilated corpses were found littered on island shores, and for weeks afterward, Philippine fishermen reported finding body parts in the belly of almost every shark they landed.

In the crescent lee of the island Elias cut the engine; we drifted toward a steep, rocky beach. Though the day was near windless, there was a heavy swell, which smashed to broken foam on the red cliffs seaward. It was not much of a place—five hundred yards long, crested with stunted coconut and banana trees, with a high-tide scurf of plastic sandals and bleached aluminium drink cans and hard-dried seaweed.

"Iguana Cay!" Arturo shouted, standing upright in the prow. We nosed toward the beach, pitching in the swell, Elias behind me yelling instructions—when to jump, remember to take the rope. The water was warm here, a generous turquoise, opaque with sea life.

Grabbing the rope, Arturo jumped for shore, disappearing to his waist, paddling his arms against the suck of the swell, making it to the dry rocks soaked and breathing heavily. He beckoned me to follow, ordering Elias to stay out, drop anchor, and set the bait lines. Arturo was grinning now, as if just pleased to have made it this far. While I hesitated on the bow, wondering whether to launch off heedless, or lower myself more gently and swim for it, he held the rope loose, letting the dugout rest easy a few yards offshore. When I finally leapt forward, expecting a last-yard flounder to land, I sank to my neck. Something brushed my calf. I kicked into breast stroke, fired with panic and the certainty that, in this warm gloop, I'd get no warning of a shark, just that bleak numbness as my leg went.

"Shark," I panted as I crawled onto the beach. I struggled breathless to my feet, tried to smile.

"If you'd come two days ago," Arturo said, ignoring my flailings, giving me his hand, "you could have had this."

He pointed to the remains of a fire, set at the crest of the beach, on flat, slatelike rocks. Scattered through the cold ashes were the bones of a hammerhead, about six feet long. The head—skin stretched tight, gray-purplish in color—looked unlike any earthly living thing, an alien mutant with smoked-glass eyes set at the far edges of an airfoil skull. It would have been caught off these rocks by the Rama Indians, Arturo said, roasted and eaten the same day, its sandpapery hide cut into strips and used "to scrub the smoke from the bottom of pots." What was left of the spine—featherweight disks of ivory cartilage—would serve as counters on a homemade checkerboard. The smell, though the fish had been stripped clean and only its barest outline remained, was as potent as if from weeks of decay, sun-stewed to ulcerous softness. With a stick, I lifted the head and out of the scimitar mouth, frozen ajar, crawled fat flies, too lazy to take to the air, their wings and feet wet with feasting.

Arturo was up at the far end of the beach, trousers rolled to his knees, the material drying in streaks. He'd cut himself a spear from the bush and was sharpening one end to a pencil point.

"Iguana," he said. "Sharks eat anything, but they love iguana." This cay, he said, was thick with them, hence its name; they had been stranded here when the island split from the mainland. He grinned, confident in his mastery of history. "Millions of years ago this was the coast." He stabbed his spear into the red-clay cliff. "Come. Let's hunt."

He walked ahead, negotiating the narrow strip of dry rocks under the cliff, and I followed. We left the beach behind us as we headed for the point. Further on, the rocks became boulders, black as lead and coated with white deposit. Every few yards Arturo would stop, hold his spear above his head, and lecture me, the sea warm as tea about our ankles. For centuries, he said, the cay had been Rama property. The Indians cultivated bananas and coconuts, hunted shark and, rarer these days, the hawksbill turtle, with its perfect, mottled carapace. They'd be out here every three weeks or so, whenever the weather allowed, fishing from two or three dories, onto which they'd heap their plunder and paddle hard, on uncertain seas, back to the mainland.

Iguana Cay, Arturo believed, constituted the most abundant fishing area of the whole Miskito Bank. And, so far, it remained his and the Ramas' secret: even Maximo, when I'd asked him to name the best sharking grounds, had cited Punta Gorda, a rocky promontory some way further south. So: given all this, I wanted to know, why did the Ramas let Arturo—a Miskito with Creole blood, hardly a natural ally—fish these gold-dust waters?

"How can they stop me?" he said, spearing into the shallows, after a darting of color. "I'm here and then I'm gone. I have an engine—not one of them has an engine. This is the way it is. There's nothing they can do."

Further on, as we came out of the lee, Arturo gave a little holler and fell to his knees. "What did I say?" He was speaking as much to himself as to me, chuckling like a happy-fed animal. As he stood up again and I came alongside I saw he'd speared a lizard of some sort. It hung limply and smelled poisoned, as bad as the hammerhead on the beach.

"It's dead," I said, meaning that it had been dead a while, surely too long to be of much use to us. "It stinks. What is it?"

Arturo looked at me sorrowfully, as if amazed all over again at my failure to learn. "Iguana."

"I thought they needed to be fresh."

"Sharks eat anything." He gripped it by the tail, lifted it off the spike, yelled across to Elias in the dugout. "Catch this!" And with one broad arc he slung the iguana nose-first, high into the sky. It flew a perfect trajectory, diving legs out toward Elias, who waited, arms wide, a good forty yards from our rocks. It was a near-flawless throw, missing Elias's lap by inches, hitting the gunwale and smacking the water, waiting there a second before coughing out bubbles and sinking into the blue. Elias dropped his line, plunged in his arm, and caught the iguana, water drooling from its open jaws.

"Keep it," Arturo shouted. "There'll be more."

At the point, where the high-tide mark was a spine of plastic debris and the sea wind felt more muscular, scurrying low through the banana trees, I came upon something far odder: a bag made from what looked like burlap, no bigger than two cupped hands, hung from a low-jutting root. It was weighted full, and was greasy to the touch; inside was a honey-colored mass.

"Shark liver," Arturo said, coming from behind, knocking it with the end of his spear.

"From the hammerhead?"

"Probably." It had been left here, some way from the carcass, to discourage rodents. Shark oil, Arturo added, setting off again across the rocks, "cures asthma, lots of illness we don't know about."

He was relishing this chance to act the guide, to work me over with his knowledge. Observing me balk at the very fact of garbage in a place this remote, he turned sensitive environmentalist. "This," he shook his head gravely, "is the modern face of paradise." He played to my weakness for shark lore, summoning wilder and ever-more-implausible stories, watching with pleasure as I gaped, incredulous. When we startled to flight a covey of leather-winged birds, big and black as ravens, and I asked him what they were, he led me away from the shore, toward the banana trees, and at every step would pick up a leaf, or a seedpod, and list its medicinal uses and aphrodisiac properties. Young coconut leaf, he said, made fine tea. Another—"bird wine"—was "medicine for the liver: when you drink it, your pee is like water."

In a clearing, he cut a sapling, long as a jousting lance, and lunged upward into the canopy of a coconut palm till three coconuts thumped to earth: hard green ovals, the size of rugby balls. He picked up each in turn, ground their points into the base of the tree trunk, then tore away the husks. "Who needs knives?" he said, taking a rock to the first, naked-whiskered nut, passing it to me, holding it up like a goblet. "Go on, drink."

This small cay, he said, had everything a man could need: palms for roofing, a type of year-round grape, even a tangled ground cover that produced whorls of cotton. The seaward edge was a shallow slant of red rock, graveled with the shells of tiny crabs, up which the ocean hissed and moaned. And at this point, growing tired, Arturo tried to cut back to the beach, but here the plantation was at its most overgrown, the banana trees choked with creepers and underbrush grown hard as wire.

"The morning's getting hotter," he muttered impatiently, as if it were somehow my fault. "We've got to get on."

▼ ▼ ▼

As we came round the point once more, back into the lee of the island, Elias was standing in the boat, waving and shouting. He wanted us back on board and was yelling at us to run. He waved an arm at the water immediately around him, barked a further flurry of indecipherable yelps, and Arturo, shouting something back, broke into a run, leaping from boulder to boulder.

The tide had risen steadily, making the way back to the beach treacherous, with few dry footings, but he moved fast and lightly, one hand against the cliff for balance, standing, finally, in the shallows on the beach, hauling on the anchor rope. I was slower, and less sure, and by the time I reached the beach Arturo was already aboard and Elias had restarted the engine.

We anchored mid-bay, fifty yards offshore, the westerly gradually building, pushing us hard against the anchor, making the lines sing. The bait lines were nylon, with lead sinkers, with a single-barbed hook skewered through the pale jelly flesh of two prawns. Elias and Arturo lassoed theirs out effortlessly, and it took me a little while longer to learn this, how to have the line flying weightless through the palm, how to draw it back through the water at that certain depth, how to strike—knowingly, not too fast—and, just as crucial, how to play the part of the gnarled sea dog, impassive, none too easily impressed, unchanging as the sun.

For ten, fifteen minutes, we hooked fish as fast as we could get the lines out. Even I, the novice, whom Elias and Arturo eyed uncertainly, could do no wrong; I'd strike too early, or not at all, and still would haul up catch: red snapper, whitejack, hammering their tails in the oily slop about our ankles. The snapper, Arturo said, playing in another, just feet from the boat,

was Jesus' fish, the one that fed the five thousand, and still bore
his fingerprints: twin dark smudges, either side of the spine,
just behind the dorsal fin. And he clasped the fish between flat
palms, its gills still flexing, looked hard into its bleak ball-
bearing eyes, and spat into its oval pout.

"That's good luck." He winked and tossed the snapper,
mouthing furiously, into the squirming hull.

When I was a kid," he said later—soaked through but beaming, big hands paying back the line as delicately as a seamstress,
having just landed the biggest snapper so far—"all the creeks in
Bluefields, the whole lagoon, all down this coast, all were
infested with sharks. You couldn't swim nowhere. But then, in
the fifties and sixties, they started to buy them for their fins and
meat and the sharks started to get wild, to disappear."

"You mean the sharks somehow knew what was happening?"
We'd both hauled in and were just sitting there, growing stiff on
our haunches, rocking in the swell, the sea knocking hollow
against the hull. "They understood?"

Arturo held up a finger. "In certain ways," he said, turning to
check on Elias's line, then testing mine too, "they are smart animals. They have a way to survive just like we do. Whenever you
kill the animal, and it bleeds, it never goes to that place again."

"But here?" He'd returned to this cay many times: why had
the sharks not yet worked this out?

"Some places"—he tapped a finger against his nose—"they
will always come back to." Iguana Cay, with its unique confluence of marine life, the way the undersea shelf rose up here,
delivering abundance and variety on a scale unknown anywhere
else along the Miskito Coast, would always prove irresistible. He

leaned forward. "Let me tell you something. Listen to this, then tell me what you think."

He talked, keeping his line taut. "A few months ago, I was out here, in this very spot, with Elias." He nudged Elias with his mahogany fish club; Elias, looking down, smiled. Arturo was baiting up again as he spoke, and as he stood to cast his line I noticed dark movement beneath the surface, midway between us and the shore, working transverse, closing on us.

"Arturo," I said, wanting him to look too, but he was warming to his story, and would not be diverted.

"So we were here, four in the morning, we'd spent the night on the cay. Very dark, the moon was new." He was watching his line now, but dreamily, only half focused. "And all of a sudden, after an hour of nothing, we hook a shark of a hundred and fifty pounds. Big enough, I tell you, but not a monster. I've got it on the rope, it's hooked well and good, and it fights a big fight. I'm on my knees, Elias is keeping the boat steady. . . ."

At the edge of my vision I saw the dark shape again, and this time nearer the beach; Elias, whose line was paid out that way, jolted upright and started round. Arturo, oblivious, talked on.

"Did you see that, Arturo?" I blurted.

Arturo stopped still, let his line hang loose in his hands. "What?"

"A big fish. Shark?" I pointed to where I'd seen the movement, but now there was nothing; now I was seeing shadows everywhere, the surface of the water splintered into sky, beach, red cliff, its own deep turquoise.

"Shark?" Arturo repeated, looking across my head to Elias. "Shark?"

Elias nodded. *"Creo, pero no estoy seguro.* I'm not sure."

"Muy bien," Arturo said, softening. "So we haul in. We've got

enough bait." There was a sudden shimmy on his line, a guitar-string quiver, but he continued at the same pace, hand over hand, and started where he'd left off, playing out the story as he wound in his line: unhurried, deliberate, conscious.

"So, after fifteen minutes, perhaps twenty," he went on, "I'm getting the shark close to the boat. I can see him down there, diving and fighting, but I know he's getting tired. I've got the rope, I'm sitting down, he's getting closer and closer. And then—" He clapped his hands together, opened his palms to the sky; his voice rose, rapturous. "Then the water gets BIG, I can't see what's happening, everything goes white and churned up and when it calms down the line's gone slack." He paused. Elias was motionless, turned toward Arturo, his line loose over his knees, mouth open.

"So what do I do?" Arturo continued, his eyes enormous. "I can feel weight, but no movement. What's happened to this shark?" Again, that pause. "Only one way to find out: pull on the rope, hard as God allows." He grinned at Elias, who snorted into the back of his hand. "It comes up fast, oh my God too fast, and the sea turns from blue to red and at the last moment, just when I realize, just when it's too late, the whole thing is flying out of the water toward me."

"The whole shark?"

"No! Just the head! The whole rest of it was bitten off. Just the head is left on my hook, just the head flies out of the water and lands in my lap."

Elias was shaking with silent laughter. "Just the head," he repeated, in a hoarse whisper. "Just the head." He reached across, knuckled Arturo in the ribs.

At that moment, no more than ten yards ahead of us, the sea

turned to milkshake. Arturo, in the middle, jolted forward, threw an arm against the gunwale to steady himself; his bait line sprang free of the water, loosing drops all down its length. Then it snapped. No whip crack, no dramatic high note, just a tangle of soggy nylon thread, half in the boat, half out. The water, still again momentarily, broke one last time: a sharp, dark outline cut free, then disappeared into foam of its own creation, like a diver's flippers, giving one last kick.

"*Sangre de Dios,*" Arturo breathed. "Get those shark lines out."

Yet for the next half-hour, with all three lines baited with snapper, all was quiet. We said little, Arturo and Elias convinced a strike was imminent. Arturo laid his red glove over the gunwale in front of him, and from time to time touched it with reverence.

"Arturo?"

"*Sí?*"

"What happens if we hook a three-hundred, four-hundred-pound shark? What good's your glove going to be then?"

"My glove," he sighed, "is so the rope don't burn my hand. A big shark will haul the canoe round and round as he looks for deep water." He smiled, guardedly. "We're going to have to play him really hard." We'd fight it to the beach, land and kill it there; after that, somehow, we'd heave it into the dugout and make for the mainland.

Two pelicans were circling us, almost colorless against the sky, cutting low over the cay and back again, making an odd clicking sound; they moved their wings little, setting and readjusting to the warm updrafts, passing between us and the sun, maintaining their distance.

It was getting hotter: I had only a baseball cap for shade and kept shifting the peak round, trying to protect my neck. Unused to such intense direct sun, my face and neck liquid with sweat, I tried to scoop up seawater to cool me down, but at the surface it was almost blood temperature and the salt when it dried made me even thirstier. Arturo, seeing me struggle, offered coffee from his flask: "Hot is good, it cools you down." Which was fine in theory, but didn't take into account the quantity of sugar he'd stirred in; so I sipped, and thanked him, and handed it quickly back.

Arturo speared the iguana onto an extra hook, its belly splitting easily as soaked paper, a guff of bad-egg air as the innards bulged through. He threw it from the bow and it hit the water heavily, floating tail-up for a few seconds before sinking abruptly, in a cough of bubbles. He looped the line around the plank on which he sat.

"It's really going to go for that?" Here, where there was no shortage of fresh snapper and succulent whitebait?

Arturo turned, smiled. "Well, we'll see."

In my imagination, the monster I'd glimpsed out there in the shallows would have had no problem with a putrefying iguana, could indeed, if the mood struck it, have swallowed the dugout, all three of us, the outboard and gas tank, whole, with one dilation of its industrial-sized gullet.

Ever since childhood I had feared and been drawn to the ocean, its unseen depths, and when long ago had learned of *Carcharodon megalodon*, the prehistoric shark, this fear seemed nothing less than reasonable. Here was a fish whose fossilized teeth were six inches long; whose gape, face on, measured a good ten feet in diameter; whose length, nose to tail, reached well over a hundred feet. Or "reaches," rather, since it is argued that *megalodon* is no more extinct than "megamouth," a soot-colored plankton sifter unknown to science until 1976, when a fourteen-foot specimen was snagged in netting by a U.S. Navy research boat. The evidence for *megalodon's* continued existence is inconclusive, but certainly plausible: early in this century, some four-inch incisors were dredged from the bottom of the Pacific—"real" teeth, not fossils—which could not have been down there for long, since early dredging equipment was only robust enough to scrape the shallowest trench. So, I imagined, somewhere down there, beyond the tropical cays and reefs and turtle grounds, the great fish lurked still, seldom surfacing from the very deep, and only then for swift, spectacular meals: whole lines of shrimp pots, half a seal colony.

However, neither Arturo, gazing out across the water, nor Elias, lying back against the engine with his cap pulled low over his face, seemed to share any of my sense of foreboding. This was Arturo's livelihood and, over the decades, as shark had become scarcer and the price of fins had risen, he'd turned ever more wily, lying to the other fishermen when they'd pressed him for his favorite spots, setting deliberately misleading trails, dropping clues that led his rivals in the exact opposite direction from the one toward which he was headed. And as the business had changed, so had the fishermen: in the 1960s, when fins were plentiful and were off-loaded for a mere twenty-five cents a pound, they all worked together, secure in the knowledge that there was enough for everyone. Now, with fins scarcer, and fetching upwards of thirty-five dollars a pound, the fishermen operated alone, suspicious of one another, jealously protective of whatever special knowledge they had acquired, drying their catch in secret, smuggling the fins to Maximo under cover of darkness.

With the heat of the sun and the slop of machine oil and rotten water, the fish in the hull were beginning to smell; the snappers were blanching, their eyes gone puffy, tiny whorls of excreta trailing out behind. Arturo, in a low murmur that had almost sent Elias to sleep and was close to achieving the same effect on me, was reminiscing about the old days of plenty, mentioning names I'd never heard, places I'd never been.

It filled me with sadness, this downward curve in fortunes that had been his working life, this struggle to eke a living from ever-diminishing resources, but whenever I started to offer sympathy, he shook his head, stopped me with an upheld hand. Just listen, his silent gesture instructed me. Hear me out.

Suddenly, with a yelp, Elias was awake. He'd tied his line round his wrist and now, desperately, was struggling against pressure to work it free. "I've got one, I've got one," he jabbered, the line tight toward the beach. Eventually he managed to untie it and throw it loose, but the slack disappeared in an instant. He wrapped the engine rag round his hand and braced himself, the line flexing into deep water off the stern, so tight it shivered the surface.

"What is it?" I was leaning over, trying to catch its shadow. But Elias didn't seem to hear; he was focused, taking line as the fish stalled, paying out again as it cut underneath us. When it surfaced—Elias arched against it, his back bowed with the strain—it came very fast, thrashing against the side of the boat: sinewy, black, a big cobra's jaw, straining at the hook.

"Barracuda!" Elias shouted, jubilant. He ordered me to stay back, and he and Arturo wrestled it aboard. It was three or four feet long, thick as a fire hose, with a wolf's fangs and a menacing underbite. Its tail pounded our legs; its teeth snapped at the air. Arturo gripped the club, about to complete the kill, but seemed suddenly as mesmerized as I, immobile, watching the great fish slowly die. It seemed unlike anything I'd ever seen or imagined, an unholy hybrid of serpent and mile-deep sightless groper, distorted almost to humanness by its great vampire mouth.

As it lay there, sucking in ever slower, its gill leaves breezing smaller and smaller flutters, I felt my line tug once, then twice: persistent, heavyweight fumblings.

"Arturo . . . ," I said, testing the tension, unsure. "What's this? What do I do?" Strike? Leave alone?

Arturo, up in the prow, didn't answer. He was holding his line between thumb and forefinger and concentrating hard. I saw his hand clench, unclench, and he reached for the glove, forced in his fingertips and yanked it on with his teeth.

"Shark?" I said, speaking as much to myself as to him. I'd had a heavier take, then a deadweight, not what I expected it to feel like.

"Possibly." He grinned, toothy as the barracuda. "Oh, yes, just possibly." His line was running fast through his glove, slack spooling from his lap. And then again, harder this time, I felt my line go, burning my skin as it ripped away.

"Let it run!" Arturo shouted at me, still focused hard on his own. "Let it take it and tire itself out."

I tore off my cap, forced it flat into my hand as protection, but in the half-second it took to change grip I lost my last five meters of line and it sprang hard against its backstop, the plank seat, out of my hand.

"What now?"

"Take it up," Arturo said, doing the same himself, hand over hand. "It won't take long."

Mine played erratically—compliant, then brutish, sometimes almost teasing. Shark, Arturo said: we must have hit a number, all hunting, all at the same time. We'd have got three if Elias hadn't been struggling to untangle his line. I wondered about his diagnosis, though: I was no strongman, yet was able to fight it with my own hands.

Elias, in the stern, had dropped his line and was instructing me, miming the necessary actions, how much pressure I should be applying, when to tighten up and when to play it easy. He ran salt water through his hair, pasted it flat to his skull, and leaned close to me; I could feel his heat, the smell of last night's beer and frijoles.

"There!" He pointed off the stern, no more than ten yards: a pale racing of color, like a seal's back, just below the surface.

"That's it." Arturo beamed. "What did I say?" His fish was hard by the boat now, his line plumbing vertically into the sun-slanted water. I stole glances at him, realizing this might be my only lesson, but every time I did so I lost grip of my own line, letting run too much slack so that the fish dived fast the next moment and slammed hard against the gunwale. Arturo seemed able to watch both at once—checking on me, following his own weaving line as he drew it ever nearer—and when he swept his fish into the boat it was with a simple, unbroken movement.

It hit the bottom writhing: a four-foot shark with filmy cat's eyes and a tail that smashed about wildly, soaking me with fish-scaly water. The extra weight sank us perilously low and at every swell now we were shipping water. Elias grabbed the bailer; the water he slung out was dark, smeared with prawns and entrails of snapper and tubercular clots of engine oil.

"You, now," Arturo said, ignoring his own shark, which lay agasp in the hull, hook still through its bottom jaw.

"What do I do?" It felt as though it was directly below us, switching direction like a caged animal.

"It's getting tired." He leaned forward, shielded his eyes from the sun. "Bring it up. Slowly."

I could have drawn in quicker, but I could feel my muscles cramping. Arturo was right: the fish did seem to be slowing, and only once did it draw away strongly enough for the line to pull through my hand. As I brought it closer, it seemed almost to be cowering from us, pulling the line back under the hull as it stuck to the boat's shadow.

"Bring it in now," Arturo said, hands braced on the edge of the boat.

"But I can't see it."

"It's there. Lift it out."

I half stood, just enough to see where the line entered the water. The shark was there, split lengthways by our shadow, hanging motionless as if it knew exactly the way this was going. I could feel it trembling down the wire, and knew it could feel me too, both of us new to this, both anxious rookies. After all my dreams of hooking a monster, this one seemed disappointingly small, something of a consolation prize, docilely waiting.

I wrapped the line round both hands and pulled hard. The shark was heavy, and its head tilted stiffly, rucking creases across its back. It was so still, and the underside of its throat and belly was pale as linen in the sunlight just below the surface. The hook glittered as I hoisted the fish toward vertical.

"Finish it quickly," Arturo muttered. "Get it out."

But I couldn't. I leaned harder against it, my knees on the gunwale, but could bring it no further than the surface. Maneuvering it underwater, weightless, had been easy: hauling it aboard, fighting its true weight, felt impossible. The shark itself, half comatose, did nothing to help: basking in the warmth, sun on its back, bewildered and exhausted by the struggle, it was resting against me, its weight against the hook.

"Give me a hand," I said, but Arturo, anticipating, was already at my shoulder, ordering Elias to the other side of the boat.

"Come on," he said. "Now! You pull!" And he knelt in the boat, in the blood and oil and fish scales, and plunged his arms into the water. With his face almost submerged he grabbed the shark round its middle, shouted at me to lift and together we hoisted it clear of the water. "Now in the boat!" he shouted. "Quick!"

Halfway over, the shark hammered sideways, knocking me to the floor. Arturo still had a hold on its tail, but it was flailing crazily now, its jaw locked open, strips of snapper caught in its teeth. I tried to stand, but the boat was rocking and taking water and I was dizzied by the knock, so I stayed where I was, certain they were both about to land on me. The shark was corkscrewing through Arturo's grasp, like a too-big child not wanting to be dressed. Arturo trod backward and slumped into the prow and the mess of netting and, forced back by the weight of the fish, sat down heavily, the shark kicking away from him. For a second, it lay still on the bottom of the boat. Elias, looking up from bailing, hooted.

"Bastard," Arturo breathed, his chest heaving.

"How are we going to get back?" Elias said. The stern was leaking fast. Left much longer, the shark would have been able to swim free.

"Take in the anchor," Arturo snapped. We'd pull onto the beach, off-load nonessentials. "Where's my club?" He groped behind himself, through the heap of netting, scooped a hand through the hull-slop. I saw it before he did: floating near Elias's feet, half-submerged, clean and dark as a bone. I hooked it with my foot and lifted it out.

Arturo knelt in the hull between the two sharks. His, landed ten minutes earlier, had stilled; mine, startled momentarily on capture, was now beating about wildly again, one arching muscle, drumming the side of the boat. Its head was up, showing the hook and the bloodless wound through its underjaw, torn ragged by its fighting. It shouldered forward, then slid back toward the stern, and its skin against my calves was like emery paper.

"Hold it there," Arturo ordered, twisting round to get an angle on its skull. I tried to steady it round its middle, leaning my whole weight forward, but it surged and pounded. Arturo forced his knee onto its back until only its tail was moving and struck it on the snout, between the eyes; through its body I felt a shiver of electricity. Again and again he clubbed it, until and beyond the point when it was clearly dead and had ceased to even twitch. There was no blood, nothing to suggest pain, no rolling of the eyes, just a soft indent where he'd hammered it repeatedly. He closed his eyes halfway through, and when he handed back the club, his head was still bowed. He lay back in the bow, on the rubbish and bottles and netting, pulled his cap down over his eyes and folded his arms tight across his chest. His hands were shaking.

▼ ▼ ▼

We left the anchor buried in undergrowth and drained the dugout on the beach as best we could. It was after midday now, and too hot to continue fishing. Yet, just off the cay, heading for the mainland, Elias hooked another. He'd been trailing his line experimentally, using the last, most fetid snapper as bait. The shark he hauled in was bovine, almost comatose, though a good foot longer than the other two. It was a nurse shark, Arturo said—the color of the seafloor, freckled with pale spots. Arturo reached over the side and he and Elias heaved it aboard.

He shook his head, disappointed. "Not dangerous. He lives in the rocks, eats lobster, crabs." Yet, stranded at our feet, half the snapper still in its mouth, it clung on longer than the other two, its gills whispering in and out until we were almost home. Seeing it there, purblind, helpless, I wished we'd put it back, since its seal-soft fins were worthless and its meat was fatty and cloying, but Arturo wanted to show it to his neighbors' children, let them tug its fleshy whiskers and run their fingers along its milk teeth, so we wedged it in the hull. Arturo sharpened his knife on its side, flipping the blade in the sunlight, his eyes unfocused, shoulders heavy.

It was hard to imagine, having witnessed the ease of Arturo's baited-hook technique, that shark fishermen had ever practiced anything else, but in Micronesia, until midway through this century, hunters used snares woven from plant fibers. Tied like a noose, the snare was lowered from a canoe, and seashells were rattled in the water to draw the shark, which was then teased through the loop by the lure of bloody meat. It took time, this method, and patience too, since any panicky movements startled off the fish: slowly, with a steady hand, the noose was drawn over the head, and was tightened as it passed the gill slits. Maoris, who prized unchipped center teeth as earrings, perfected the method: hooks, they knew, wreaked dental mayhem.

Early hooks were of bone or wood. Hawaiian chieftains bequeathed their skeletons for the carving of hooks, although, throughout the islands, bones of great fishermen were judged equally propitious. To prepare wooden hooks, young ironwood branches were lashed into tight Us, and released only when they'd hardened into shape. And always, whatever their constituent materials, the hooks were speared with the oiliest and bloodiest bait fish. Sharks can sniff food at five hundred meters—one part mammal blood, according to researchers, in a hundred million parts water—and even their eyesight, once thought weaker than that of most fish, was, in poor light, a good ten times more sensitive than man's.

We took a different way back, a shorter route to shore, heading for the south entrance to the Bluefields lagoon. We rode with the swell, which had strengthened since we'd been fishing and now tipped us firmly back, with a sense of barely contained power. In part this change of route was of necessity, since to return northward would have meant taking the swell side-on, but in part it was because Arturo wanted to fish for prawn alongside the mangroves again, and these southern mangroves were the best.

Pelicans followed us, watching for floundering fish where the water shallowed and boiled. With each swell, each shove toward shore, the sea lost its luminous turquoise and became darker and muddier.

Arturo, up in the bow, was shouting back orders to Elias: keep straight, hard left now, that's it, steady. The shallower we got, the more opaque the water became. Arturo tried to avoid riding the waves, but at points this was impossible, and we'd crest with a great howl as the outboard reared out of the water. And then, beyond the bar, in an instant the water was deep again and I smelled the dirt of the warm land, saw once more the grackles overhead above the forest and felt relieved, more than I'd ever guessed I'd feel, to be heading for the safety of streets and buildings.

Through the lagoon mouth, into the lagoon itself: the water was a mile wide here, and with forest so brightly green the color looked painted on. Above the canopy towered spikes, like out-size telegraph poles—all that remained of the coconut palms that had survived the hurricane, a decade earlier.

"Everything you see," Arturo said, indicating the new forest, the way it crowded the water's edge, "all of it has pushed up since the big storm."

"Even the mangroves?" They seemed so sturdy, immovable, their claw roots thick as a man's legs.

"When the hurricane came," he answered, turning back to face the front, "everything went down. Only five houses in Bluefields remained standing. And the forest—all that was destroyed. From the town you could see straight out to sea—no roofs or walls stood in your way."

Ahead I noticed three dories, smaller than ours, struggling under tarpaulin sails. They scarcely seemed to be moving at all, and their sails sagged motionless.

I watched all this half-dreaming, aware that soon I'd be moving on, tracking the bull sharks south, to the San Juan River, and beyond. I wanted Arturo to join me—had wanted this, in fact, ever since he'd said he had family there. San Juan del Norte, the settlement at the river mouth, was by all accounts a pirate town, not much different now than it had been two and a half centuries before, and I figured Arturo could ease my way. He'd intimated more than once that he'd been planning just this trip for a few years now, but the opportunity had never arisen. I suspected something else: a wound, some rift let fester. As we closed on the dories I asked again. How about it, I said, casually as I could manage, why not? Here's the chance you never had. He knew I'd help with the travel—that much we'd discussed already.

He turned back to face me, smiled as if he hadn't heard. "See those boats?" He hooked a thumb across the bow. "Rama Indians."

They looked a scanty lot, in tattered clothing, sitting two to a canoe. They stopped their paddling to watch us approach.

"Morning," Arturo called out, in English. Elias cut the engine and we coasted level. One of the Indians reached out a hand to grab our boat; the dories slid together, swollen timbers creaking. Two of their boats were empty, but in the furthest, a slug-fit in the hull, was a considerable-sized shark, half on its side, its long-muscled tail fin dragging in the water. It was the color of clay shot with lead, and its mouth, ripped sideways by the hook, was clamped shut: ugly, pitiable, like a prizefighter being stretchered from the ring. In a final show of disrespect they'd heaped their netting and old bait on top, and sat with their feet up on its hide.

"Some shark," Arturo said, kneeling up to see better, his eyes wide. "Where did you catch it?"

They glanced from one to another, suddenly fidgety. "Out there," one said.

Arturo grinned. "Out where?" He scanned their faces, acting blithe, as if it was all a big joke.

"To sea." This was the first man talking, the one who'd pulled us alongside. He rested his jaw in his hand.

"To sea—that so? We've been out all morning. Never saw you all." Arturo was sizing up the big shark, muttering to himself. No one answered him; I could sense them steal glances our way, comparing the catches.

"Iguana Cay? You been out there?" The Rama was smiling as he said this, chewing something in his cheek.

"No, no," said Arturo, too quickly, but they were all eyeing him now, hands on their paddles, laid flat across their dugouts. "What you going to do with the shark?" he added, flustered. "Take it to Maximo?"

"Take it home first." The Rama laughed and was echoed by the rest: mouthfuls of broken teeth, blackened, holed, mostly missing. He picked up his paddle and dug the surface. "Show the ladies."

I asked Arturo why he'd lied, especially since, by his own admittance, the Rama well knew he fished their cay, but he did not answer. We rode the hour back in silence, and not until we reached the wet mud landing at his house, and were unloading the sharks in front of the children, did I try him again.

"How long," I began, as we dragged the dugout from the water, into the same mud furrow from which it came. "How long's the weather going to last? How long will it be good for?"

He straightened, leaving mud prints on the gunwale. "Have fun today? Consider yourself a shark fisherman now?" Elias, fuel tank in one hand, gas line in the other, was mumbling good-bye, ignoring Arturo.

"Yes," I said, to them both. Elias turned to go. "I'm off too,"

I said to Arturo. "Perhaps tomorrow. As soon as I work out how to get to San Juan del Norte." He was leaning over the sharks, measuring them in hand spans. I spoke to his back. "And you, Arturo? You coming?"

"Ah," he said. "The question." He laid a hand on my shoulder, pushed us out of the sun, under an overhang. He screwed up his eyes, roused phlegm in his throat, spat noisily at a garbage pail. "You don't worry about me. I'll be there."

6

A hundred and fifty years ago, San Juan del Norte was a great port in the making, at the strategic mouth of a river that was destined, so the world believed, to become the much-heralded Pan-American canal, an engineering work of fantastic ambition that would link, for the first time, the Atlantic with the Pacific. Such a canal, it was thought, would transform Nicaragua from a peasant economy into a crucial world power. Hardly surprising, then, that the port at the river mouth became the focus for competing strains of colonial greed.

In 1848, the British foreign minister Lord Palmerston ordered its seizure, arguing that it belonged to his ally the Miskito king, despite the fact that the nearest Miskito Indian lived in Bluefields, sixty miles to the north. The British forces raised the Miskito flag, a peculiar confection thrown together for the occasion, and, after being routed, and gaining the town again, signed an armistice: San Juan del Norte—rechristened Grey-town, after the governor of Jamaica—would remain British.

The British could not have stepped in at a more propitious time. That year, prospectors struck gold in California and U.S. East Coasters, unwilling to hazard the long trek overland, sailed for Greytown from ports all up the seaboard, taking passage from there up the San Juan, across Lake Nicaragua, then by coach over the narrow ribbon of land to the Pacific, and finally north to San Francisco. Greytown, the necessary staging post, boomed: American citizens, foreseeing many golden years to come, began to settle; an American steamship company built offices; dance halls, billiard clubs, gambling parlors, and whore-houses were all fashioned from the native mahogany and cedar; fancy ladies in crinolines and bustiers took ship from New Orleans.

America, never able to understand how it had lost such vital hegemony, raised official complaint, argued continually, once even bombarded British warships at anchor, but never once suc-ceeded in wresting it from the British. U.S. envoy Ephraim G. Squier visited in 1849, and his distaste for the hierarchy was nakedly undiplomatic. "The thing is too absurd to be contin-ued," he wrote, arguing for American stewardship. Greytown possessed "low, monotonous scenery" and a "limited stock of amusements"; the ragbag of races—Europeans, Indians, blacks, mestizos—"all mingle together with the utmost freedom," enjoying "general drunkenness and indiscriminate licentious-ness." There was even a scorpion whose sting "causes the tongue to swell so as to render utterance difficult, or impossible," and a flea that laid its eggs under the skin of unfortunates' feet. There were man-eating alligators, and, he added, for the first time stat-ing simple fact, the harbor was "infested by sharks."

Those less politically jaundiced saw it differently. Thomas Belt, an English naturalist passing through in 1868, though half in love with the plentiful white cranes, jacana, toucans, and tanagers, also found time to praise the "neat, white-painted houses," the soft-grassed streets and squares: it was, he later remembered, "one of the neatest tropical towns I have ever visited."

Business at the quayside was continuous, with schooners, late into the evening, loading, in Squier's words, "manufactured goods of every description"—cooking pots, spices, weaponry, axes, rum—in return for what the land still possessed in abundance—coffee, indigo, sugar, rubber, mahogany, turtle shell. But it was the animal life that most astonished Belt: alligators that "bellowed like a bull," that buried themselves in mud to ambush wild pig, that brought down men and horses with equal ease; and the freshwater sharks that patrolled the turbid waters of the river mouth (and that, four years later, accounted for the lives of seven capsized canal surveyors, eager Americans looking to carve a way west through this continent).

For decades, the canal appeared a certainty: up the San Juan, where English pirates had foraged in the seventeenth century, where Horatio Nelson had sailed a century later, now would pass the trade of all the Americas, even the world: Louis-Napoléon, writing in 1846, believed Nicaragua would become "better than Constantinople, the necessary route of the great commerce of the world," and that it was "destined to attain an extraordinary degree of prosperity and grandeur." There were problems—a succession of rapids that, in places, lowered the draft to barely a foot, and the raising of the $270 million that the project would consume—but against the potential benefits, these were felt to be merely inconvenient trifles.

Powering it all onward was American business; the Nicaraguan government, well able to imagine the consequent bonanza, allowed itself to be swept along. When a top-level U.S. commission finally, in 1876, chose the San Juan route over all other Central American possibilities, and this was ratified a year later by the International Canal Congress in Paris, the canal decision looked irrevocable. From then until the end of the century a succession of surveying teams would jostle alongside the merchants and whores and export clerks of old Greytown, setting off every day into the jungle with their caravans of porters and equipment, calculating everything precisely: the exact siting of the six necessary locks, how deep and far the lower-section cutting would run, where to build the dam.

That the canal was, in the end, cut through Panama was most commonly blamed on a set of Nicaraguan postage stamps depicting the country's volcanoes. The Panamanian delegation lobbied furiously: how could a country pocked with volcanoes, it demanded, possibly be safe for world trade? The Americans, long set on Nicaragua, could find no counterargument and, on 2 June 1902, authorized construction of the first stage of a canal through Panama. For Greytown, the long slide into history had begun.

Few photographs remain of Greytown at its peak. A home-printed history I unearthed in an old man's backyard showed only snapshots, gone blotchy with dampness and time: a three-story warehouse, U.S. flag hoisted; sleek piebald mares tethered outside a great Southern mansion; European women carrying parasols, lost in conversation; men in white linen three-pieces

being taxied down wide boulevards in shady landaus. . . . "Quite
some place," as I was regularly reminded. By 1970, the date of
the last photograph, the same broad-stooped mansions had
become broken-windowed and roofed only scantily, with ill-
fitting strips of corrugated iron. The manicured grass walkways
had turned to dust and the people that remained—two hundred,
if that—now had little but nostalgia to sustain them. Finally, in
the mid-1980s, Sandinista soldiers, suspecting the town of har-
boring Contra guerrillas, torched what few buildings still stood.

The new settlement—San Juan del Norte once more—was
not built until the civil war had ended, at the beginning of the
1990s, and then at some distance from the old, a fifteen-minute
boat ride through the mangrove shallows, far enough away, they
figured, to wipe clean and start anew. Jungle had reclaimed the
land where Greytown stood, and not even the water onto which
it gave remained the same. Silt had changed the shape of the
estuary and further narrowed the bar mouth: what had once been
Central America's most prized natural harbor was now hazarded
by only the most experienced of fishermen, in the subtlest of
craft, on the calmest of days.

In all this change, there remained only two constants: the
rainfall—plentiful enough down the entire Atlantic coast but, at
San Juan del Norte, a formidable 260 inches a year, more than
anywhere else in Central America—and the sharks, which
despite decades of exploitation in the lake, two hundred kilometers upriver, here at the mouth still sustained a considerable
presence. And it was not just at the bar, with its ranks of hump-
backed breakers and its daily changing riptides, where they lay
at wait, but up unflustered side waters too: bull sharks can laze,
and comfortably attack, in three feet of water, and when one day

during a brief rain break I mentioned to the mayor that I quite fancied taking a dip in the river that eased past the new settlement, he wagged a finger in my face and said, with no hint of a smile, "Not while I'm mayor, you won't."

It took me well over a week to reach San Juan del Norte, a long time to cover sixty miles. Most direct, and quickest, would have been by sea, but boat services between Bluefields and the Costa Rican border had long since ceased to be regular. At the jetty I was given conflicting information: this old hulk might be able to drop me off; another, bound for Puerto Limón in Costa Rica, might be loading supplies for the San Juan. But nothing concrete materialized and so, after two days of such false leads, I decided to head inland.

I could, in theory, have walked the beach—though near-unpopulated, battered by wind and rain and driving black sand, it was at least straight; provided I rose with the sun on my left, and kept going, I should eventually make it to the river mouth. But I didn't want to chance it alone, and could find no one prepared to act as guide. Again, all those I approached asked the same thing: why San Juan del Norte? If I really wanted to see it, they joked, I'd arrived at least a century too late.

Inland meant a dawn boat up the Río Escondido to Rama, then ten hours by American school bus along broken roads to the capital, Managua. Leaving here, two mornings later, on the Pan-American highway heading south, I was shocked again by the dilapidation: low-rise squalor, built cheaply as possible amid the dead dogs and diesel slicks, no one trusting much to nature anymore since 23 December 1972, when the earthquake—El

Desastre—had torn down every art deco movie house, ice-cream parlor, and hotel, gobbling up whole streets and factory complexes, killing twenty thousand and unhousing five times that, creating an overnight repair bill of $772 million.

At the Costa Rican border, for four hours, our bus was searched minutely, every bag rifled through, the officers moving with a painful, deliberate slowness so that it was past midnight by the time we crawled into San José. And here, again, a long wait: three days this time, for a seat on an eight-man Cessna down to the Atlantic Coast: Barra del Colorado, the Costa Rican side of the San Juan delta.

Every Costa Rican, those few days, had asked the same: Why my interest in Nicaragua? Why, especially, the Atlantic Coast and the Río San Juan? "You do realize," they'd say, "that Nicaraguans live on the river?" "So?" "They're robbers. And murderers. And kidnappers." At Barra, where during breaks in the rain you could almost see clear to Nicaragua, the same suspicions persisted. "We're peaceful this side, man," an old Creole, leading two goats across the airstrip, stopped to tell me. "Nicaraguans want to fight. Dey drink rum and get tricky. Not here, man, not in Costa Rica."

And all that day I waited, while the rain, this "dry" season, swept off the ocean every half hour, filling track ruts, sluicing brilliant off the iron roofs. Fishermen, with an eye for an easy dollar, began offering me rides. "A hundred and fifty bucks to San Juan del Norte." Why so much? "Twenty gallons of gas," they'd say, straight-faced, "and gas is expensive."

So, in the end, worn down, near dusk, I took the best offer: fifty dollars, to a man going most of the way anyway, who accepted the notes with bright eyes and a shaky hand and who tillered slowly for two hours, in deferential silence, as the forest turned to night. And when he dropped me off, watching me scramble ashore in absolute blackness, he said, raising a hand, smiling for the first time, "Have a good time, *Inglés*. This place is a shithole."

Dawn, after a night of rain, revealed a town of some forty houses, many half-built, lacking roofs or whole walls. Most were square, two-room boxes, on stilts, made of timber dragged from the forest that backed the town. On the other side ran the Río Indio, a hundred yards wide, so full that at points along the town's edge it was overlapping the bank, causing men to haul their canoes yet further onto land. Two long concrete paths served as streets, and up these I walked slowly, sensing myself the object of some curiosity: old men watched from darkened rooms, waving back cautiously; cows, lying between houses, turned their heads to see me pass, jaws working on automatic, tongues afroth.

At the far end, the houses gave way to jungle again: just a few last fresh-cut stumps, still shiny with resin bleed, then the concrete ended and the path disappeared into tangled bush. Debris was scattered throughout: tin cans in the remains of a fire, bottles smashed in the grass, a mound of Cerveza Imperial empties—Costa Rica's national beer, clearly the town's major import. Between the rubbish and the jungle and the houses was barely grassed mud, the color of ground coffee, pecked with dog prints and chicken shit.

I walked back along the water's edge, past upturned dugouts tethered to half-drowned trees. Exactly halfway I came to a large, open-sided shed. Underneath were three outboard engines— shiny, 80hp Yamahas—and a twenty-five-foot fiberglass hull, up on blocks as if in midconstruction. With the drizzle firming up to rain again, I stepped under cover, onto a carpet of sawdust. Netting was heaped on two gasoline drums; there were fluorescent buoys, flag markers, a jumble of oilskins. But I was most intrigued by the machinery: these engines were a few thousand dollars apiece, unlikely money in a place this down-at-heel. The metal was cool to the touch, dewy with wet.

"What are you doing?"

I started round. At the far edge of the shelter, under loops of netting, was a low-slung hammock. An arm was signaling in my direction.

"Me?" I said, though there was no one else. Into the silence came the noise of the other man's breathing. I moved a step closer, till I could just make out his outline, heavy in the hammock. "I've just arrived," I added. "What are you doing?"

"Waiting." He swung a leg out, lifted his bulk to sitting. Under the hammock were six or seven Imperial empties, hand-crushed. He held another can in his fist.

"Waiting?" The dawn light on the river behind him threw his features into shadow. "What for?"

"To go to sea."

"What's the problem?" Here were boats, engines, gasoline.

He snorted, shook his head, looked me up and down. "Wind. Waves. There's a big sea out there."

"Today? It's not too bad today." Which was true: after the rain the trees were still. I could even catch birdsong, from far across the forest. He raised his eyebrows, looked away.

"When did you last go out?" I asked him.

"A month, maybe more."

"And when will you next go out?"

"Who knows?" He drew up his shoulders, thrust out his bottom lip, squinted into his beer can. He tipped back his head, emptied the last dregs down his throat.

"Drink?" he said.

Arturo was not here, and the whole of that first day, as I cautiously wandered the town, attempting conversation, I tried to find news of his family. The women were friendlier than the men, asking why I'd come, where I'd been, what I planned. The men would stand in twos or threes, or lie back in their rockers on their porches, and nod surly acknowledgment: it was always I, the newcomer, who was forced to introduce myself, never they who approached me. To my questions about Arturo, and my sketchy description of him and what I guessed his two sons to look like, I received the blankest, most bewildered looks.

Only at the end of the day, as I sat alone on an upturned dugout, staring out across the river, did an old woman, washing clothes, suggest I try the coconut plantation. Many of those who worked the plantation, on the far side of the Indio, had grown up in old Greytown, she said, before it was razed by the Sandinistas. They, unlike the immigrants who largely comprised the new settlement, would know all the families and would be able, if anyone could, to locate Arturo's sons.

So the next morning, as the township was waking, I found a boatman who could take me, and for the next hour we paddled upstream, hugging the bank, the dugout slipping silently through the dark water. Traveling like this, on the smooth river, we could have been far inland, on some quiet jungle tributary. Only a faint radio hiss, of breakers on the Atlantic shore, served as reminder that the coconut plantation beside us occupied only the narrowest strip between river and ocean, and though we couldn't see it, it was never out of earshot, and I could taste the salt on my lips and hands. Egrets and broad-winged eagles startled from the canopy as we passed, arching over the river, settling in treetops on the far bank. Then, suddenly, coming from behind, gunning past us, leaving the dugout rocking in its wake, powered a fiberglass dory, nose planing high above the water. Its driver stood in the stern, one arm on the outboard tiller, staring straight ahead.

"Fisherman," my boatman said, shaking his head. We both watched him go, me wondering where he was going, hammering through the jungle at such speed, burning all that expensive gasoline, but, more than this, how fishermen stranded on land for such long periods could ever—legally—make this kind of money. He passed, the waters behind him stilled again, he disappeared into a long bend. The howl of his engine receded to echoes, then nothing.

The entrance to the plantation was a shallow-sloping mudbank, and here, for the first time, the undergrowth had been cleared and I could see some distance under the dark plantation canopy. The boatman paddled till the prow wedged the mud, and motioned me to jump out: he was going back. I sank to my ankles, struggled up tractor ruts to harder ground, and when I looked back, the canoe was already gone, taken by the current.

The plantation was almost deserted. It was mostly cleared at this point, with well-spaced coconut palms, but further off to each side untouched scrub encroached again. At the base of a nearby tree a Creole was husking nuts. He'd driven a steel-capped stake into the sandy earth and was working from a mound of green coconuts, taking one at a time, driving each onto the stake till the husk cracked and he could tear it off with his hands. He worked hard and rhythmically, one every seven or eight seconds, building a heap like cannonballs, each still hairy with husk whiskers. He was barefoot, with trousers rolled to the knee, and shirtless: sweat ran from his back and chest, darkening his waistband. He was working with such rhythm, such natural choreography, that I would have thought it noble, had I not been later told how little he earned: fifty dollars a month, at best.

I made to move on, but he noticed me and stood straight, a coconut weighed in his palm. He grinned, nodded nervously.

"Hard work," I said, in English. "How's it going?"

"No, not so hard," he laughed, in rich, inflected Creole. "As long as dere is coconut, I can do it. I like de work."

I moved closer to him, feeling uncomfortably like visiting royalty. "You like it? It looks very tough to me."

He looked at me gravely, shook his head. "Oh, no, sah. It's good work. It give you power. In de mornin when I wake up I feel straang."

I gave him my hand, intending straightforward friendliness, sensing he saw me perhaps as some kind of management spy. Where was everybody? I asked quickly. Was he the only one around? He frowned, pointed further on, to a couple of tumbledown shacks, and the break in the trees that gave on to open sky.

To my back, as I turned to go, he said, "And de pay is good. You work hard, you get de money. Oh, yes, I's happy enough. You can tell them that."

At the huts, with a view across low, coarse beach scrub to the ocean, there was a cluster of people in poor clothing, motionless in the shade, and a man and a woman, dressed more expensively, standing slightly apart, he with a briefcase, she with a clipboard. White drug bottles stood on a table between them. The woman picked one up.

"One a day," she said, looking at the label, then at the woman at her side. "You, Juanita, you've got fourteen children. You don't want any more, do you? Use these."

She was speaking broken Spanish, using the simplest diction, as if to a child. As I moved closer, the man with her lowered himself wearily onto a bench in the corner, laid his briefcase across his knees.

"It's true," he added, flipping the catches. "You're not going for the record, are you?" He laughed to himself, then noticed me watching. "You looking for someone?"

Everyone turned. I tried to keep it simple. The people here on the plantation were said to know everyone, all the families, the whole history of the place. I was after Arturo Ramirez, I said, a Bluefields shark fisherman.

"Well then you need Thomas," he said. "This is my plantation. Thomas has been here longer than anyone. Come, let's walk."

As with most other landowners, he'd spent the Sandinista years in exile. Now, having returned, he was building a house on the beach. "Wind power!" he shouted above the whip of the sea. "That is one thing we are guaranteed never to run out of!"

Restarting the coconut plantation was not, however, proving straightforward. He'd requested an army post, he explained, in the hope of intercepting most of the washed-up cocaine before it reached his workers. This had succeeded, but at a cost. Now it was the soldiers who collected the drugs, who themselves were selling at least half, and who were sliding visibly into addiction.

▼ ▼ ▼

Thomas, when we found him, was deep in the plantation, talking to a man on an ancient tractor. The plantation owner left me, explaining he had to find his builders, and I waited for Thomas, clearly some kind of foreman, to finish his orders. He greeted me with a handshake—long fingers that, despite his age, felt strong as wood. He was Creole, the color of domino blacks, and the whites of his eyes were red from the sun and the salt.

"Arturo?" he said, sucking in air so that his lips flapped inward over toothless gums. "Arturo from Bluefields, you say?"

I nodded. Thomas rolled his head, pressed fingers to his brow. "I was there seven years of the war. I know the fishermen." He opened his mouth, and the breeze shimmied his lips. "But Arturo?"

I described him as best I could, his squat muscularity, his fondness for brown slacks, in particular that flying-buttress nose, his defining feature. Thomas shook his head. "Arturo," he repeated. "I'm getting old. I don't remember so well no more."

"Perhaps," it struck me, "he was in the jungle at the time, fighting. You might have run into him there?"

Thomas laughed. "Oh no. You know how old I am? Seventy years. They wouldn't have wanted me fighting." And, forgetting for a moment the reason we were talking, the reason he was being asked to dredge up his past, he took my elbow and said, "Let me tell you how much fighting I did in the war. I was here, working even then on the plantation, and at five o'clock in the evening the soldiers come. They tie me up like a pig, leave me on the ground. At nine o'clock they carry me to old Greytown. Five days I'm in jail and then they take me and some other men in a helicopter. All the way as we flew up the river there was a young boy with a rifle pointing at my head. He kept saying, 'I feel like a little killing today.' That was the end, I was sure of it."

We looked at each other in silence—he smiling benignly, as if too old and wise for hatred, I feeling far more uncertain, shocked more than anything by the everyday nature of his story: one man's horror, uniquely terrible, yet, in this country, also perfectly ordinary. "That's, that's," I heard myself saying, "an awful story."

He fanned out his hands, an evangelist's gesture. "Yes"— he grinned—"but look at me now. I'm back where I started, the war has ended, I'm old and most of my family is still alive." He had a scar down his forearm, ridged and worm-shiny. "Well," he said, setting off for the cleared center of the plantation, "there's work to do. We walk together?"

At his side, approaching the huts again, I remembered Arturo's sons: Thomas would surely know them, even if Arturo himself had slipped from memory.

"Two brothers?" he said, standing at the edge of the sunlight, one foot in the tractor ruts. "There are two brothers here, two fishermen."

"They live here? On the plantation?"

"No, in San Juan."

"You know them?"

"One, yes." His previous warmth had gone.

"His name?"

"Lloyd. Big man."

"Is there a problem? With them, I mean?"

"Those fishermen. Be careful with them." He had his hand on his jaw, half-covering his mouth. "They are young men, head-strong. I can't explain. You'll see."

▼ ▼ ▼

I stayed with Horacio, an eighty-year-old Creole, who'd set himself up, in this place of zero tourism, as the town's hotelier. He had three rooms, and welcomed me eagerly, beating dust off the mattress, explaining how I must never open the mosquito window screen, nor use too much water—since it was he who had to hand-pump it from the well—nor pilfer from his supplies of rice and sugar, whose levels he'd check each evening.

With no electricity, he went to bed early and rose at dawn, warbling Negro spirituals as he clattered about the kitchen till I too was forced from my bed. His accent was exaggerated almost to the point of parody, and he spoke Spanish with the same eccentric inflections that colored his Creole patois. Much of the time he talked to himself, and I could hear him making himself laugh, clapping when he reached his punch line, giving girlish, high-pitched titters. "I'm in de mood for dancin," he'd croon most mornings, slow-waltzing his large enamel mug full of instant Presto coffee across the boards. "I'm in de mood for lurve."

Horacio was born in Greytown at the end of World War I and, until the Sandinista revolution, had traveled little, working first on the dredge for the canal prospectors, then as a pilot, guiding traders over the treacherous bar. Come the destruction of Greytown, he, like most others, had fled to Costa Rica, returning as soon as the war was over. Costa Rica, he held, was "a dangerous place to live right now. Too much badness—violating and killing and smoking of drugs." He was unrepentantly reactionary: the young knew nothing, would not listen. To counter this, he talked constantly, and on afternoons when the rain came down I'd encourage these reminiscences, while at the same time struggling to unravel meaning, so skewed and folksy was his delivery. "Horacio," I'd say, "that's a great story. Could you tell it again?"

He was a fine-looking man, almost aristocratic. With age, his face had not collapsed, but become more angular, skin stretched tight over his forehead and cheekbones. He wore plastic brogues without laces and brown flannel pants that I never once saw him wash. Though skinny, he had a wiry strength, and his eyes did not yet seem an old man's eyes, the whites not yet turned to milky coffee—all of which he credited to his daily slug of shark liver oil. "It's good for the asthma, good for the cold," he'd say, taking down a jar of syrup the color of sunflower oil. "Keeps me young."

In early middle age, after "Hitler war," with the canal prospectors finally gone, Horacio, like most other men, turned to shark fishing. He'd worked with his brother, laying lines from the beach through the night, and one record morning they arrived at the shore to find a shark on every single line: fifty fish, which it took them three days to skin and bleed of oil. Because there was such abundance, the dealers in Bluefields and San Carlos could dictate the prices, and took only what the market wanted: fins, hides, liver. Hides were sold to shoemakers, and each fisherman had racks of sharkskin pumps: slip-ons, lace-ups, shufflers. The carcasses they buried in the sand. "Back then"— Horacio shook his head—"nobody used the meat."

They fished from dugouts, too, but this was less straight-forward. Sharking in the delta was easy enough, but to get to sea meant braving the bar, its rip currents and shallow-backed breakers, and the certain patrolling sharks. Horacio spoke wistfully of these years, as if the danger was precisely what had made them significant and memorable. As a boy, he'd once stood on the beach and watched the boat his father was piloting turn turtle in the surf and the white-skinned captain disappear with a crazy thrashing. Thirty years earlier, his grandfather, skipper of a shallow-draft freighter—an "iron boat"—that shipped men and cargo between Granada, on the lake, and Bluefields, on the coast, had capsized in the exact same spot, midway through the channel. "Out of thirty-three person, three get saved." Horacio rolled his eyes. "My mother's father, Richard Brown, and Johnny Chambers." The clue to his own longevity, he believed, was divine intervention. "No shark ever touch me. Two times I went down to the bottom of that bar, two times my boat capsized, and no shark touch me. It is the history of my life—I am a lucky man."

With age had come an unswervable certainty. "No young boy going to tell me how to handle my boat in this bar mouth," he'd say, meaning the fishermen. Though a good fifty years older than most of them, he possessed what they, with their big outboards, derided: technique. As a pilot, he'd worked for three different shipping companies, and always with just "paddle and pole," and always alone. He could tell the depth of the water on the bar, he claimed, by lying flat on the sand spit and calculating the height of the surf. The bar had silted up considerably over the decades, but back then it reached thirteen or fourteen feet deep in the center channel, and it was through here that Horacio would lead the nervous freighters and schooners. Incoming ships would anchor offshore and sound their klaxons for him to come; those heading downriver would disembark and seek him out, pay him to lead through first. Several times, he said, he'd capsized while piloting. "But then I just fight the boat as quick as I can and turn it back over."

Throughout this speech, unprompted, came his distaste for

the younger fishermen, whom he knew I was interested in. Most hurtful of all, it seemed, was their ignoring of him—"These young boys they don't speak with me"—though this he presented as their loss, and not something which he let trouble him much personally. He saw them as foolish and headstrong, and scorned their belief that all that was needed to beat the bar was a fiberglass dory and a large outboard. "They say they don't need to be careful because their boats can jump the waves, but what happens when the engine breaks down?" They didn't, in short, heed his advice and would, he felt, come badly undone. "Plenty of them don't work with God's spirit; they believe in their own strength, in just what they know. This is not enough. You can't do anything without God's will. That swell, that riptide, even them sharks—that's God's power."

At the boat shed, next day, midmorning, I found the fishermen: ten or more, most at work on the raw fiberglass of a new launch, or *panga*, three of them playing poker on an upturned chest, each with a can of Imperial. It had rained steadily all night and the river was the highest I'd seen it: backwashing up the muddy boat ramp, tugging at tethered canoes all along the village edge, carrying with it uprooted trees and tangled nests of vegetation. The fishermen barely noticed my arrival: a couple looked up, nodded slowly, then bent to their work again.

I attempted a casual opener, judging it best to approach slowly. I moved near the hull, which stood on blocks, upsidedown. The fishermen were hammering away with chisels at the fiberglass skin—uneven, bubbled, near translucent—splintering and sanding, working in silence.

"Building a new one?"

They stopped, looked up. A large man, his paintbrush dripping resin, said, "You looking for Lloyd?"

I laughed, astonished, then, seeing him begin to smile, nodded, glimpsing myself suddenly through all their eyes: white man in the tropics, sleeves rolled down against the sun, sweating even in the shade, my questions to Thomas no doubt already passed on round the whole village, my every movement debated and analyzed.

"Well," he said, passing the paintbrush to the man beside him. "Lloyd is me. What do you want?" He gripped my hand and shook it hard, as if it were some piece of salt-seized fishing equipment, needing to be loosened off. He was broader, fatter than Arturo, his neck hung with gold chains, a look-alike Rolex ostentatiously loose on his wrist.

"Unnh," I groaned, wrestling my hand free. He smiled as I massaged my knuckles, then landed a hand on my shoulder.

"Come," he said, propelling me forward. "We can talk outside."

He held me close, and I smelled aftershave on him, an oversweet eau de cologne mixed with sweat and alcohol. In one hand he carried a clip of Costa Rica colones, which he fingered continually. His mouth was full of gold, the typical Nicaraguan dental job, each incisor framed in metal. When I mentioned Arturo he withdrew his arm, fell silent.

"It sounded," I suggested, "as if he was going to come here, to San Juan del Norte. He didn't say when, but soon, I'd guess."

"No, no." Lloyd began walking again. "I don't think so. You know when I last saw him? Nineteen eighty-five. I was just a kid, fighting the Sandinista, and when I come back home my mother tells us he's gone. Since then, nothing."

"And your brother?"

"Costa Rica," he said, with a toss of his head.

"What about your mother?"

"San Carlos." The settlement at the mouth of Lake Nicaragua, where the San Juan began its long run east to the Atlantic.

I persevered, explaining that I'd fished with Arturo off Bluefields, that we'd planned to meet again here. I told of my fascination with bull sharks, that I wanted to follow them upriver, across the lake. Lloyd listened, head bowed, stroking the banknotes with the back of his fingers. I threw in a sketch of the day we went fishing together, how Arturo had taken just a woolen glove as protection and how, seemingly against the odds, the dugout had carried us and three sharks safely back to shore.

He expectorated loudly in the direction of an old, glue-eyed dog. "Dugout, eh? He still uses a dugout, my old man?" His guffaw tailed off to a snarl. "You see what I have? *Panga* and a big engine—a real engine."

"Arturo's not a rich man," I said, suddenly feeling myself cast, uncomfortably, as his defender. "He doesn't catch as many sharks as he used to. How come you're doing so well?"

Lloyd turned, began to head back toward the boat shed. "He's old, that's all." He paused, tapped the side of his nose. "Lobsters. That's what he needs to try. Good days, I can earn three hundred dollars, maybe more: fifty or sixty kilos, straight to Costa Rica. Hawksbill, too."

"But the hawksbill turtle's banned, isn't it?" Over the decades, it had been hunted to dangerously low levels for its mottled mahogany carapace. Now, by law, villagers were allowed to take only what their family could eat.

He laughed, dug me in the side. "Yes, well, the law says one thing. . . ."

Two men passed us, slowed up, stared at me. They carried axes; their feet and hands were pale with sawdust.

"Perhaps," I suggested, turning back to face Lloyd, "I might come fishing with you." I was curious to witness such bounty, was particularly curious why the fishermen here should have been so much more successful than those in Bluefields, just sixty miles up the coast.

He looked at his watch. "The sea's too rough."

"But there's no wind."

"Have you seen the bar?" He gave a half smile; sunlight flashed on his bridgework. "It takes two weeks after a storm for the bar to settle again. You know what happened two years ago?"

"No." We were back at the boat shed now and were being watched: sloe-black eyes, the *tssk* of a fresh beer, the idle prowl of large men, guarding their territory.

"I'll tell you sometime," Lloyd said, casting his voice wide. "Not a happy story."

I wanted to mention Arturo again, but from Lloyd's dismissive sweep, I now saw the older man's appearance here was unlikely: if Arturo had put it off for twelve years, then surely he'd find some reason to delay again.

Lloyd thrust out his hand. "Back to work," he said with a grin, with the air of a man who had just the opposite in mind. I nodded back, agreeing to continue our conversation sometime later, and, looking round the knot of men, added, "What are you doing here, anyway?" The way they'd drawn together, and now stood close, in silence, made me suspect some kind of conspiracy, though I couldn't imagine what.

"Yesterday," he said, indicating the hull, "we started building a new *panga*. Yesterday, also, the beer arrived. We made some

mistakes. So, today, we have to get back to where we started and
do it all again."

Of the old town, old San Juan del Norte, or Greytown, razed
by Sandinista soldiers a decade earlier, I imagined a romantic
wreckage might remain: the ribs and roof timbers of the houses,
scorched but still standing; grass pushing up between the floor-
boards and covering, once again, the main wide boulevard in a
lush, silvery sweep. Horse-drawn buggies would be left, reins
akimbo, where they'd been abandoned in the last-hour panic to
flee; tram doors would be swinging open, nests of parakeets in
bellied-out bench seats.

But no one would take me. The old town was down the Río
Indio and across the lagoon—not the short hike I'd pictured
through the forest—and, to most, my curiosity seemed eccentric. Why go there? Had I family buried in the cemetery there?

In the end it was two boys, no more than seven or eight, who
ferried me. They were the new generation, wholly mestizo, who,
unlike the older residents, spoke no English. All morning they
scurried about the town, borrowing paddles and gasoline, somehow cadging an outboard and a canoe, and at midday, under the
hottest sun, we set out. This first stretch—down the Indio to the
bar mouth—I'd done in darkness on my arrival, and so now
watched with interest as the river slowly widened and we came
to a great confluence, the water turning from languid green
through brown, whipped by crosscurrents. The boys, suddenly
tour guides, pointed out the ocean far off to one side, and I could
just pick out the tops of the breakers over the sand spit, a haze of
spindrift.

We turned inland, entering a broad lagoon, with jungle on

all sides. In my mind were old maps, sketches of this mile-wide natural harbor from the boom days, and, against these, what we saw now was unrecognizable. Before, the bar mouth had been deep and wide; now, with every passing year, the San Juan deposited ever more silt along its lower reaches, creating unexpected islets and oxbows, constantly altering the draft. In the middle of the lagoon, halfway to the old town, we ran aground and had to heave out the engine and pole forward with the paddles.

There were no other boats on the lagoon. Just us and, in the distance, a relic from another age: a huge skeletal piece of ironmongery, corroded blood-purple, a ghostly industrial-age structure for dredging, which would have been abandoned here, ankle-deep in the lagoon, when all hopes of the canal finally died. It stood a hundred feet high, about to stride off into the jungle. Rust stain, like paint, trailed from its legs.

At the far side of the lagoon, approaching banks of rubberweed—called *lechuga*, though it was nothing like lettuce—the boys slowed the boat.

"It's in there." They pointed ahead, across twenty yards of weed, toward the edge of the jungle.

"The old town?" There was nothing to indicate what this had once been, just a narrow wooden jetty, half-obscured by creepers, and, deeper in, a flagpole with no flag. It was quiet, windless, very hot.

"We have to get through the *lechuga*," one of them mumbled. "I've never seen it so bad."

"And it's boring when you get there," the other added, looking at his knees.

"Really boring," the first repeated. "Even *you* wouldn't be interested."

"Yes," the other nodded. "Just mud and mosquitoes." He paused, shot a glance at his friend. "And poisonous snakes."

"All the same," I said, "we've come this far."

"*Lechuga*'s horrible," the smaller one groaned, slapping his paddle petulantly against the water. "It will take an hour to get through it."

"An hour?" It didn't seem that far.

"Yes." They both nodded vigorously. "What do you think, mister? We go back?"

It did take an hour, and as we hauled through the swampy morass, tearing out fistfuls of methane-belchy stalks, trying to dredge a path of clear water through to the jetty, the *lechuga* closed behind us as completely as if we'd never come. I lay over the bow, trying to pull enough weed from our path to enable the boys to inch us forward, and could feel my old pants, already soaked, begin to tear against the rough planking. At points, the boys tried to drop the engine, but on the first howl of revs the propeller would snarl a football of weed, which took another ten minutes to untangle. When, finally, we reached the jetty, I stood to haul us alongside, and both my pant legs, soft as blotting paper, tore clean away.

"Oooh, mister," they cooed, clapping their hands. "Lucky mosquitoes."

I looked at them, at their own flimsy shorts and torn T-shirts, then at my own raggedy cutoffs. Out here on the jetty there was a slight breeze, and no sign of mosquitoes. We'd be all right.

"Well," I said, mainly just relieved to be on dry land, "we're all in it together now, aren't we?"

Further in, though, on the path that led away into the forest, we lost the sun to the canopy, a hundred feet up. The breeze died and in the dark water through which we trod I sensed the stirring of hard-backed, slimy things. In places there were broken bricks, laid when the building of the new settlement began six years earlier: this road and the jetty were to have provided easy access to the old town, to the cemeteries that held all their histories, but no one had counted on the speed at which the jungle can push back: with no caretaker, the forest had reclaimed everything, turning it again to swamp, breeding mosquitoes big as thumbnails.

Only in the center, on a slight rise where the ground was firmer, was there any sense of how the place might have looked. The boys, too young to know firsthand, pointed out where the main street had run: from jungle at one end, under our feet, into jungle again. Here the trees were sparser, the noise of the insects less overwhelming. Now that we'd slowed, however, the mosquitoes were catching up: I flattened them where they were feasting, overripe against my thighs, the backs of my knees.

The boys were swatting them away from their eyes. "You want to see the graves?" Through the sudden mist of bugs I was finding it hard to tell them apart. "Yes?" I heard one of them say.

"Fine," I muttered, inadvertently squashing a mosquito inside my ear. "Let's get moving." At my feet was an old tin kettle, half-filled with leaf mulch. I kicked at it, by now failing in my attempts to gouge the mashed insect from my cochlea, and it rolled heavily on to its side, oozing pale green slime.

There were, so I'd already learned, three separate graveyards here. One for the British over the centuries—from Nelson's doomed 1780 campaign, when more than eight hundred men had perished, through to the last priest in the 1950s—another for American tradesmen and canal engineers; the last, supposedly, dedicated to the British Masons—St. John's Lodge—who'd once dominated Greytown commerce. In the clearing only one graveyard was visible, ringed by broken iron fencing, as well as a distant scattering of other headstones, splintered or lying on their backs. When I managed to flee the cloud of bugs long enough to examine a headstone, I could see that the names were Anglo-Saxon: Ellen C. Pottner, Robert Craig, Susan Forest, Louisa Coulson. One stone listed the dead from a shipwreck—the *Joseph L. Potts*, which had gone down, like so many others before and since, just off the bar.

Nothing else remained. Just the bones of the dead in the ghost of a clearing, fast surrendering to jungle; fearless mosquitoes turning my arms and legs to burning lesions; a sense that, whatever romantic notions I might have entertained, the death of this place was going on largely unlamented, and perhaps this was only right. There was life here—rampant creepers and screeching egrets, even the moss that was swallowing the gravestones—far more than there had ever been in the final fifty years of Greytown's actual existence.

When I looked round, the boys were setting off at a run, shouting at me to follow. "Or you can stay here if you like, mister," they yelled, snorting with laughter, "seeing as how you like it so much."

I ran after them, by now desperate to escape the tormenting mosquitoes. I chased at speed through the underbrush, but the bugs stayed hooked in my flesh, snouts down, plump abdomens aquiver. Only at the jetty, with the breeze once more on my skin, did I manage to rub them clear.

The boys were snickering at me, shaking their heads. I could feel sweat running into my eyes.

"Okay then," I said. "Let's go."

They glanced up at me, attempted to sober themselves a little. "Your trousers?"

I looked around. My shredded pant legs lay discarded near the boat. "What about them?"

"You can't go back like you are," they whimpered, succumbing once more to helpless giggles. "You've got no clothes on."

Grinning gamely, I picked up what remained of my trousers and threw them to the stern. Looking over the water it was clear that the *lechuga* through which we'd struggled had already closed over; it was going to be a long claw back.

"Right then, you two," I said, sensing that the time was right for a little discipline. "Get in the boat."

They looked at the canoe, then at the expanse of *lechuga*. Silent now, they climbed back into the canoe. The day was suddenly very still, the sun directly overhead.

A half hour in, we'd gone ten yards and were stuck fast, our energy mostly gone under the afternoon sun. I suggested getting out of the canoe and tearing through the weed by hand.

"Good idea," came the voice from behind me, near breathless, choking with suppressed laughter. "Good idea if you want to be eaten."

7

Here at the river mouth, a month on from the start of my journey, I kept hearing one name, more than any other, over and over: another *extranjero*, a white man like myself, whom it was assumed I knew since he too had been interested in bull sharks. To locals he was "Torso"—Thomas Thorson, an American zoologist who, throughout the late 1960s, had caught and tagged bull sharks up the length of the San Juan and Lake Nicaragua. He hired local fishermen and paid them not for salted hides nor for fins but for the live fish, each of which he tagged at the base of its dorsal fin and released.

Received wisdom at the time was that the sharks in the lake and those at the river mouth were distinct species. The former, it was said, were landlocked, stranded by volcanic uplift and prevented by successive racks of rapids from moving downstream—a view set out by a U.S. paper in 1877: "The numerous rapids of the river discourage the idea that the species have voluntarily ascended the river and entered the lake." Archie Carr, an American naturalist who spent much of his life in Nicaragua and Honduras, argued, as late as 1953, that it was the earthquakes of 1630 and 1633 that had finally and irrevocably severed the lake's bull shark from its maritime cousin. To Thorson, too, the lake shark was a unique species, the only shark he'd ever seen taken more than a hundred meters inland. Black-tip, nurse shark, tiger, hammerhead—all, he knew, were common just offshore, but none had ever been spotted in freshwater lakes. He returned to the San Juan and Lake Nicaragua again and again; the quest became an obsession. He wanted proof, answers, data: unshakable facts to answer this biological oddity, the only man-eating shark that thrived in freshwater, far inland.

Over the intervening thirty years, Thorson had become an unlikely legend among the older fishermen, revered as much for the respect in which he'd held the locals as for the cash his tagging program had injected. They judged him eccentric, certainly, for why would any man not only choose to sacrifice the income from butchering shark, but pay generously to have each fish released? I sensed they saw him as a kind of grand-scale sport fisherman, only with an additional, unexpectedly compassionate interest in his prey. Whatever the truth, the man and his methods were still enthusiastically discussed—hardly surprising in a place this remote, which saw so few outsiders.

The river mouth was, as so many had warned me, truly the end of the line. In the week I'd been there so far, there had been just one arrival: a trader from the Costa Rican side of the San Juan delta, who'd slewed to a halt on the bank in a *panga* loaded to the gunwales with canned fruit and cases of beer, sacks of rice, and a king-size, flamingo-pink wardrobe. For two hours he'd bartered hard, a safebox of Costa Rican colones on his knees, and when he left it was with a boatload of passengers, yodeling their farewells as if delirious just to be in movement.

I became friendly with the customs officer—he, a government transfer from Léon, was an outsider too. He ran the customs post single-handed, a less impressive appointment than it sounded, since this week he'd had only the one passport to check. Yet he kept his uniform clean and pressed and was even trying, without much success, to grow a beard. Most days he sat at the open door of his official shack, and often, midafternoon, I'd pass by for a chat, only to find him fast asleep, head heavy on the desk, his official stamp gripped tight in one hand, snoring so loud the window frames rattled.

Yet compared to the rest of the town, his lassitude was nothing extraordinary. The pace of things—especially now, with the ocean "too high" and the fishermen unable to work—was typically slow; the simplest of conversations took half an hour, with long spaces of silence; even the cows walked faster than most of the menfolk. The only hurried movement I remember seeing in those first few days was the passage to and fro across the river of two men in a canoe, loading up bags of coconuts and heaping them this side, under shelter, beside their shack. I approached them one day, curious to hear their story; after all the plantation owner's talk about theft, these two had made me suspicious. When they saw me, they immediately dropped the sack they were carrying and strode away in the opposite direction. Fifty yards on, they sat down on the grass and continued their conversation. When I reached the edge of the township and turned back, the sack was gone.

To this kind of everyday thievery, and to much else besides, the mayor turned his blind side. He was keen to talk to me, believing that somehow I could take "messages" to the world I came from: specifically, to act as a public relations man for his town and encourage a little tourism. But as to municipal control, he was compromised and impotent. He was an elected politician, no more, and as such was in thrall to his constituents, the most powerful of whom were the fishermen. To improve the town, to mend the burned-out generator, even just to provide some kind of regular transport upriver, he recognized the need to raise taxes, yet did not dare. He dressed the part, certainly— navy slacks, black plastic lace-ups, airline pilot's shirt—and enjoyed the sense of stewardship that came from striding the township in the early morning or at dusk and having his people salute him, straight-faced, as "*alcalde*," mayor, but in truth he was absolutely one of them, and unwilling to risk his popularity.

He was third-generation San Juan, a Creole in his forties. His grandfather had come from Jamaica in 1890 to work the canal dredge, and his father, born here, had gone on to become Greytown mayor for thirty-five years. His own term of office, thus far, had focused on the settlement's rebuilding. "I am pioneer of the reconstruction," he said to me once, during one of the formal interviews he'd insist on. "We made a study with the UN, and decided to build here. Here is better than old Greytown—there's less flooding, less mosquitoes, and we have a better view." There was no finer spot for tourism, in short, along the whole Atlantic coast.

"That so?" I said, beginning to weary of the enforced formality of these occasions. "How about the crocodiles? And the sharks? Hardly perfect bathing, is it?"

He sucked the end of his ballpoint. "It is not exactly recommendable, no, but it is not too dangerous, either." A pause. "Best to keep to the edge of the river, best to swim quickly, and

not go too far in." He brightened. "Yes, that is what we will tell
the tourists."

I began to wonder whether the mayor was not, in fact, a good
deal cozier with the fishermen than he let on. The business deal-
ings of the fishermen obviously extended beyond the odd trip to
check their lobster nets; their houses were the only ones to have
reliable electric light, and for this to have been the case a regular
supply of gasoline and generator parts would have to have been
secured. The mayor had power; the fishermen had money. It was
a natural enough coalition.

Cast in this light, his protestations about drug smuggling,
and his stated resolve to clean up the town and hunt down the
perpetrators, rang somewhat unconvincing. He was frank about
the quantities of cocaine and cannabis that were found washed
up along the shore, but less so about what happened to them
afterward. "Sometimes," he explained, "we have the opportunity
to take it away from the people who find it; sometimes they sell
it before we get to them." Either way, it was no secret that,
somehow, large amounts found their way from the Atlantic coast
up into the center and, from there, to Florida and the United
States. If there was a smugglers' cartel that operated from the
San Juan delta and the southern Atlantic coast, it was clear
they'd need three things: lightweight, high-powered launches; a
working knowledge of the tides and currents and treacherous bar
mouth; and sympathetic law enforcers.

Most nights, till late, the mayor and the fishermen drank
together in a long, barnlike shed, under a bare electric bulb.
Someone had a tape machine, and over the churning of the generator came endless, tape-looped marimba, audible all over town.

They drank till blind to all else. They hollered and clasped each other by the shoulders, becoming ever more theatrical in their gestures as the night inched toward morning.

One night, unable to sleep, I went walking. At the door to the long shed were three cows, their noses shiny under the electric light. They watched the drinkers in silence, shoulder to shoulder, eyes unblinking, big tongues lolling. They stood there motionless for maybe ten minutes, grunting as if in discussion. Not once did the fishermen, abandoned to arm-flailing and high-decibel argument, look up or even notice all those eyes on them, and when the cows finally moved on to find a quieter spot at the far edge of town, I saw the fishermen turn, gaze blearily for some moments at the empty doorway, then shake their heads in silence, as if sprung by a sudden sadness: something had passed, but they knew not what it was.

Children, playing in the shallows, heard it before anyone else. Two girls, standing either side of a large woman pressing clothes against a washboard, suddenly began beating the water with their palms and ran onto the bank, splashing wildly. "*Chevvo llega!* Chevvo's here!"

I stood but could see nothing: the river waxy-smooth as ever, midmorning heat just building. Further up the village, other children came hurtling down porch steps, shouting too, heading this way. The woman bundled up her washing, stepped backward out of the water.

"What?" I said. "Who's here?"

"Chevvo," she answered, with a wave. "The delivery man."

Yet, with the gathering babble of children, I could still hear nothing. I stood on the bank lip, leaned out as far as I could, but the view downriver was obscured by an overhanging tree. I thought I heard an engine hum, but then, as abruptly, it died. Some of the children had banknotes, screwed tight and grubby in their fists, and were fighting to be first onto the small patch of beach below the bank. "Chevvo, Chevvo, Chevvo," they were chanting, beating their knees, beaming euphorically in anticipation.

Round the bend in the river, in silence, nosed the bow, then the heaped midships, of the cargo launch that had unloaded here only three days earlier. The skipper—this "Chevvo," I guessed, with his week-old stubble, laborer's gut, and too-tight soccer shorts—saluted when he saw the waiting crowd, the gesture of the oceangoing hero, returning home. He'd cut the engine and was coasting into shallow water, tillering with the tips of his fingers. He was carrying less than before, but this time was not alone: a man sat facing him, his back to us, baseball cap pulled low over his face. He was making hand gestures to Chevvo, making him laugh.

"Okay!" shouted Chevvo, leaning over the stern, levering the outboard clear of the water. "Out the way!" He pointed at the bank. "All of you—get back!" He bent toward the man in front of him, who slowly, as if arthritic, got to his feet, removed his cap, and looked across at the crowd.

I jumped to my feet. "Arturo!"

It was him, unmistakably, though he looked far from his best: slept-in, exhausted, a beer can coughing froth in his outstretched hand. I waved again, realizing I'd long ago stopped expecting him; I was planning to leave soon for the journey upriver, and had hoped that others might be able to take his place. But now here he was—louche, disheveled, eyes damply swiveling—but nonetheless, unarguably, here. He saw me and winked, but his gaze was already moving on, taking in the hitched-up skirts of the washerwoman, the shyer girls who stood further back, in the shade.

The launch grounded, throwing Arturo forward onto the rice sacks. He steadied himself, leapt ashore. Chevvo followed. Arturo, without looking back, broke into a run.

"I thought you'd decided not to come," I shouted, setting off after him.

"Well, I am here." He slowed to a stride, nudged me in the ribs, his breath warm and yeasty.

"What swung it?"

"My boys, of course." He dropped his beer can on the grass, flattened it without breaking stride. "I want to see my boys."

The rest of that day, late into the evening, Arturo spent with the fishermen. All he wanted, all he could talk about, was to see his sons again, and so I walked with him to the boat shed where we waited for Lloyd to return from upriver. Arturo hummed desultorily about his journey here—crossing into Costa Rica at San Carlos, then down the Sarapiquí to the San Juan delta—and, with more fire, about the luck he'd had in the time since we'd parted: every dawn it had been calm enough to make it to the cays, and the sharks had been plentiful, earning him and Elias close to $250, with still some kilos of fins left to dry.

Finally, Lloyd arrived. I'd expected coolness, even animosity, but they greeted each other with kisses. When they'd finished embracing they put their arms round each other's shoulders and sat down beside the river. They didn't have to do much else for me to know that, right then, I wasn't required.

▼ ▼ ▼

Until Arturo's arrival, with my gradual acceptance that, not-withstanding his promises, he'd opted to do the sensible thing and stay home in Bluefields, I'd become resigned to setting upriver alone. I was apprehensive about this—river transport sounded uncertain and the population scattered and lawless—but I was, by now, prepared for it. The river was not exactly uncharted, and I'd be sure to find other shark fishermen able to continue the bull-shark story for me. Further up the San Juan, I guessed, there'd be men who would be able to provide me with the jigsaw's missing pieces, not the least of which were the hows and whys of the last three decades of the shark's existence in these waters, which had seen such havoc wreaked on its num-bers. Traveling alone up this great pirates' waterway might even, I told myself, have advantages—I'd have no guide, but would, at least, be able to roam unencumbered.

Now, though, with Arturo here, it seemed I could readjust my expectations: we could travel together, he on his return loop to Bluefields, I on my way to the lake. In recent days there had been whisperings of the arrival of a boat headed for the coconut plantation, but since there was no telephone in San Juan del Norte, no one was exactly sure when it would steam in, nor how long it would take to load up, nor how many passengers the cap-tain might be happy to take when he did finally leave for the return run upriver. He'd radioed the day before from San Carlos, saying he'd be leaving just as soon as he'd filled the oil drums with diesel, but he had omitted to mention how long this would take, and now the radio had thrown a transmission valve and could only pick up incoming messages.

I decided to sit and wait. I'd not pressure Arturo, hoping

that, by the time the coconut boat came to leave, he'd be only too keen to start again for home. Meantime, I wanted to walk the shore, to rekindle some sense of the rawness of that steep black coast, to see for myself the infamous San Juan bar, before taking ship upriver. Earlier, Lloyd had promised me a ride across to the coastal strip, and now, midafternoon, I set off to find him.

I heard the fishermen's whooping halfway down the riverbank, a cacophony of voices that seemed to echo out across the water, and wash back, twice as loud. As I drew closer I saw two of the fishermen with their fists raised, bouncing on tiptoe, as if braced for an old-style boxing bout. The others circled them, hollering instruction, encouragement, at least one brandishing a wad of notes; all of them, as ever, clutching cans of Imperial.

Arturo was the first to see me. *"Amigo!"* he shouted, clapping his hands. The rest quieted, looked round.

"I was just—" I began, but Arturo broke in: "Where've you been so long? Join us. Take a beer, have a seat."

One of the fighters handed me a can—warm as pee, with an explosive ring pull—and looked around again for his opponent. But the other had let his fists drop and was watching me. A couple of the fishermen moved away toward the half-resined hull, picking up their brushes and pots. The rest, too, seemed to have lost interest in the fight. The man with the cash folded it double and palmed it into the bum of his jeans.

"Come on then," Arturo said, scooping the air in front of him. "Meet the boys."

I sat on an upturned chest, offered my hellos, guessing this wasn't the perfect time to demand a taxi ride. A handful of the fishermen—Lloyd, Lewis, Melvin, as well as Arturo—looked around for seats. The others were already back at work on the boat, silently smoothing on glue thick as honey, as if they'd been at it all morning.

"Tell us something," Lloyd said, leaning forward, his hand heavy on my knee. "How rich are you?"

I hedged, explaining that my earnings were at best unpredictable. "But you," I added, "you seem well off. All this time you're not working. How can you afford that?"

"We have other ways of earning money," put in one of the men varnishing the boat. "Like this. To buy a boat costs five thousand dollars. Making one's only two thousand."

"How many do you sell?"

He laughed, squeezed the brush against the lip of the can. "Oh, we don't need to sell them." The other men, even Arturo, were smiling too.

"So it's just fishing, then? Just lobster?"

Lloyd picked up a rattle of fishhooks, shook them for emphasis. "You know how big our lobsters are? Up to four kilos. Their whiskers"—he stretched out his arms—"are that wide." He and the others, he explained, would set gill nets, buoy them to the surface, and tether them by anchor, and the next day would ride out to the ocean and haul in their catch.

It was, I could not help thinking, terribly wasteful: here were fishermen, who should have had a greater understanding, acting woefully casual with resources they knew to be dwindling and on which they depended. The nets, as much as five hundred yards long, were indiscriminate killers, and brought up all kinds and sizes of fish, shark, and turtle.

With lobster prices so high—six dollars a kilo—none of these fishermen bothered much with sharks. They cut them free and hoped the tide carried them away from land. They treated the lobster with equal disregard. "One part of the year they are here, then they are gone. They migrate. We catch a lot, but most of them escape." Pregnant females, the fisherman added, were thrown free, though sometimes—"Okay, mostly," he conceded—these were dead when they were hauled up.

The fishermen were less lackadaisical when it came to "the Spanish," on whom they blamed the state of most things on the coast—the economy, education, the rape of their land, even the decline of the bull shark.

"And how about the drugs?" I said.

Lloyd twisted to face me, legs set wide. "Yes?" No one spoke. Twenty yards down the pathway I could hear footsteps approaching.

"What happens when they land on the beach?" I felt something go in my voice; I was almost whispering. "Who sells them?"

Lloyd rolled his eyes, gave a stagy laugh. "The policemen, the army. They're out there all the time."

"True enough." I nodded, relieved.

"Last month," he went on, "they found two packets on the shore. You know how many got handed over at police headquarters in San Carlos?" He paused. I shook my head. He bent for another beer. "One." He broke off, looked up. The plantation owner was standing in the doorway, briefcase in hand.

"I need a ride to the plantation," he announced. No one answered. The boat-glassers dipped their brushes, bent to their work again.

"Lloyd?" he broke in. "You free?"

"Sure." But Lloyd planted his hands on his hips, made no move toward the boats.

"I'd like a ride too," I added, spotting my chance, guessing I could negotiate the return trip once we were on our way. From the plantation I could cut through to the shore, and then all Lloyd would have to do would be to pick me up at the bar.

"Okay," the plantation owner said, nodding at Lloyd, then at me. "How much?"

"Oh . . ." Lloyd grinned, looking round, waiting till a couple of the men had caught his eye. "How about beer? A six-pack will do just fine."

I'd not been on the beach long when a soldier, no more than a boy, uniform loose on his bones, ran shouting after me. I'd seen him as I'd passed, squatting on a twist of driftwood at the beach lip, staring out across the ocean. Now he was standing, yelling above the crash of the breakers.

Ahead, the beach was straight and black and steep, with wind-buried coconuts and faded detergent bottles sticky with salt. Three miles on, into the haze, was the bar mouth, where Lloyd had promised to meet me with the boat. I pretended not to hear, put my head down, pushed on faster.

"*Señor!*" He was running now, right behind me. "*Señor!*" He pulled at my elbow. "Where are you going?"

His hair was frosted with salt, his teeth stained and broken as an old man's. In one hand he swung an automatic rifle. To the bar, I said, where the river joins the sea.

He shook his head. "It is not safe for you to walk down this shore." He lifted the rifle under his arm, began to toy with the safety catch. Beside us, a wave smashed bigger than the others, sinking dark orange into the sand. We started round as one, jumped clear.

"What do you mean?" It was not proving an easy walk, certainly, with the sand soft and littered and the salt wind slicing sideways off the foam. But it was a straight line south, and empty, just the grackles and pelicans overhead.

He stood above me and pointed down the line of the beach, into the distant haze. "See that?"

My eyes were gluey with salt, my mouth drier than sand. All I could see was the disappearing edge of the plantation, peeled back and salt-stunted, and a spotlight of sun, far out to sea.

"There," he repeated. "A mile, no more. Two men."

"Two men . . ." That far off, the horizon shimmered like a heat mirage; there were breaks, disturbances, but those could have been birds or driftwood stumps, lying sideways. All I'd noticed were footprints ahead of us, already filling with sand.

"They look for drugs. They live out here, travel the beach at night."

"So?" If this was true, they'd be unlikely to trouble me. And, besides, I was running late; if I missed Lloyd, I'd surely be stranded here all night.

"They've got guns," he continued, and I noticed the whites of his eyes, scratched and bloodied, the pupils shrunk to pinpricks. He'd become increasingly edgy, twisting his rifle butt in the sand, round and round.

"Yes," I muttered, suddenly seeing his paranoia for what it was. "Yes, I understand."

When I walked on again he made no move to stop me; with a bleary wave he turned, half stumbled, sat heavily in the sand.

"Don't say I didn't warn you, *hombre*."

He said more, too, but his words were overtaken by the wind, by the screech of a vulture that cut low between us, by the whine of the blown sand across the beach scrub.

▼ ▼ ▼

I walked on. I was on a leftward curve, gradual into mist, where all the landmarks looked the same, or had occurred many times already: broken propellers, spirals of frayed fishing rope, Cerveza Imperial cans dulled to pewter, a punctured buoy disgorging seaweed.

Slowly, something was beginning to emerge into sight: some kind of shelter, open-sided, zinc-roofed, a ragged fire hurrying smoke toward the coconuts. Near the fire a figure disappeared under cover, bending double to clear the roof edge. Nearing, I saw another, stretched back in a hammock, one arm hanging free. Beside him, a tangle of lobster nets. Inside the shelter, a torchlight stabbed on and off; from my feet, a bundle of dried scrub cartwheeled up the beach, spinning wildly. Close now, I slowed up, keeping as low as I could. Abruptly, the man in the hammock swung down, stood beside the fire, and stretched a full yawn: like the first, he wore a soldier's uniform. I wondered whether to stop, unsure how to read the actions of boy soldiers, as nervous of their knee-jerk bonhomie as of their need to dominate. I edged on, wishing the sand was not so molten, but sensed him notice me, start to wave.

"Hombre!"

I looked up, forced a grin. He threw his arm in the air. *"A donde va?"*

I repeated my earlier explanation, tapped the face of my watch. "See you, then. I've got ground to cover. It's getting late."

He grinned back, knocked me a mock salute, bent toward a box at his feet. He pulled out a bottle of Victoria and dusted sand from the neck. In one movement he raised it to his mouth, wedged it tight between his teeth, and bit off the cap.

▼ ▼ ▼

Alone, out here, I had time to think properly for the first time in days. The moan of the wind in the coconut palms, the haze of spindrift from the breakers, the steep black beach, the cart-wheeling inland of a thousand tiny splinters of shell and beach scrub and sand—all this become almost meditational, one long mash of noise. I turned over and over what Arturo had told me, the pieces that made up his life. It now seemed clear that he would not join me upriver—the coconut boat was due any day and he was just beginning to settle in, to really enjoy himself. But he'd been making up for this as best he could, explaining all he knew about the river and the lake, the giant shark of legend that cruised the deep off the southern shore, the island further north where Indians used to throw their dead to the bull sharks. As for San Carlos, the "hellhole" at the lake mouth, he advised me to stay well away, even though, for a whole picture of the state of fishing today, this old shark-fishing center would be crucial.

From Lloyd, subsequently, I'd gleaned a little more, the missing piece: San Carlos was also home to his mother, Arturo's estranged wife, and her new husband, himself an old shark fish-erman, a former rival. That I'd heard none of this from Arturo made perfect sense: the last thing he'd have wanted would have been for me to dig up a past he was trying to forget; worse still, take seriously a man who now shared a bed with his wife, the mother of his boys.

Behind me, as I waded on, my footprints were blurring, smoothed over with a mud of sand and water. I was walking along the tidemark, since the sand was harder there, and could feel the light begin to fade as dusk approached. There were ghosts of other footprints—an occasional, deep heel mark—and other signs that men had passed this way: bamboo shavings, fresh ax cuts in a log, fruit husks. Further on, nearer the plantation edge, I could just make out the outline of a man, working rhythmically, possibly cutting wood, the motion reminiscent of a lone oil derrick, hoisting and falling. A black-eyed eagle was working the space between us, landing claws out on the crest of the beach, lifting into the wind again when I approached too close. The man did not look up, and I did not disturb him: I needed to make it to the bar before nightfall; Lloyd, I felt sure, would not wait for long.

By now, I was more than happy to be leaving San Juan del Norte. Life in the township had become claustrophobic, every day an exercise in avoiding those who'd decided that friendship with me would secure their own particular goals. For the mayor, this was tourism, and all I had to do was spread the message that the town was up for the influx, had boats and guides and sunny-faced ladies prepared to launder safari suits and toss together tropical salads.

For Félix, the pastor, my presence was proof of God's mysterious workings: that his prayers for outside help had at last been answered. When I sat in on mass one Sunday morning, after the usual half hour of high-decibel exhortation—"The trumpets are sounding! Prepare yourself! Renounce flesh! Turn to Christ!"— he made me stand while he explained to his congregation exactly why I'd come and what I could do for them. "Ask him anything you want! That's what he's here for!" After the service they clustered round, pressing me for lightbulbs, candles, batteries for their flashlights. Félix, though, had greater ambitions. As he walked me out of the church, he put his arm round my shoulder and whispered, "An airstrip. That's what we really need. You will help?"

By the time I reached the bar I was flagging badly, barely able to lift my feet through the sand. The breakers, pale fleeing foam in the dropping gloom, were booming, echoey, as if I'd just entered a small room, not a wide, bleak seascape with sky as big as the earth.

Here there were lone orchids, and the remains of a wrecked dugout, the wood bleached white as bones. South across the Costa Rican border were tiny figures: beachcombers, edging across the horizon. And, as I climbed the last, desolate dune and came out over the bar mouth, I saw the breakwater stretch far behind the beach surf, cresting and splitting, rolling furious.

Standing there, my face and chest soaking in the driving salt mist, it was not hard to see why the fishermen had spent the last weeks ashore, drinking, their fiberglass *pangas* tethered and outboards under cover. This bar, where the San Juan met the sea, was rightly feared, and was attempted only in the most benign conditions. Not only was it the coast's most treacherous stretch of water, but here the bull sharks had bred and hunted with a ferocity that was as much a part of village life as the villagers' burned-out generator and endless days, their very isolation.

Two hundred years earlier, the bar had been an open harbor mouth, and the old maps showed a navigable U facing clear to sea. But silt had long since narrowed the mouth and raised the bar, and by the turn of this century schooners were anchoring offshore, their crews only braving the bar in smaller launches.

Today's fishermen, as Horacio had often repeated to me, did

not have this kind of respect for the bar. "I can lie on the sand
and tell you how many feet of water the waves break in. These
boys now, they think they have more strength. But they know
nothing." And I guessed it was Arturo's son Lloyd, as much as
anyone, whose strutting confidence the old Horacio so despised.
Lloyd, with his gold-rimmed teeth and clanking gold pendants,
who—since escaping the shipwreck on the bar two years ago
when sharks devoured sixteen others all around him in the boil-
ing sea—now believed he was untouchable.

There was no sunset, just a gradual fading to a steely sky and a
slight quieting of wind, enough that the sand stung a little less
and the salt was not always in my eyes. I guessed by now that
Lloyd, well into his second or third six-pack, had forgotten me. I
looked about, wondering where to settle down, judging it best
to find shelter before night came in. The coconut plantation
that backed the beach would break the wind, but I'd often
been warned about the snakes in the underbrush; the beach,
windswept though it was, might be safer.

Standing on a high sand ridge, my back to the ocean, I
watched the light fade over the forest. From here, the river
worked its way over rapids and through encroaching jungle,
climbing for two hundred kilometers until at last it reached
Lake Nicaragua, the country's old heart. Up here beat pirates,
murderous English, French, and Dutch, intent on the plunder
of Granada; up here, with less success, came Captain Horatio
Nelson a century later, a soft-chinned youth struggling to control his first expedition; then, in 1848, the Gold Rush East
Coasters, hurrying through to California. It was to have been

Central America's great transcontinental canal, but had ended up, these last twenty years, a poxy battleground: on either bank had been gun emplacements, Sandinista against Contra, brother against brother. And, throughout it all, the bull shark, cruising in the wake of all this troublesome humanity, twitching for the offal.

With dusk, a distant cloud of egrets, like butterflies, began dropping from the sky, settling to rest against the far riverbank, jostling the mangroves as they grabbed for footholds. I sat to watch, laying my pack beside me in the sand. This would do: in the lee of the dune, enough breeze to deter the monster coastal bugs. The sea seemed louder now, without the wind-rush in my ears, and beat upon the shore with a bassy whop and hiss. I cleared the shells and smoothed where rocks had been, tore away a creeper that dug into the sand like ivy, and lay back and closed my eyes.

And sat up straight, the next minute, straining to pinpoint what I thought I'd heard: the irritable whine of an outboard, from somewhere through the coconuts, the direction of San Juan del Norte. I listened. Silence. Then it came again, swelling louder, and I caught the hollow slap of fiberglass on broken water and barely had I stood up to yell out, "Over here!" than round the bend toward the bar came the biggest of the *pangas*, nose reared up, throttle fully open, skidding on the turn. I grabbed my pack and ran toward the water, yelling out and waving. In the almost-dark I couldn't see who it was, just the luminous hull as it banked in my direction, fifty yards now and closing. At twenty yards, with the prow still up and howling in,

I leapt aside and hollered out one final warning. In the moment before impact, before the boat ploughed deep into the sandbank, I saw just this: a mad cut of grin, wolfhound white.

In the sudden quiet afterward there was just the ticking of the engine and a deep, pained groaning from the bottom of the boat. "Mother of God," I heard; then, softer: "Holy Jesus Moses. Where am I?"

"Hello?" I looked over the edge of the *panga*, and was hit immediately by the rancid tang of the late-night beer hall. A large man was sprawled full-length across the bench seats, face down, a half-crushed can of Imperial in his fist. With his free hand he was pushing against the floor of the boat, yet seemed unable to raise himself even an inch off horizontal. "Lloyd?" I said, offering my hand, reaching down and waving it in front of his face.

"Oh yes," he said, managing to roll on to his side. "That's me." He scrabbled round his neck for his pendants, shoved them back inside his undershirt. With a great clatter he heaved himself upright, held the beer can up to his ear, shook it, then tipped the last drops into his mouth.

"Thanks for remembering me, Lloyd."

"You think we forget?" And this time his laugh flashed more metallic than enamel: each tooth picture-framed in gold. He climbed out of the boat, tested the gunwale with the weight of his backside, and walked to the prow, gesturing to me to help him push. Yet, as hard as we tried, it was only our feet that moved, struggling for footholds in the wet sand. The boat seemed wedged fast, hammered in against the grain.

It took a good half hour to heave it free. In the soft sand it was near impossible to find purchase, and we slipped and scrabbled against the deadweight of the boat, sinking yet further in. Lloyd, smelling strongly of beer and the acid-sweet reek of long-time inactivity, appeared unflustered, content to lean his bulk against the prow, hopefully, rather than exert his full strength. In between heaves—and before we'd decided that it might be quicker to remove the outboard and rescrew it again once afloat—Lloyd would gaze out toward the ocean, his eyes following the breakers on the bar, the line of crests still visible, fizzing with luminescence.

"The sea was very rough," he said, so quiet he could have been talking to himself. When I didn't reply, he turned to face me. "That day," he repeated. "The sea was mighty big."

"When?"

He shook his head, disappointed at me, and suddenly I remembered: he'd hinted at this story before, the capsize of the Bluefields cargo boat, two years earlier.

I pointed toward the bar. "Out there?"

He took a deep breath. "Twenty-eight of us. Sixteen died. You see over there?" He waved his arm toward the edge of the rollers. "We were coming in that way, because from where we were looking it seemed an easier way in. But the waves were bigger than we thought." He rubbed his hands together. "The sea took us, turned the boat over."

"What did you do?"

"I swam, hard as I could. It was daylight, so I could see the shore, not like now."

"And the others?"

"I see them going down, one by one. I see their eyes"—he prized his eyelids wide open—"their eyes were very big. Then they were gone."

I looked across at the bar, the angry, tumbling, endless breakwater, its voice raging loud against the night, the barrier between the ocean and the land, these half-salt waters of zero visibility where the great shark lurked. I could understand why it was so feared, how it had become emblematic of the place's isolation, and why this fear had become almost necessary, even a source of cathartic release.

We stood side by side for some time, listening to the pulse and suck of the waves.

"For days after," Lloyd said, staring straight ahead, "pieces of liver, pieces of hands and feet, came up on the beach." He put his big hand to his face, covered his eyes.

Quietly, I said, "And you? How come you survived?"

He raised up both hands, palms outward. "Praise the Lord, it was not my time."

8

Twenty thousand coconuts lay in vast mounds at the entrance to the plantation, and at midafternoon one day, almost a week after first expected, the coconut barge pulled in. I'd returned to the plantation this time in the hope of securing myself a ride on the barge—this, I reasoned, was its only certain stop—but I needn't have bothered. After loading the coconuts, the barge returned back down the Indio to the dock at San Juan del Norte, and there moored up for the night.

Next morning I arrived at the dock early to find forty or fifty people, luggage at their feet, already waiting to embark. Having been the first yesterday, at the wrong moment, today, with departure finally imminent, I found myself at the back of the line. And there was limited space: a second covered barge had been chained to the first and only this one remained empty of coconuts. I tried to jostle forward, but was elbowed firmly back.

There was no shortage of freight. The men—sweating heavily, despite the early hour—carried purple plastic suitcases and wore shirts with collars and cuffs. Each woman hefted two huge red buckets—clothes, food, shoes. The moment the boat hit the dockside everyone elbowed to the front and began lowering down their children into the empty barge. The kids hit the deck and scrambled for a stretch of free bench, lying full-length to secure their territory. Men followed, throwing open hammocks that they slung from the rafters, jumping up into them and feigning sleep.

Fighting onto the barge, I remembered that I too had a hammock, but rafter space was fast disappearing. I began to dig in my pack, guessing that by the time I found it I would probably be too late, wondering how many nights on the river these men were expecting. I located it finally, bundled at the very bottom, and hauled it out in a tangle of dirty underclothes. I scanned the roof: at the far end of the barge, directly above the engine, was what looked like one last space. Getting there was a struggle through bodies, past women setting up kerosene stoves and men dealing cards on beer crates, headroom perilously restricted by the hammocks.

Eventually I reached the stern and began stringing mine up. The man in the nearest hammock, just six inches from my face, leaned toward me, took a drag on a home-rolled cheroot. The engine was directly under us, and the stench of sweet diesel almost overpowering. "Hot, eh?" he said, and lay back, smiling.

It took another half hour—extended farewells, babies and last sacks of chicken legs being passed down, hands clasped through thickening exhaust—for us to pull away. The captain drove the engine so hard the planking rattled, one whole board leaping loose. Smoke from the tailpipe lay thick on the river; from the side pipes, just above the waterline, streamed rainbow-oily water.

We could see the whole village waving until we rounded the bend—all of them, even the fishermen, gathered for the send-off. Arturo was down by the riverbank, giving me a clenched-fist power salute, a gesture that he held till I gave one back and then, grinning to himself, he turned away for the last time.

Our farewell, the night before, had been held in the fishermen's shed, Lloyd and the others drinking raucously all around. Then, for the first time, Arturo seemed genuinely sorry not to be coming, and sorry, too, that he'd led me to expect the opposite. But he wanted to stay on with Lloyd, he said, to spend some time together as father and son, and guessed it might be a while before he returned to Bluefields.

Later on, he'd handed me a scrap of paper—a page from a school exercise book, muddied at the edges—on which he'd scrawled a number of words. His writing was poor, a jumble of upper- and lowercase lettering, and he'd had to help me decipher it.

"San Juan, beautiful. Beware Costa Ricans," the first line read. After that it was harder to work out.

I pointed to the next line. "What does that say?"

"I'm telling you what I know," Arturo said, leaning over my shoulder. "It says, 'El Castillo—Spaniards.' Then the next is, 'San Carlos—*peligroso.*' "

"Dangerous? Why?"

"It is not a good place. I advise you to spend no time there. It is important for the shark, yes, but a good many bad people live there."

I looked down the page. The next line read, "Solentiname—hippies." Then, "Ometepe—pirates."

"Is there nothing else you want to add? Names, people I should look up?"

He tutted, shook his head. "When you get to these places, you will understand. What else is there to say?"

There was one more scrawled line, blurred illegible by damp. "And that?"

"That says, 'Granada—where all the money went.' " He narrowed his eyes.

"I don't understand."

"You will, my friend. You will."

Now, pulling away, I touched my hand to the pocket where I'd put Arturo's piece of paper. I'd wrapped it in plastic, and folded it with care. Without the man himself, these few words were all I had.

With my hammock up, and my pack stored, I stood at the edge of the boat and watched the iron roofs of San Juan del Norte recede, to be replaced by unbroken jungle. Where the Río Indio met the San Juan the captain throttled harder still. In the center of the current, the river twisting fast and strong toward the bar, we drifted in a long eastward loop. Only at the far side, in stiller water, did the barge steady and fight back against the flow. Here, rather than cross the heavily silted lagoon, we nosed into a deep cut-through, a canal sliced into freshly forested silt banks. We entered the narrowing water at a crawl, one barge lashed behind the other, the men hollering conflicting instructions, all of them poling hard against the bank.

▼ ▼ ▼

For centuries, these very waters had constituted Nicaragua's most vulnerable, least defendable highway, a magnet to bandits and pirates from across Europe and North America. Every buccaneer agreed: the San Juan was the route to the country's heart, to the measureless treasure that Granada held. These were brutal gypsy men, committed only in their greed and their heartlessness. First, they'd sniff out women. "At the price of a knife, an old axe, wood-bill or hatchet," wrote the Dutch pirate John Esquemeling in 1670, "everyone has the liberty to buy himself a woman. By this contract the woman is obliged to stay with the pirate all the time he remains there."

Once the hunt for gold was on, however, the women were abandoned as swiftly as they'd been procured. Throughout the late seventeenth century, with Jamaica seized as a base in 1655, English pirates were hammering hard up the river, each time targeting Granada; in one six-year period—between 1665 and 1670—the city was sacked no less than three times. Most traveled by dugout: John Davis, an English pirate heading for Granada a decade later, paddled upriver by night, during the day hiding his men and boats under forest on the riverbank.

From permanent bases at Bluefields, and Cape Gracias a Dios on the Honduran border, these pirates wreaked merciless damage—not only on the Spanish colonists, but, indiscriminately, on the local Indians too. In the early seventeenth century, these lower stretches of the San Juan had been home to about a thousand Voto Indians, all of whom fled their jungle homelands forever when the first pirates came.

By the beginning of the eighteenth century, the outlaws—

backed in their subversion by English forces on the Atlantic Coast—were firmly dug in. Fifty years later, contraband trading was estimated at around three hundred thousand pesos a year. The Spanish authorities realized that something had to be done.

For too long, the Spanish had failed to police the San Juan corridor. In part this was because they had invaded from the west, and believed the Atlantic region to be monsoon-sodden, underpopulated, and, in trade terms, next to worthless. It was not for another eighteen years after Gil González Dávila's 1522 Pacific "conquest" of Nicaragua, and only following a royal edict to "continue the exploration of the river, and to determine whether it was navigable as far as the sea," that the mouth of the San Juan was located at all.

Granada itself did not qualify as a proper marine port until 1578, when three Lake Nicaragua–built warships descended the river, bound for Cartagena, Havana, and Cádiz. And from then until the catastrophic attacks of the 1660s, the Spanish were too busy accumulating wealth, loading *fragatas* with gold and spices, erecting cathedrals to the glory of their God, to worry themselves overmuch with defensive fortifications. It was only in 1666, suddenly panicked by the realization of their vulnerability, that they threw together a castle at El Castillo, two-thirds of the way upriver, and the next year completed another at San Carlos. But by then the worst of the damage had been done, and Granada was no more than a skeleton of a once-great city, smoldering in its own ashes.

Those pirates who did make it to Granada unharmed and undetected were commando-tough, fanatically resourceful. They had to be, for though there was sufficient food—in the hawksbill turtle that Miskitos from all up the coast would come to hunt during its February breeding season, in the piglet-soft manatee, in the bird life and abundant fishing—there was also no shortage of predators. Camping out at night on the banks of the San Juan cannot have been especially restful: prowling the forest were jaguars, snakes, ocelot. There were foraging ants, which hunted as massed armies; there were mosquitoes; and there was malaria, running at often epidemic proportions. In the river were alligators and bull sharks.

Against the warlike might of Nature, there was only so much preparation that an expedition could reasonably make—or so figured the youthful Horatio Nelson, readying his men for the conquering of Nicaragua, via the San Juan, in 1780. Gathering his forces in San Juan del Norte, and having encountered thus far no resistance from the Spanish, he had good reason to feel buoyant. The river was running easy, the weather looked set fair, the health of his troops, even after the rough crossing from Jamaica, was robust. He had no detailed maps, and even the Indians at the river mouth could give him only the sketchiest idea of what awaited upriver—whether savanna, swamps, jungle, or cliffs—but, to this, the twenty-two-year-old gave little mind: it could not be more than a hundred miles to El Castillo, and, he reasoned, he had surprise on his side.

Optimism, in short, ran high: the expedition physician, Dr. Thomas Dancer, figured the most likely complaint would be upset stomachs from drinking tainted water. Another expedition member, cocooned in the security of a barroom in San Juan del Norte, confided to his diary, "The mosquitoes, sandflies and other insects, the poisonous reptiles and wild beasts, of which so much is said in England, are mere bugbears to frighten children." And so, anticipating a swift, bloodless capitulation from dumbfounded Spanish forces, Nelson decreed that rations suitable for the sick—vermicelli, sugar, sago, chocolate, oatmeal—

should be jettisoned in favor of a full load of ammunition. And, on 28 March, the expedition set off upriver, the start of an ordeal longer and crueler than any of them would have ever dared imagine.

With the last of the light, and with the barges lashed together once more and heading up a broader, deeper tributary into the jungle, women set up kerosene stoves and began tearing up chickens with their bare hands, the yellow fat bright under their fingernails. They fried onions in a soup of oil and tipped in the meat, along with green peppers and tomatoes, mashing it all together with the back of a steel ladle.

On the prow, with the light on the river glowing ever fainter, I talked to the captain. His wheelhouse was set right up, almost over the water, a cupboard-room with just enough space for a high stool and the wheel and a ledge for a notepad. His face was gray as the fading day; his skin was graveled with soot specks, the squint lines from his eyes ruled in black. Above us, men were stamping across the corrugated-steel roof, cracking open beer bottles, becoming raucous. They sat down at the front edge of the roof, with a view upriver into jungle, and dangled their feet into space, obscuring the captain's vision. He reached forward through the window and grabbed one by the ankles. From above there came laughter and, a second later, a bottle of beer, lowered to within inches of the captain's face. "No!" he shouted, hammering at the ceiling with his fist. "Get off! Get off!"

When they did not, he made no more protest, crouching, instead, further down onto his stool. To me he spoke almost in a whisper, not once turning from the river.

He was from El Castillo, and this cargo barge a longtime family business; the men he'd come with were his sons. For sixteen years he'd worked the river, yet still, despite such experience, refused to guess how long our passage might take. There were so many unknowns, he said, smiling for the first time, exposing teeth rotten to the gum line. There were the rapids, smooth and deep one day and full of exposed rocks the next; how perilous they were depended on their feed from the San Juan's tributaries, and rainfall at the top of the river could be many inches different from that just forty miles down. There was the engine, and then there were the barges, both of which dated to the early 1970s. There was, most important, the speed of the river. Now, even with the screws on full, we were making poor headway against the current, and this was only a side flow, still some way from the main sweep of the San Juan proper.

During the civil war he'd holed up at El Castillo. At that time, anyone traveling on the river was assumed to be partisan, and a barge of this size, more suspect than most, would not have lasted long under competing shellfire. Quite aside from which, the coconut plantation, having been seized by the Sandinistas at the start of the war, was no longer in production. The captain's sons, youthful ideologues all, signed up for the revolution and spent most of the 1980s on the Honduran front.

In contrast to those years, memories of the decade before filled him with evident pleasure. The plantation, its operations guaranteed through the owners' links with the dictatorship, had harvested at full capacity. Back then the river was more predictable, too, and he regularly made the round trip within a week.

There were perks in all that river travel, he added, shooting me a brief, almost covert smile. From the back of the main barge he used to bait lines with tarpon and *machaca* and by journey's end would have had at least a couple of big shark to sell to the San Carlos dealers. The sharks were drawn anyway by the passage of the big boat through the water, by the grinding of the engine and the drop-through toilet that sat proud on the stern— you could see their dark shapes chasing the wake, sometimes closing right on the propeller—so it was no great leap to make sport of them, and besides it made the days pass quicker, the hours of staring out at endless jungle.

The sky was overcast, and when night fell it came suddenly and absolutely. I was up at the prow, the captain having long since lapsed to silence, and was knocked breathless by the speed of it: no pale shadow over the forest, no sliver of moon; even the electric-white egrets that had clustered along the far bank were suddenly swallowed, in that instant, by the noiseless black. I gripped the wheelhouse doorjamb, looked back down into the belly of the boat. A few candles were being lit; a man with a flashlight was helping people to their bags; the hesitant blue of the kerosene stoves made everyone seem unsteady on their feet, as if struggling against a swell. The captain cursed, pushed past me into the gangway.

"Alvaro!" he shouted, crouching to see through. "One of you—cut the speed! We're taking it slow from now." He clapped, hooted. "Alvaro!"

Toward the stern, a figure rolled out of a hammock, bent over the pounding diesel. The engine hammer dropped to idling, then inched again to a half-throttle growl. The captain, back at the wheel, was muttering, "The edge, the edge. How far? Can anyone see?" He was forcing the wheel to starboard, the chain-link to the tiller rattling down its gunwale-runners.

"Where are we going?" I asked, raising my voice above the shouts of the drinkers overhead, but the captain made no reply. In the darkness I sensed him moving toward me, then back again, smelled food on his breath—rice, beans, and a staler sweetness that could have been alcohol, or simply one too many sleepless nights.

I'd been so absorbed by departure, by the thrill of movement after so long in stasis, that I'd given little thought to how far I planned to take this ride, and on this Arturo's jottings gave no pointers. To get any sense of life on the river, I'd have to progress in stages, but so far there'd been few signs of anything even half resembling a settlement: I'd spotted only single shacks, many abandoned and roofless, already reclaimed by the jungle, and in the few hours before dark had fallen, I had noticed just one lone dugout, paddled by a man with a chalk-pale face, whom we'd left pitching perilously in our wake.

At the confluence of the rivers, where the San Juan splintered for the ocean, there was, I remembered, a police post, but little more. I'd heard that some way further up, where Costa Rica's Sarapiquí met the San Juan, there was a village; perhaps I could stop there, use it as a base to explore the lower reaches, and hitch a ride upriver the next time the coconut barge came past. All of which sounded fine in theory; what I did not know, because the captain would not tell me, was how far we'd gone already, and how much further, in this tropical blackout, with only the phosphorus of the fireflies to guide us, we were likely to travel tonight.

Back in the pit of the boat, triggered into hunger by the smell and heat of the frying oil, I bought a plate of chicken bones and frijoles. The meal came on an earthenware plate, still sticky from the meal before, and the woman who handed it to me, gripping tight to the edge of the plate till she could feel my cash in her palm, reminded me three times to return it. She held a candle up between us. "As soon as you've finished," she repeated, "back to me."

There was no place to sit. Down each side, figures were hunched over their food, and even the sacks and beer crates down the aisle had been taken over for seating. I sensed faces angle toward me, then, in silence, turn back to their food again.

On the roof a small group was gathered. I climbed up, struggling to steady myself as the barge, scraping the bank, lurched sideways.

A man offered me a beer and in the gauzy side glow of the flashlight, while he dug in the plastic foam cooler, I picked out the others: three men, one woman, all staring into space, mouths agape. The fourth man passed me the bottle and as he did so the beam of the flashlight skidded sideways. The barge, stationary now, appeared half covered with jungle. For a second, the beam settled on a spot deeper into the forest, and I saw the diamond glint of a pair of night-hunter's eyes.

As we talked, and I ate what I could stomach of my fast-congealing chicken, the captain and his sons made the boat fast to the bank. The younger men threw in anchors upstream, roped hard to the bases of the nearest trees. Having no idea where we were, I simply felt relief that the captain had decided to stop here: traveling in total blackout, with no guide lights, did not make me feel easy.

The least drunk of the five on the roof was a teacher, a sad Creole with slow hands. He didn't say much, but when he did speak, the others ceased their babbling and sat quiet. A Blue-fields second-grade instructor, he'd been visiting family in Costa Rica and had come to San Juan del Norte solely for the ride upriver to San Carlos. From there, he'd ride the bus back home. We started talking about Bluefields, and when I mentioned the problem of drugs, he groaned.

"Anywhere up that coast, you'll see men walking the beach, looking for drugs." He gazed past me, into the forest. "And each time they sell it on, the price goes higher and higher. In Bluefields, most of the young people are on drugs."

"Most?"

"Boys like my son." He leaned closer, lowered his voice. As a teenager, he said, his son had been captured by a Sandinista *brigada*, trained to fight, introduced to marijuana. From that, he'd progressed swiftly to ever-harder narcotics. The teacher indicated the satiny crook of his arm. "Yes." He shook his head. "Even that." When the war ended, his son left the Atlantic coast for a two-year billet on a cruise ship out of Miami—a new life.

"He cleaned himself up," the teacher whispered. "He bought clothes, music, all kinds of pleasant things. He was my son again. But then he came back to Bluefields and in three months all his money was gone on drugs." Five years on, unmarried and still in Bluefields, his son had fathered "six or seven" children, each with a different woman.

"I am sorry to say it," the teacher said, in a voice so soft I found myself inching yet closer to catch the words, "but this is the story of the Atlantic coast."

The drinkers shook their heads in unison. Below us, in the pit of the boat, came the shufflings and gruntings of people settling themselves for sleep, heaving themselves into their hammocks, the creaking of the roof joists as the hammock ropes stretched to take the full weight. I began to say my good-nights, guessing that if I didn't claim my hammock space pretty soon, someone else would snatch it.

The woman raised her head. "Hang on." She was swaying as if we were on a high sea, her voice slurred to a parody of drunkenness. "You haven't said nothing about you. What're you doing here?"

I explained. She listened, chin on her hand. Her elbow, positioned precariously on her knee, kept slipping. She'd slump forward, then snap upright, wiping her mouth. When I finished, she nodded several times, then several times more.

"I know all about sharks," she said. "Ask me anything."

I opened my mouth to speak, but she was already off. "San Carlos, where I live, that's the capital of shark fishing. Or should I say 'was'? *Was* the capital of shark fishing. We have a giant shark there—you've heard? And we used to be rich because of the sharks. The whole quay, every day, so many sharks."

"What happened?"

"Ahhh . . ." She threw up her arms and her beer bottle catapulted from her fist, landing with a thin splash, some way off in the river. "Where do I start? The dictator? The 1960s? The 1970s? All those shark fishermen. Too many shark fishermen."

"How about you? How come you know so much about it?"

"I was married to one of them. He disappeared. Left me with nothing." She leaned back, shoved a hand into her jeans. "It was a bad time." She pulled her hand free again, brushed it down her pant leg. "You haven't heard the stories?"

"No," I said. "Well, a few."

"In that case, my friend . . ." She laid her hand—warm,

sticky with beer—across the back of mine. "You come and see me." She tore a sheet of paper from the teacher's notepad, took my pen and scratched her name and address. "Don't leave San Carlos without coming to see me. You hear?"

I slept little that night, what with the hollerings of the drinkers on the roof, the cacophony of snoring from the hammocks. I was astonished no one yelled at them to quiet down, but perhaps, in a country that had been so long at war with itself, the expression of freedom, to whatever end, was to be embraced.

In snatches, I dreamed what was to become a recurring dream. I was standing atop an abattoir ramp—an old slaughterhouse whose floors were winy with blood, where the lighting was naked bulbs, swinging head-height from long wires. It was the Bluefields slaughterhouse, long ago closed down, beside a sewage outflow in the poor part of town. In the dream the conveyors carried not half-ton beef carcasses but sharks of all sizes, their skins turning to rumpled leather in the heat. Their fins were razored off, their hides peeled and hung up in the sunlight to dry. What remained—giant, pink, fat-streaked slugs—were tipped into a grinder and mashed for dog food.

The noise of the slaughterhouse woke me, and I pushed myself upright in my hammock, panicked and disorientated. In the next-door hammock, not eight inches from my face, a man and a woman were kissing with audible enjoyment, and the motion they'd set up was rocking the whole boat. It was still dark, and raining, and the roof was not watertight: there was a rusted hole over my knees and my pants were soaked.

Yet, when dawn came, it brought with it not only silence—

the drinkers having long since collapsed in exhaustion—but also an end to the rain, and a vast melted sun that turned the whole river red and raised everyone coughing from their sleep.

The captain had sat all night at the wheel, and looked as if he'd slept even less than I. His hands were on the wheel and his chin was on his hands and he was staring out across the water, toward a splintered tree trunk stuck roots-up in the middle of the river. The river seemed to open out just ahead, and seemed also to have risen considerably during the night: the trees we'd moored to were now underwater, the ropes disappearing into cappuccino foam. Behind us, in the low-down hull of the boat, the women were cooking again: chicken and rice, chicken and beans, hurtling offal and empty cans wide into the current.

The captain saw me, lifted his head off the wheel. "See that?" He nodded ahead. "The San Juan." Normally, he said, he'd have pressed on further under darkness, but such was the blackout last night that even he, who'd done this journey many hundred times, had begun to lose his nerve. With the rain, and the upflung trees and shredded vegetation that we could now see spiraling past us in the current, his caution had been proved right.

As his sons struggled to free the boat from the bank, the captain outlined his plans: San Carlos in two days, a day unloading, then back to San Juan del Norte by the end of the week. The plantation owner, he said, had been insistent: the plantation was stockpiling coconuts, and with the river the only workable trade route to the interior, he needed the barge on permanent turn-around. Before El Castillo, the captain had just one stop: the junction of the Sarapiquí River, on the southern, Costa Rican bank of the San Juan.

This was the river down which Arturo had come to reach San
Juan del Norte. And this, too, was where I decided to stop. From
there I could prowl the lower reaches of the San Juan and, with
luck, thumb a ride on the coconut boat on its next haul upriver.

Fighting against the ever-rising water, keeping close to the
bank to avoid the spiraling debris in the center, it took us till
midday to reach Sarapiquí. The river was well over a hundred
yards wide at some stretches, and looked at with a broad eye
appeared not to be moving at all: only drifting birds, at rest on
the water, and uprooted trees moving fast downstream, gave any
clue to its speed and power. For some time, the forest on both
banks was unbroken, just high trees with trailing lianas and
monkeys that leapt from view, howling, as we neared. Without
warning, it started to rain again, and a moment later, as suddenly, the sky cleared and for that minute, while the last rain
fell, all about us were rainbows.

We passed the Nicaraguan sentry post and two soldiers,
down to their underpants on the bank, shampooing so hard their
faces and shoulders were lost in brilliant white foam, leapt to
their feet and saluted us. Behind them, cut from a crescent of
jungle, was a box-hut on stilts and, pulled up on the mud, a
beat-up *panga*. A little way back was a flagpole, but no flag. The
soldiers watched us pass, their chests streaked with shampoo,
unwavering, transfixed, as if we were something otherworldly,
not just the regular cargo barge, once more on its way upriver.

On the Costa Rican bank, further up, small farms began to
appear: a hut by the river's edge, then, behind that, a half-acre of
burned jungle, a cow, women at windows. It was across these
stretches that Miskito and Creole and all those disaffected with

the Sandinista takeover had fled during the 1980s civil war.
Most of the inhabitants of the old San Juan del Norte came this
way, before heading further south, to safe houses deeper in Costa
Rica. What I could see now was so dawn-still, so brightly ajan-
gle with monkeys and cockatoos and oropendola birds, that it
was hard to imagine it had ever been a battleground. The only
clue to the recent encroachment of man was, as we progressed,
the ever-thinning Costa Rican forest. The Nicaraguan bank, by
contrast, was undisturbed, still-virgin rain forest.

This, however, was not as straightforward a comparison as it
appeared. Nicaragua might have protected its southernmost
stretch of forest, but elsewhere, little remained. Maps from just a
century before showed "forest" all up the eastern seaboard, across
the hills to Managua and north to Honduras. Now, most of the
central part of the country, certainly around Managua, Granada,
and halfway east to Bluefields, was desiccated savanna, the
ground dry as bonemeal, where farmers at the plough were visible ten miles away.

Six months after returning home, I learned that sixty-two
thousand hectares of Atlantic coast forest was to be sold to South
Korean loggers—ancestral property of the Rama and Miskito
Indians being offered up by politicians in the capital. Reading of
this, I understood for the first time what the mayor of Pearl
Lagoon had meant when he'd spoken of his people's hatred for
their overlords. "Violence will come," he'd threatened, and now,
with distance, this seemed anything but melodramatic. It was,
rather, just a plain statement of fact: revolution, he was warning, was the inevitable consequence of such treatment, and would
not be far away. At the Sarapiquí junction, finally, the barge
nudged alongside a mud bank, and I and three others jostled to
the prow to jump. I'd asked the captain to watch out for me on

his next run upriver, and he'd promised, though when I'd pushed him on how long this might be, he'd merely smiled and rolled his eyes. Now he was leaning forward through the wheel-house, looking animated for the first time in hours, shouting at us to leap first and leave the bags. The others—young men with cheap shoes, hefting black plastic sacks—jumped without look-ing back, and were striding up the slope toward the forest before I'd even hit the ground.

As I looked round, at the huge sweep of the river curving into the distance, at the wall of jungle facing me, I felt a tug of pure loneliness, and when the captain raised a hand in farewell, and the drinkers on the roof hollered their good-lucks, toasting me raucously, it was as much as I could do to look up and meet their eyes. For ten, fifteen minutes, the barge remained in sight, toiling against the current, and when it finally merged into the forest, round the furthest bend, the noise of the engine carried for some while longer, a far-off murmur that I focused on as if everything depended on it, until finally, and long after it was really gone, I let it go.

9

In the United States, a land where rogue nature was regarded almost as an affront to hard-won science, a shark had only once, in recent memory, hunted inland. It was the summer of 1916, and the result was panic all up the eastern seaboard. In the space of twelve days, two swimmers were taken off the New Jersey coast, and three more, in an unprecedented attack, near the small town of Matawan, whose only link to salt water was a meandering, eleven-mile tidal stream.

The first Matawan victim disappeared on 12 July—a boy, who had been leaping into the stream from abandoned dock pilings, and who was pulled under, never to resurface. Within the hour, the shark struck again twice—first to be hit was the boy's would-be rescuer, who died of his wounds; then, a half mile downstream, another boy who, despite a leg torn half to pieces, survived. Shark attacks in the region were not new—but they had never before happened inland.

To a community that had believed itself inviolable, a swift revenge was clearly called for. All that night, the men of Matawan lined the creek and set dynamite charges, hurled pitchforks and harpoons after every shadow that crossed the water. They hoisted lanterns and stalked the banks, spraying the creek with buckshot. At first light, as the tide began to ebb, they waded in with knives and sledgehammers. Over the coming days, having cleaned out the ammunition stores in Matawan and Keyport, they made nets out of chicken wire and still, for almost a week, dredged up nothing but mud and rusted bits of farm machinery, strips of dynamited fish.

For six days, no shark was caught in the creek and, when one finally was, this seven-footer—despite the ten-cent "Come and See the Terror of Matawan Creek" sideshow that was immediately erected, despite the clamor from the people to put a shape to their monster—turned out to be a convenient patsy. The real killer, it turned out, had been captured four days earlier, by accident, by a fisherman some way offshore. That fish was an eight-and-a-half-foot great white, in whose belly were wads of half-digested human flesh. It had invaded man's territory, wreaked mayhem, and escaped to the sea again.

In the frenzy for explanation, some fairly wild theories were put about. The U-boats, some argued, in preventing the sailing of passenger liners, had deprived sharks of their ritual pickings of galley waste, so forcing them to hunt closer to shore. The bombing of Europe, others believed, had scared sharks to the far side of the Atlantic.

Advice on avoidance was equally eccentric: dive underneath

an onrushing shark, *The New York Times* instructed, as sharks cannot chase prey upside down. A dancer wrote to another paper claiming balletic high kicks had frightened off her predator. The tourists, however, voted with their wallets, and a million dollars' worth of hotel reservations were canceled. Shark experts, who had previously claimed that a shark would never kill a man, now conceded that Matawan had proved them wrong. As one lamely admitted, "The nearest I can come to accounting for the sudden preying of these fish is to say that this is a 'shark year.' "

The people wanted answers, and there were none. They felt hunted, afraid even to dip their toes off shores that had long been their holiday homes, and the best advice was conflicting and confused. And then, as suddenly as the sharks had come, they were gone, and gradually, with the ending of the war and the promise of a new future, the episode drifted into history: it became myth, the inspiration for a thousand newspaper articles, one best-selling thriller, and a series of Hollywood blockbusters, and for the descendants of Matawan, a vein of darkness, never forgotten.

Late that night on the riverbank, I shared a meal with a family whose house, just away from the water, lacked doors, half its roof, one whole wall. We ate round a fire, and they made me huddle in close: San Juan mosquitoes, they warned, were especially partial to pale skin. Come midsummer, when mosquitoes were at their most virulent, cattle had even been known to suffocate, their nostrils clogged black with insects.

They were grilling slabs of white meat on a steel mesh. The meat oozed fat and moisture that sparked the flames higher, charcoaling the underside. A young man, Salvador—father, I guessed, to the two small boys who stared at me across the fire—passed around enamel plates, and on each heaped a fistful of cold rice and a square of meat that he lifted from the flames on the end of a long machete.

"Today's," he grinned, as he sat down with his own. He stabbed the knife into the ground beside him.

"Tarpon?"

He laughed, displaying a half-mashed mouthful. "Shark, my friend." At the water's edge, just behind us, he pointed out the remains: barely three feet long, its sides filleted hollow, hook still through the jaw.

"But it's just a baby." Not that it didn't taste good—like rich, steaky tuna.

"If you live here," he said, sucking oil off his fingers, "you eat what you can get."

When the clouds cleared from the moon, the far bank became visible and the river itself appeared like poured satin. In the distance were what looked like hills, and somewhere in between, during the civil war, there had been a permanent encampment of Contra guerrillas. Between the Atlantic coast and El Castillo, there had been four Contra camps on the Nicaraguan bank of the San Juan, and these people I was now with, like every other peasant family along the river, had been forced to take sides.

"We weren't interested." Salvador chewed as he spoke. "Not our war. Dirty Nicaraguans fighting dirty Americans. You walk in the jungle, you get shot. So we stayed here, kept quiet. For ten years we held our breath."

Being white, I was beginning to understand, was in itself enough to trigger this kind of talk, for to be white was to be seen as American, and about Americans few felt neutral. So I explained that I was English, and as I did so the woman arched her back, shook herself, yawned, looked round for her children. Salvador, mumbling inaudibly, began to polish his machete on his shirt.

"The river," I said quickly, sensing that political discussion was the last thing they wanted. "The river—that's what I'm interested in. Tell me about the river."

He reached out, gripped my elbow. *"Muy bien,"* he sighed. "The river."

We talked for three hours, till well past midnight, and, from fatigue, my Spanish grew elliptical, verbless, incomprehensible even to myself. He'd been born on the river, he said. His wife was from further up the Sarapiquí and he'd had to work mighty hard to sell the San Juan to her. Who, she'd demanded, would willingly trade a peaceful, fertile hill town for a low-down jungle river on the front line, a river where children weren't even safe to paddle? In reply he'd offered the simple truth: that it was his home, that he loved it, that he was a fisherman and knew nothing else.

"Besides," he added, picking at his teeth with the machete tip, "I told her shark tastes good."

In the twelve years they'd lived here, survival had become increasingly difficult. They'd cut into the jungle behind the house, but his efforts at gardening had been halfhearted. It was being on the river that excited him, working the deep dark places for the fish that he was sure still lurked there. To begin with, he blamed his falling catches on himself—the wrong type of bait, fishing too late in the morning—but gradually other fishermen began admitting the same. Big shark were becoming scarce. People out fishing still disappeared, sharks were still slit open to reveal body parts, swollen smooth and pale as china. But, compared with just twenty years before, their numbers were well down.

"Why?" I asked. "Why has this happened?"

He smoothed the embers with the flat of the machete. "Chinamen in Bluefields. They buy the sharks and cut off the *aletas*, the fins. Before the Chinamen, sharks used to swim up the river. Not anymore."

"Some people," I suggested, "say it's because of all the shark-men at San Carlos. They took thousands every year from the lake. That's what I've heard."

"Who tells you that?" The knife tip glowed orange; he flashed it across the darkness.

"People in Bluefields. Along the coast."

"See? Chinamen, black men. What do they know? Have they ever been up here, up the river? Have they ever seen the lake?"

I could think of no answer to this: how to reply to prejudice, grown inflexible as bone from years of hard grind and disaffection? So instead I nodded, and murmured, "Tell me about the lake, then. When were you last there?" Did he distrust its fishermen as much as those on the coast?

This time he laughed. "Seen my boat? It would take me a week to get to the lake in that. And then there are the rapids. And my family. What would they do?"

"People up there used to think the sharks were trapped in the lake."

"That's only because they never came down the river." He turned toward me, his eyes, one whole side of his face, lost in shadow. In the absolute stillness I could hear him breathing, hear his wife coo-cooing their children to sleep, and at that moment I wished I was still on the coconut boat, riding amid the boozy hubbub to El Castillo, cocooned in movement, far away from here.

I stood, looked round for my pack, wondering where I could sling my hammock. "I should get some sleep," I said.

He slapped the side of his face, showed me his palm, fruit-splattered with bug blood. "It's okay. Tomorrow you come with me."

Those next few days, paddling the lower reaches of the San Juan, I lost all sense of time, distance, direction; the only reminder of east and west was the constant unspooling river, its mile-long, broad sweeps oceanward. By dugout, travel was interminable; often, when Salvador was fishing, I'd ask to be left on the bank, where I'd try to draw people into conversation—attempts that ended, most often, with their staring at me in bewilderment, eventually making some excuse and wandering home along the riverbank to their huts and black-earth gardens. I had a map, and would ask the older men to point out where we were, which tributary we'd been taking all morning, but they'd shake their heads, amused by my need-to-know. "Don't recognize that," they'd chuckle, turning to their friends for agreement. "The river is a snake—it changes all the time."

Further downriver, after another morning's fruitless fishing, we came to a spot where the river narrowed, then opened up wide again. Twenty yards back from the bank was a shiny-roofed shed in a grassy clearing. Behind that were small farms, some cattle. I could hear singing—voices raised, a shrill metallic echo—and in the pauses a guitar, woefully out of tune. We pulled the canoe onto the bank, and I set off across the grass. When I looked back, halfway there, Salvador was still bent over the boat.

"You're not coming?"

He sat down on the edge of the canoe, paddled a hand in the air. "The American. I'll wait here."

As I approached, the singing swelled, reached a warbled crescendo, then died to silence. The guitarist, overshooting the ending, hit an extra, dissonant chord. I crept to the open door, peered round.

Inside were ten, perhaps fifteen people—mostly women, a handful of children, and an oversized adolescent girl who stood facing the gathering, a Bible open in her hands. At the side, across from a trestle-table altar, was a tall white man with a pendant crucifix. A guitar, tattooed with "CND" and "Make Love Not War" stickers, leaned against the altar.

The girl whispered the reading, each verse punctuated with *"Nombre de Dios," "Sangre de Dios."* As she warmed up, her voice rose, and she lifted her eyes from the page and tilted her head back and began to shout out. "Amen!" she cried, at impromptu moments in the text. "Amen! *Nombre de Dios!*" She laid the Bible on the altar and raised up her arms, fingers straining heavenward. She began to sing and then, as suddenly, she stopped, beamed beatifically at the congregation, took a deep bow, and stepped back to her place.

"Grassyarse," the white man said. He picked up the guitar, then noticed me. "Come on in!" he called out in English. "Come in! Join our worship!" His voice was the voice of a fat man, a

Deep South tremolo. I slipped in at the back, feeling I'd been here before, seen this whole scenario many times: white preacher in the jungle, his gathered crowd of innocents. The preacher continued in Spanish, adjusted his guitar strap, positioned his fingers over the fingerboard.

"No time to waste," he cried. "Christ is coming. No time to waste smoking cigarettes, drinking beer. Not a second to spare." We were all children of God, he said, and should sing to His glory. He hit an open G, grinned broadly, ran his fingernails across the dead strings. Taking a deep breath, he launched himself into "She'll Be Coming round the Mountain," replacing *she* with *he*, a bold substitution that kept him beaming right up to the final, discordant flourish.

I'd arrived close to the end. Laying his guitar across the altar, the preacher bowed his head, clasped his hands before him, and recited first the Lord's Prayer, then two extended blessings. "And of course," he finished, "we must not forget our neighbor—poor Antonio. He is not a bad man. He is not to blame. Have mercy on him."

He strode down the aisle, shaking hands with each in turn, thanking them for coming, reminding them to return the next day. The sun was on the roof and it was hot and close inside the shelter. I could hear the shouts of men on the river, birdcalls from the forest. As the women walked past me, out into the full heat of the day, I saw their faces were slick with sweat; their dresses clung to their spines.

The priest double-pumped my hand. "And you are?"

I told him, explaining that I'd stumbled on his church by mistake. "To be honest," I said, "I'm not that sure where we are."

He smiled, tilted his head to one side. "Who is? Isn't that the whole point? Isn't that why God has brought you here?" He paused, wiped his wrist across his brow. "Truth is, we don't get a whole lot of visitors. Kinda off the beaten track, here. You staying a while?"

I slid my hand out of his hot-sweat grip. "Wish I could," I mumbled, "but I'm with him." I looked round. Salvador was pacing up and down the bank beside his canoe, a banana leaf umbrellaed over his head. He noticed us, nodded.

"He'll want to get on the river again," I added. The white man's gaze was drifting; in his pupils I saw myself reflected, a tiny pale chessman against the dark river.

"Perhaps," I went on, "you could tell me one thing. That Antonio you mentioned in your prayers. Who is he?"

"Ah." He crossed himself. "An unhappy story."

He related it, however, with some relish, sighing theatrically and wringing his hands. Antonio was a fisherman from further down the delta, whose home was the wedge of jungle between the two estuarine forks of the San Juan. He'd been out hunting one afternoon on the Nicaraguan bank when he'd been jumped by a jaguar, a full-size, adult male, eyes peeled wide, ravenous. Antonio had shot from the hip, clipped the animal's shoulder, and with his second cartridge and the jaguar almost on him, had blown a hole in its head.

His next move was more complicated: jaguars were a protected species, and anyone caught poaching was guaranteed a long jail term. On the other hand, a good pelt was worth several thousand dollars—enough to buy a *panga*, an outboard, to set up as a lobsterman and make some real money. So Antonio skinned the beast and paddled home. To the soldiers who later tracked him down, and entered his hut to see the great skin stretchered and salted, Antonio's plea of self-defense rang more than a little hollow. This was a month ago. Right now, said the preacher, Antonio was behind bars in El Castillo.

"Will he have a trial?"

"Unlikely."

"How many years will he be inside?"

"As many as they feel like." He walked out into the sunshine, waved an arm across the view before him. "Beautiful, huh? Crazy world."

Down these lower stretches, among the older fishermen, I had taken to using the name of Thomas Thorson, zoologist, as a way of introducing myself and my own journey. Still, fifteen years after the last of his researches into *Carcharhinus leucas*, Thorson was remembered with extraordinary fondness; sometimes the very mention of his name caused the men to look more kindly on me, too.

Thorson first came to the San Juan in 1963. Random reports from adventurers, naturalists, and the occasional roving government envoy had triggered his curiosity. Was the bull shark confined to the lake, or did it migrate freely to and from the Atlantic? Until he began his tagging program, most fishermen on the lake believed their shark to be a unique species, cut off from its maritime cousins many centuries before. Others, a minority, spoke of the existence of an underground passage that linked the lake to the Pacific—feeding Cocibolca, as the Indians referred to the lake, not only with a constant supply of bull shark but with the infusion of salt water they surely needed to survive. Thorson's preliminary findings established that the shark could, and did, thrive in both the river and the lake.

The handful of fishermen that he hired on this first expedition hooked nineteen shark in four different locations: at the lake's northernmost end; at San Carlos; halfway down the river; and in the turbid waters at its mouth. All, Thorson claimed, were the same species. Two years later he witnessed with his own eyes what he'd expected to see for some time: shark fins, cutting upstream. "There is [now]," he wrote, "no real basis for the belief that the shark population is landlocked."

It may have been, albeit with no scientific evidence, that the lakeside dwellers had always believed this to be the case. To them, there were two distinct species: *"tintoreros,"* so named because of their dark undersides, and the paler-bellied *"visitantes."* "Visitors," then, though why, or from where, no one had ever agreed. For Thorson, extending his research into the late 1960s, the evidence was building. To those who said the shallow rapids that punctuated the San Juan's middle passage would prevent the migration of sharks, he simply pointed out that barges of three-foot draft regularly made the passage. "If, as observed, vessels of the size of barges can make their way up the river, it seems completely indefensible to assume that the rapids present a barrier to the movement of strong swimmers such as sharks." In 1969, shortly after he began his program, three sharks, first hooked on the Atlantic shelf, were recovered in Lake Nicaragua. And the traffic, it turned out, was two-way: not long afterward, nine fish tagged at San Carlos were all recovered at Barra del Colorado, three of these having covered the two-hundred-kilometer stretch in just over seven days.

Thorson had come to Nicaragua at the turning point in the life of the bull shark. Between the mid-1960s and the early 1970s, the years of his researches, the shark-fishing industry was at its peak: each year, from several different locations—the

river mouth, San Carlos, Granada, the Solentiname Islands—
between ten thousand and twenty thousand sharks were caught
and butchered. Clearly and indisputably, this was unsustainable,
whatever the fishermen's protestations about nature's ability to
effortlessly right itself.

In his concluding report, written in 1982 after one last, vale-
dictory survey, one detects a leaden mournfulness that this great
fish, his life's work, should have been so thoughtlessly exploited.
In 1969, he noted, a great shark-processing plant had been
installed at Granada, and fifty San Carlos and Solentiname fishermen had been contracted. The shark, as a result, had been
brought near extinction.

But there was hope: already, Thorson wrote, reduced shark
fishing had seen a modest revival in numbers. Not, however,
that the shark was safe: another threat loomed, in the shape of a
transcontinental canal, one of the most resilient of Nicaragua's
glory dreams, newly resurrected with the Sandinista victory.
Thorson, near despair, did his best to sound sanguine. The
canal, and consequent damming of the river, "may well benefit
Nicaragua economically, and make a port of Granada, and perhaps later of Managua; but if so, these benefits will be exchanged
for the unique distinction, presently enjoyed by Nicaragua, of
having within its boundaries the classical population of sharks
existing in an inland body of freshwater. An era, extending from
the *conquistadores* to the present, will have come to an end."

To date, these prophecies had proved unduly pessimistic.
Desire for an east-west trade route remained fervent, at least
among government officials, but the focus had shifted from
the San Juan corridor to Monkey Point, a coastal promontory
between San Juan del Norte and Bluefields, from where it

was hoped it would be possible to carve a "dry canal" direct to Managua, lay a railway, build a port. The river itself—undammed, winding free—no longer broiled with the entrails of many thousand shark, and supported a good deal fewer shark fishermen than it once had; but the shark was slowly staking a comeback, and those fishermen that remained were wilier, more cunning, pathologically secretive.

Some days later—endless, fruitless days toiling the river in search of fish, shark, anything to feed Salvador's family—we were heading back upstream, close to the bank, approaching a curve of stiller, peat-dark water. The river had fallen a little, and a high-tide scurf of sun-bleached grasses and nest-tangled twigs, three feet above the water, marked its previous high. Once in the still water we began to make good headway, paddles in perfect time. We came out into the sunshine again.

"Buenas! Hombres!"

A man with an ax stood on the bank. He was small, and gray-haired, but there was a honed-down wiriness to him. *"Hombres!"*

We lifted our paddles, felt the dugout twist slowly in the current. He called out for us to land, to pull the canoe up on the mud. "Sure," I heard Salvador murmur. "Why not?"

The man stood where he was, just observing, as we hauled up and laid the paddles in the hull. When we began to walk toward him, he waved an arm and turned for the hut.

Salvador glanced at me, and in his arched-eyebrow shrug I recognized my own weariness, my own readiness to have this decision, at least, taken for me. It had been a long morning—a long few days, in fact, almost a week since the coconut boat had gone—and the sun on the back of my neck had begun to tinge everything a faint chlorine blue. My legs felt unsteady too. I followed last, picking my way across the rough ground, the earth like molasses, split by felled trees.

The hut itself looked as if it dated from far earlier, though its corrugated steel roof was so new it appeared lacquered, flashing off the water. The man climbed the steps and waited by the open doorway.

Inside it was dark. The hut consisted of a single small room, barely twelve feet square, and the only light came from the doorway; as I stepped through I blocked out the sun and only when I was properly inside, and seated on the floor beside Salvador, did I see that every last inch of wall space was hung with the jawbones of sharks—jawbones of every size, dried and prized open, smaller specimens fitted inside the gape of monsters, most of the incisors still intact, brilliant white against the leather yellow of the jawbones.

I followed the walls around, trying to guess the total—sixty, seventy? They were hung floor to ceiling, secured to the wood with twine. There were so many that they almost ceased to feel macabre; if I half closed my eyes, and squinted till my vision was blurred, they appeared a grand-patterned wall covering. There was little else in the hut—a bundle of fishing nets, some polystyrene buoys. The floor was covered in fruit husks and a fine grit that felt like crushed shells. When I looked again at the old fisherman I found his eyes already on me, his arms folded, an expectant smile on his lips.

"How many?" I said. "How many is this?" Beside me, Salvador was grunting to himself, fighting hard not to be impressed, I guessed: against this, his own recent poor-luck run looked even more paltry.

The fisherman spoke through his smile. "To be honest, I've never counted. But if you're asking me how many sharks I've caught in my long life . . ." He paused, cupped his chin in his hands.

"No." I waited. Silence. "But do tell," I added. "How many?"

"Ahhh!" He knocked his forehead with the flat of his hand. "Many thousand. And not once did a shark even scratch my skin." Again, that weighted pause. "Though I did have two dogs, two fine hunting dogs, that were not so lucky."

He had worked for Thorson—not the coincidence it might have seemed, since Thorson's approach, which was to pay only for shark brought to him alive, meant most fishermen from these shark-rich lower stretches would have come into contact with him at one time or another. The man claimed Thorson had given him a new respect for the sharks, even though, after the American had left, he'd hunted as voraciously as before.

"I was," he sighed, "a rich man. House in Barra. Boat with engine. Beautiful wife."

"What happened?"

He uncrossed his legs, inched forward on his haunches, lowered his voice to a baritone whisper. "Drinking." He back-angled his thumb toward his mouth. "The great devil alcohol."

"And now? Do you still find there are many sharks? I mean, Salvador and I haven't had much luck these last few days." I glanced at Salvador; he was staring out the door, expressionless.

"Well," said the fisherman, rubbing his hands, checking from me to Salvador, then back again, "they're still there. But you have to be clever. They know we're here. So we fishermen have to know where to find them. I know where to go."

"I know where to go as well," Salvador coughed. He was

still focused on the doorway, on the open sky beyond. "I don't find any."

"There may be all kinds of reasons for that," the fisherman said, his voice softer. "I've been here longer, all my life. I'm an old man." He cleared his throat. "I caught one yesterday."

Salvador started round. "Yesterday?" His voice trembled. "Where?"

"Ah," the older man murmured. "You know how it is. I'd love to tell you, really I would. But I can't. Sorry."

Despite the bravado, the quiet assurance that no one knew the river as well as he, the older fisherman led a cautious life, conscious that though the numbers of bull shark were down on the boom years, the sharks were still there—prowling, invisible, potent as ever. He'd even begun washing in the river, which he'd never dared to as a child, but would venture in no further than knee-deep, and then only for the briefest moments, his eyes on the water ahead, scanning for movement, for that infinitesimal flutter of turbulence that indicated the onrush of a big fish. He'd shown "respect," in short, which was why, he believed, he'd made it to old age unscathed.

That night, inspired by the old fisherman's example, I took to the river to wash. It was the first time my body had felt soap and water since Horacio's hand-cranked shower in San Juan del Norte, and afterward I felt strangely chilled, as if I'd just sacrificed a vital layer of insulation. As the fisherman had directed, I stood in the shallows, using one of Salvador's enamel mugs to ladle water across my back and chest. Mud squeezed up between my toes until my ankles were stuck fast. Thus trapped, I watched the river with an extra, near-paranoid acuteness. Halfway out, a tarpon whiplashed clear of the water, an explosion of jeweled spray in the dying sun, and I panicked backward, lost my balance with my feet still glued, and sat down heavily in the tea-warm shallows. With mud all down my shorts and the backs of my legs, I sat on the bank and attempted to dry myself.

Night came noisily: only the river, it seemed, was still, fireflies and their quicksilver reflections like tiny neon sparks, far off across space. With the breeze coming off the land, curling northeast for the Atlantic, I didn't hear the *thuddathudda* of the diesel until a half minute after I'd spotted the coconut barge itself, on its way back to San Juan del Norte. It was sweeping fast downriver in the darkness, the erratic skitter of handheld flashlights at the bow. There were shouts, but the barge kept its course against the far bank. I stood and waved and yelled out, hoping they'd at least notice, remember me for their return, but no flashlight turned my way. Wombed in its own small-world hubbub of diesel and stewed chicken fat, the barge passed on into the night: at that speed, emptied of coconuts and running with the current, it would be in San Juan del Norte before the small hours.

The next day I stayed behind when Salvador left to go fishing. Gazing out on the river, reluctant even to turn around lest somehow I miss the coconut barge passing, I found myself dreaming of the historical freight this river carried. Now, a time of peace, it was hard to picture the past shellfire between these banks, but so much of the river's history consisted of just that.

For the most part, the instigator of hostilities had been either Britain or America, and when it had been the one, the other would pontificate loftily about colonial greed. When Britain captured the mouth of the river in 1848, it despatched sorties to where I now sat, near the mouth of the Sarapiquí, in an attempt to secure the entire lower stretch; one year later, Ephraim Squier, the U.S. envoy, came this way and could barely contain his disgust. The British, he claimed, had slaughtered twenty Nicaraguans at Sarapiquí—brave boatmen who "had made their stand against the English after the capture of San Juan," the station he believed was rightly America's, now known by "the ghastly name of Greytown." As his boatmen paddled his party upriver, the envoy's words betrayed an entire nation's jilted ambition. "The whole affair was a wanton act of aggression, and worthy only of pirates. No wonder the sailors hissed 'Death to the English' through their closed teeth as we swept past the scene of their humiliation."

Some seventy years earlier, another, substantially larger English invasion had come this way. When Horatio Nelson left San Juan del Norte on 28 March 1780, heading upriver, his train of boats was chaotic, ill-planned, and poorly suited for river passage, resembling nothing so much as some ramshackle procession from the Middle Ages. First off were Indian canoes carrying his pilots, then his cutter, then the boats carrying his officers, after them a slew of pitpans and *pangas* with troops and rations and arms, and, finally, trailing badly even after the first hour's headway, the heaviest craft, loaded with gunpowder, provisions, and troops.

The river was low—this was the dry season, and there had been no freak rains to raise the levels—and the ships grounded again and again as the pilots tried to guide their retinue out of the estuarine shallows to the main sweep of the San Juan. That first day, eyed by alligators, harried by low-screeching parakeets and egrets, they covered a mere six and a half miles. The second day, walleyed with exhaustion, they rested. The third day, with the heaviest craft still stuck fast, Nelson ordered back *pangas* to salvage provisions. The fourth day, by mistake, the expedition hit the Colorado fork of the San Juan and began heading down-river again. Never again, Nelson swore, would he take instruction from his pilots.

It took them two weeks before they even sighted the Spanish fortifications at El Castillo—two weeks of unfit soldiers wilting from heat exhaustion, of nervous nights' camping at the edge of "these horrid woods," of dining on such local delicacies as stewed howler monkey. The twenty-two-year-old Nelson, too much of a greenhorn to feign indifference, suffered as much as his men; though starving, he refused the monkey stew, pale to the gills at the sight of the swollen head, the glazed-fruit eyes, the child-sized limbs. He was less squeamish when it came to iguana, wild duck, and turtle, but was careless at crucial moments: within sight of the Spanish positions, and momentarily jubilant at having almost made his goal, he bent to drink from a jungle pool. Within hours, he was wracked with dysentery.

He was more circumspect when it came to the river itself; warned off by his Indian scouts, he wisely refrained from swimming. The San Juan, they claimed, swarmed with sharks as well as smaller, barracuda-type fish that would thrash the water to foam after even the smallest fragment of meat. And it was not just loose scraps that drove these fish crazy—they'd go for anything fleshy and bite-sized. In such waters, the Indians informed their soft-chinned commander, a man would not remain a man for long.

With the San Juan such a long-established corridor for

invasion, it was perhaps surprising that the most spectacular of all the U.S. attempts at conquest was pitched not at the Atlantic but at Nicaragua's better-defended, and more populous, Pacific coast. But then the invader—self-styled "Presidente" William Walker, whose name today still held a bogeyman's power, hurled as a curse by children—was no run-of-the-mill megalomaniac. Nicaragua belonged to him, he believed, almost by divine right, and he came breathtakingly close to succeeding in his ambitions.

From early photographs, it was hard to picture the man of destiny he was to later become. Here, instead, was a sallow, rheumy-eyed adolescent who had lived, according to one biographer, a "monastic" childhood. To his Nashville, Tennessee, schoolmates he was something of a joke—"Honey," or "Missy." He was fully grown at five feet four, and, by the age of twenty-two, lone and friendless, was already multiqualified—a degree in classics, another in medicine from the University of Pennsylvania, yet another from the Sorbonne. A trained lawyer to boot, he became, aged twenty-four, the editor of a radical New Orleans periodical. By 1855, a decade of anti-Establishment posturing having roughened him to a lawless maverick, he set sail with his fifty-eight-strong band of "immortals" to capture Nicaragua.

His justification was energetically argued: Nicaragua was run by conservatives, based in Granada, who were on poor terms with the United States and were threatening to impound, for nonpayment of dues, the United States's San Juan passenger barges. Walker marched in, allied himself with the liberal opposition, and within six months had seized Granada. He appointed himself president, announced that English was henceforth the official language, and introduced slavery.

The whole misbegotten episode he recorded in a book. As

told in his own words, the story of this renegade band of *filibus-teros* is self-serving, blind, fantastical, but seldom less than grip-ping. To the end, his moral certainty remained unwavering. "The filibusters had the will to administer justice and would, when they had the power, protect the weak and the innocent from the crimes of the lawless and abandoned," he wrote. His men were "Americans in the service of Nicaragua," and their eventual ejection at the hands of Costa Rican and British forces filled him with righteous bitterness.

In retreat, after nearly a year in power, he dynamited and put to the torch most of the center of Granada, conducting sum-mary executions—"politic and humane," he would plead—and, finally, was routed for good. The rump of his force, fleeing down the San Juan for the open ocean, was snuffed out at El Castillo. To his former comrades he promised, in revenge, "a return to the land whence we were unjustly brought." And, sure enough, he was back again just months later, for one last push.

Round midnight, sixteen hours after I'd spotted it heading downriver, I heard the barge again. This time, nose into the cur-rent, hammering at full whine, the noise of the engine reached me some ten minutes before I saw the spidery grab of flashlight beams at the bow. I held my breath, praying they'd remember me: over a week had passed, and evidently, by the speed of the turnaround, they were up against the clock. I'd stuffed my pack, was ready to leap aboard and go. I stood up, then sat down again, realizing I was invisible against the dark bank of jungle and would not, however hard I waved, be able to attract their atten-tion if they were intent on pressing onward.

Salvador, silent these past few days since our visit to the old fisherman, sat behind me on the steps of his hut, grumbling incoherently, looking down when I twisted round to talk to him. He, who'd seemed so concrete a presence that first night, had gradually dissolved before my eyes the more time we'd spent together. I guessed it was family problems, as much as his own failure at the hunt: five days ago his wife had left up the Sarapiquí with the children, and since then he'd spoken barely a word.

For a few minutes more the barge inched across my vision, hugging the far bank as it had on its hurry downstream, then, gradually and unmistakably, and just at the moment when it looked as if it might pass on by, it began to alter its course. Two flashlights swept the midsection of the river, and as the barge loosened into the current, it appeared to hover motionless, then slip sideways, pressured by the weight of water. The moon came out, then was swallowed again by cloud, and in that instant, with the barge well over halfway across, I spotted two men at the bow. At their feet were plastic sacks, slick black in the moonlight. Behind them, lit sporadically by jerking flashlight beams, scuttled three or four men, leaning wide from the gunwales, shouting as they ran from stern to bow and back.

At twenty yards I heard Salvador's name being called, and Salvador, suddenly keen as a puppy, jumped down the steps and ran to my side.

"They've come," he stuttered. "They've come."

"Don't they always? Anyway, they knew I was here. And I asked them."

He squinted toward the boat, as if suddenly myopic. He rubbed his palms down his shorts. "Not for weeks, sometimes." His breath came quickly. "Sometimes they never stop by here."

The pair on the bow had hoisted up their bags, as if preparing to jump. The barge was just three or four yards away now, parallel to the bank, and I could see full-weighted hammocks, like pupae, strung from the rafters. One of the men lifted his sack with both hands, yelled across to Salvador.

Through the darkness, knocking Salvador to the ground, came the first of the sacks. The men followed, trying to make the bank in one leap, stumbling forward in the shallows, dragging themselves almost on all fours finally onto the dry. I watched them as they hefted their belongings onto their shoulders, wondering what route they'd taken, what contraband they were carrying that had brought them back so fast. They nodded in my direction, grunted thanks at Salvador, cut round the back of the hut, and disappeared into the forest.

I took up my pack, turned to Salvador to offer my thanks for his help and hospitality, even though both of us knew he'd barely noticed me these past few days. He nodded, bounced from hand to hand the bottle of rum I'd just given him. "Okay, my friend," he said, shaking my hand. *"Que le vaya bien.* Go well."

Behind me came the juggernaut growl of the diesel, a snarling of gears. I dropped my pack. "Hey!"

The barge, under half-moon light, was moving again up-current. I ran up the bank till I was parallel with the wheelhouse. "Hey, Captain!"

A light snapped on, flashed across Salvador, then paused on me. I shielded my eyes, pointed at my pack. "Hang on a second!"

"Who are you?" came a voice. "Police?"

"Police?" I cried. "No! I was with you last week. I'm going to El Castillo, remember? I need a ride."

There was a quick exchange, then the engine slowed off a little. I could hear laughter, a couple of men at first, then a ripple down the length of the boat. Another flashlight came on.

"Ah, yes," came the captain's voice, dropping, with perfect timing, into the silent dark. *"You."*

In the small hours, toward dawn, I climbed out onto the gunwale and struggled to the stern to take a pee. I'd not slept: the barge this time was even fuller than before, and all the rafter space was taken. I'd laid my pack on the floor and tried to wedge my back between sturdy calves behind, but had been forced to give up and spend the night crouched forward over my knees, forearm as pillow. With a sporadic moon, the captain had decided to press on, and throughout the night the barge labored hard against the current, the grinding of the diesel setting up a persistent, parallel hum inside my head.

From the stern, with no handrail, I wavered unsteadily, watching the wake twist white, then settle into the black river. I could just pick out treetops, silvery in the moonlight, and the grooves of the wake. I was glad to be moving on. Underpopulated, with everyday life a set of obstacles to be struggled with or simply endured, these lower waters had felt like the dead heart of the river, and I was looking forward once more to bigger communities, places that did not feel so utterly finished, so incontrovertibly the end of the line. I was also thinking of the sharkmen up this higher stretch of river, of stories I'd heard of sharks caught off the El Castillo foreshore by men who spurned dugouts to wade barefoot into the rapids. With Arturo's warnings of the lakeside fishermen still sounding in my ears, with his cryptic scribblings burning a hole in my pocket, I was experiencing a growing thrill of unease. I did not know what to expect, since so much I'd heard had been contradictory and folk-

loric. I knew of the giant shark, of lakeside Indians who'd sacrificed their dead to the bull shark, of the age-old enmity between
the shark men of the lake and those of the Atlantic coast. I also
knew that I was not American, and in the regions into which I
was heading now, that was a distinct advantage.

Coming back from the stern, I ran into the captain. I waited
for him to swing down from the gunwale, and on the flat-back
stern, our feet ashiver with the thrum of the prop shaft running
under us, we stood and faced each other.

"Good trip?" I said. "I never expected you to be back so
quickly."

"Eh, well, you know." He spoke at my chest. "The pressure's on."

"But you'd forgotten me, right?" I meant this to sound easy-
going, as if it had just occurred to me, but it came out petulant.

He patted my elbow, made to move past. "We'll be in El
Castillo by the end of the day." He planted himself at the very
stern, legs set wide, his back to me. I heard him unzip.

"You'll be pleased to get there," he said, with a chuckle. "You
can buy some soap, have a wash."

Dawn brought low cloud and mist, which hung in the windless
forest like smoke. It was hard to guess how far we'd come during
the night—ten, twenty kilometers at best, judging by the
length of time it was taking the scenery to change.

Through the rain I could see small farms. In places, where
the gradient was steepest, the land had peeled away from
itself—landslips like claw marks, red-clay scars. Soft land, easily
fissured and fractured.

"See that?" said the man next to me, pointing. "That's what happens when you take away all the trees." He spat into his hand, rinsed it overboard. "Costa Ricans—what do they know?"

He was from Managua—originally, many years ago—and the sight of this crumbling hillside triggered memories of the night of 23 December 1972, the night of the earthquake. The ease with which he fell into the story made him seem like El Desastre's very own ancient mariner, and certainly he swung on me as if worried I might escape, one hand over mine, face pressed close.

He'd been working as a servant back then, as chauffeur for a rich trading family. The first shock had come when he was asleep in his watchman's hut at the end of the drive. It had been a normal enough night until that point—coolish, even, for the time of year, and he'd been sleeping under a light blanket—but after the first tremor the air suddenly thickened and grew hotter, and he threw off the blanket and walked in his underpants into the street. People were on their doorsteps, fanning themselves with newspapers. Downhill toward the lake and the Mombacho volcano he could see a faint spreading glow, like a backyard bonfire. He was just about to go inside when the second shock hit.

"It was just before midnight, cars rolling by with their windows down, people playing music, and the whole road just opened up like the end of the world had come."

He was wheezing now, as if right back there, amid those first seconds of confusion. His employers' house had folded in on itself and the pavement he was standing on buckled like hot plastic; fire exploded out of front doors and blew out windows. He ran barefoot up the gravel sweep, scarcely daring to think of the children, knowing all too well where their bedrooms were.

"And then I see the Cadillac!" He squeezed my hand harder,

sighing as he remembered the make and model, a sleek black limousine now stamped flat by a concrete girder. Every day he'd buffed that coachwork; now its roof was the same height as the hood. He'd spent the next two hours in the debris of the building, he and the other servants screaming at each other through the falling dust, emerging finally with only two out of seven bodies—the two youngest, boy and girl twins.

"Look," he said, throwing back the last of his coffee, nudging the mug hard in the cook's backside till she turned and took it back. "I'm no fan of the rich, but what I saw that night made me see that none of us stand a chance, not when God's made up His mind."

"What did you do then?" I said.

"Took the boat to San Carlos." He leaned back, ran his hand in the water. "Became a shark fisherman."

"Shark fisherman?" From chauffeur?

"Managua was destroyed. San Carlos was where the money was. So they said."

"Were they right?"

He swept a hand from his chest to his knees. His trousers were shiny with dirt, his shirt rose up over his waistband, the cotton worn muslin-thin. "What does it look like? Do I look like a man who made his fortune?"

We talked a little more. He had a brother in El Castillo; the two of them, he said, could show me around.

Midafternoon, we came to our first set of rapids. Idling the diesel, the captain stepped from the wheelhouse and ordered all passengers into the *panga*: to unweight the barge enough to climb the rapids he wanted an empty boat. Loading all thirty took three trips to and from the bank while the barge balanced in the current just below the white water. I wondered how necessary this whole maneuver was, since the side barge, with a full load of coconuts, was freighted far deeper than ours had been. More than anything it felt like an opportunity to strut a little seamanship—the captain's sons ordering us from boat to boat, powering the *panga* away afterward, to pilot the mother ship up through the rocks and slip channels. We waited, watched the boats pass out of sight.

In the quiet, gathered like refugees in the shade of trees as wide as houses, the men began talking noisily about other rivers they'd traveled, comparing methods of navigation. No man with any experience, one said, would have used an engine up the Río Coco rapids; the others nodded, one eye on the river. The old shark fisherman stood alone, some way back, scratching at his belly, mumbling to himself.

On and upriver, our progress slowed by two more sets of rapids, by being again made to wait ashore while the barge was piloted through without us, people began to settle into their hammocks once more. The captain had promised El Castillo by dusk, so I'd made no claim on any rafter space, but the light was already beginning to fade and we were still, by most estimates, an hour or two off.

It was these final miles, approaching the Spanish defenses for the first time, that had been so crucial to Nelson. His expedition had struggled over each set of rapids, the Indian scouts dragging the canoes through the shallows while the expedition waited on the banks. Each time he'd stepped ashore, he had expected an ambush.

The first Spanish fortress was sighted ten days after leaving San Juan del Norte—a feverish claque of soldiers on an ellipsoid island just above the Bartola rapids. Under darkness, Nelson ordered the cutter upriver, escorted by a flotilla of Indian canoes. It was an interminable night: at points, every soldier was up to his waist in the river, hauling the cutter through the broken water. At dawn, they were fully exposed when the Spanish opened fire. Nelson shouted his men forward—sailors grabbed cutlasses, soldiers their muskets—and, shoeless in the scarlet mud, ran hollering toward the battery. The Spanish threw down their arms; the island, Bartola, Nelson rechristened St. Bartholomew, a change of name that lasted barely a month.

Yet things had not gone too badly: so far, he'd had just one casualty, and that from natural causes: a soldier bitten in the face by a tree snake. "He was found dead," Nelson's physician recorded, "with all the symptoms of putrefaction; a yellowness and swelling all over his body; and the eye, near to which he was bitten, all dissolved." But by that time, Nelson's attention was elsewhere. He was corralling his men for the final push, the assault on El Castillo; was already moving on, confident of victory.

The sky was turning salmon as we passed Bartola—now a tangle-brush landfall, some two or three hundred yards long, in the middle of fast-flowing shallows—and the forest on the Nicaraguan bank, unbroken until this point, began to peel back to reveal rough grazing, and homesteads cut into sections of high, ancient forest. Where the trees ran to the water's edge colonies of egrets had gathered, as if to roost, and in the pale light, viewed from far off, I guessed at a thousand, so closely packed as to blur into one solid wedge of color.

From the roof, with the captain's sons, two gauchely flirtatious teenage girls, and the old shark man, I glimpsed El Castillo at the same moment as the captain, below us, sounded his approach bell. Against the forest-fire glow of the sky the castle stood out in silhouette, raised above the skyline on a hill so perfectly conical it appeared man-made. Around its base the lights of the town streaked the dark water like clown paints. This final approach was a good half mile, and sentries atop the battlements would have been able to spy even further still. Of the twelve Spanish garrisons along the San Juan during the eighteenth century, El Castillo was the strongest, the best equipped, the most naturally impregnable.

Nelson first sighted it on 10 April 1780, two weeks after starting upriver. He understood immediately that there was no chance of a direct attack, and so ordered his men ashore. Ahead, freshly whitewashed, El Castillo de la Inmaculada Concepción had gleamed totemic, a hundred feet above the rapids, armed with twenty cannons, a brass mortar, and a garrison of seventy, something less than half of Nelson's total.

Hacking through the forest to the south of the fortress, one of Nelson's soldiers was pounced on by a jaguar; only the howling of the Miskito advance party saved his skin from being torn from his back. With the weather worsening, Nelson, shaky with dysentery and stuttering feverish from malaria, ordered a lightning bombardment: he'd seize it, tear down the Spanish flag, and this "inland Gibraltar of Spanish America"—in the words of the Jamaican governor, John Dalling—would belong to Britain. "By our possession of it," the governor had predicted, "Spanish America [will be] severed in two."

El Castillo," sighed the old fisherman, edging up close to me. "It's good to be home."

I nodded, exhausted. It was almost dark, and the outline of the forest was merging with the night sky. He put a hand on my shoulder.

"You know what happened here?"

"I was just thinking about all that." We were traveling close to the southern bank now, away from the broken water that marked the central channel, slowing in preparation for landing. "You know—Nelson, all the British pirates."

He knocked his palm against his forehead. "What about our Rafaela? You've heard of her, yes?"

"Of course," I said, but he ignored me, lost in his reverie. "Rafaela Herrera, 1762, daughter of the garrison commander. The English attacked El Castillo, the commander was killed. Rafaela took command, fired the cannon that sank the English ship. You've seen her face on the banknote?"

I nodded, dug in my wallet. She was there, on the ten-córdoba bill, a seventeen-year-old in what looked like a billowing nightdress, holding the taper to that fateful cannon.

He took the note from me, kissed it noisily, thrust it back at me, warm and wet.

"Now she—she is the real Nicaraguan. She is the reason why we will never be conquered, why the flag of no other country," he pronounced, pointing into the night sky, "will ever fly over that castle."

10

In appearance—blunt snout, wide-set eyes—the bull shark is markedly different from other sharks. Like an actual bull, it squares up thickset round the shoulders and midsection—"very heavy-bodied," in the words of one scientist. Its eyes are smaller than those of most sharks; its tail fin, unlike most, is flattened off, back-angled, thickened with one long ridge of muscle. Wet, its underside seems pale as clouds, its spine the color of the seabed, although once hauled onto land, with the hide dry in the heat, the beast will fade to gray, to become special no longer.

For, undeniably, it *is* special, and it was not hard to understand the fearful reverence in which it was held. No shark but *Carcharhinus leucas* possesses the ability to transfer from salt water to fresh, and for years, even to those who sacrificed their lives to its study, its secret remained obscure. All sharks, after all, are geared to marine life, their excretory systems especially adapted to prevent dehydration by retaining nitrogenous waste—urea—in the bloodstream, thus maintaining an osmotic balance with the surrounding salt water. For the bull shark, many thousand years of lying in wait for turtle and manatee and tarpon in the brackish water at the mouth of the San Juan and, eventually, of following those prey upriver had triggered its key adaptation: the ability to shed salt from its bloodstream the further it penetrates inland. In short, it had developed a built-in, self-righting buoyancy vest, good for all conditions.

Unique, then, but not beautiful. Its jaw is wider and squarer than any other; its incisors are proportionately more fearsome; its eyes are tiny, since sight, in turbid waters, need not be perfect. And those purblind eyes stalked this river: steel ball-bearing eyes, set deep in the sides of its skull. But overwhelming them, in terms of power, is its formidable, tank-armored snout, shielding olfactory sensors common to all sharks but in none so refined as in the bull shark. *Leucas* will swallow anything—squid, sea urchin, sandbar shark, porpoise, tuna, stingray—but tease it with just a couple of drops of fresh blood and, far away downriver, that great head will set still, twitch like a Doberman, and the chase will be on.

On the El Castillo foreshore, something like fifteen years before, depending on whom I talked to, just such a scent had been laid down. I heard the details first from a very old woman, who lived in a clapboard two-room on a hill by the overgrown graveyard at the top end of town. I'd been passing, and had waved; she'd called me over, and then she'd started talking.

She claimed to be a hundred and three, though her back was still straight and her skin good. Her eyes, however, betrayed great age: cloudy, scabbed, liverish, they strayed all over my face. She'd outlived all her brothers and sisters, as well as every one of her six children. Two of her three grandsons had been killed in the civil war. She recited this on automatic, as if she'd told it many times before. Then, one arm on the front rail, she lowered herself back into her rocker. "So tell me, young man, what is your story?"

I talked a little about my journey, my fascination with the freshwater shark, with those communities that had had to adjust to life in the constant presence of such a predator. She listened, eyes swiveling, fingers caressing her turkey-wattle dewlap. A crowd was gathering behind me, and the more people that stopped, the more flamboyant the old woman's gestures became. In a nearby yard a rooster crowed. She held up her hand; abruptly, the noise ceased.

"Fifteen years ago," she said, rocking herself into motion again, "when I was a young woman and my family was still alive, God rest their souls, I was passing the day with my good friend Gloria." She paused, breathed deeply, and crossed herself. From behind me came a mumble, then a hissed *shhh*. The old woman looked up again, pressed two fingers to her brow, fixed on a point far over my head, and continued in a low monotone.

"It was a fiesta, the wedding anniversary of Gloria's son, and I was helping prepare the feast. We were having pig." A gasp from behind. I looked round. Two women had their hands to their mouths. I smiled at them, suspecting that this melodrama was being laid on for my benefit, but they coughed and looked past me, focusing hard on the old woman.

"Pig," she repeated. "Gloria lived by the river and she had reared this beautiful pig in a pen under the house." It was easy to picture—the buildings lining the El Castillo shoreline were all raised on stilts, and underneath, in the soft ooze and amid detergent empties and the hard-caked froth of the last high water, hogs and bitches rooted for leftovers.

This particular pig, raised for the occasion, had been garroted at dawn. By ten, the two old friends had collected their cleavers and chopping boards and had heaved the carcass onto a low table and set the table in the shallows. Like washerwomen, they shoved their sleeves up over their elbows and set to work. They began with the entrails, sweeping them riverward with a broad sideways wipe, letting blood from the split guts sluice the surface clean. They gossiped, they laughed, they reminisced about how good life had been to them. Behind them, from the house, came the early-morning shouts of children, the clatter of plates, happy-family chaos.

I could sense what was coming, and guessed, to judge from the absolute quiet as the old woman paused again, that those around me had heard this story many times before. The old woman waited again, touched her handkerchief to the corner of her eye.

"And so, I tell you," she went on, "there we were preparing the feast. We'd almost finished, I was leaning forward to clean my hands, and suddenly there was a crashing in the water in front of us and Gloria was grabbed by the legs." Her audience gave an appreciative murmur; the old woman pressed the handkerchief to her mouth, let out a low moan. "She was a small woman, Gloria, smaller than me, and the shark thrashed its big tail and took her down whole." She paused. "I've never been near that river again."

"No," I said, sensing the crowd behind me disperse. "I can see that. What a terrible thing to have witnessed."

"Yes." She began to fold the handkerchief, concentrating hard on the exact creases. "It quite spoiled the party."

She looked up at me. "Oh, don't look so serious, young man. It was terrible, of course it was, but life must go on." Her eyes, momentarily still, caught mine. She smiled.

"That shark," I said, holding her gaze. "What did it look like? Did it ever come back?" For, I knew, a shark that had hit lucky would haunt the same stretch of water for weeks, months afterward. Sharks did not possess huge brains—the whole cortex was not much larger than a clenched fist—but their memory for blood was unerring.

"We never saw it again. And you know why?"

I shook my head.

She leaned forward; her knuckles whitened as she gripped the arms of the rocking chair. "Because it was special. A once-only."

"How do you mean?"

"It was red. A red shark."

"Red?" I laughed, then checked myself. "Red from all the blood, perhaps?"

"When I say it was red, young man," she growled, "I know what it is I'm saying. It was not gray, nor green like bad vegetables, like other sharks look, but dark red." She looked about her. "Like the color of the dirt on the path you're standing on."

"Red. I see. How do you explain that?"

"There is no reason. Every fifty years, maybe more, God sends us a red shark. That is why I do not worry. That is why I know Gloria has gone to a good place."

Every morning at first light, before the heat of the day closed in, I'd climb the long red path to the graveyard, but I never again saw the old woman. Her rocking chair was there, tear-dropped with dew, and one morning I even saw her dainty handkerchief, folded where her hand had lain, but it was as if she herself had never existed, was as much an invention of my overcurried imagination as the red shark, I was sure, was of hers. But then, one day, I heard talk of the red shark from someone else, a man who had no reason to blindly sign up to baloney.

He was a bar owner for whom business, with no beer to sell, had gone markedly quiet. All day he sat at a plastic table in the middle of the bare room, on the wall behind him a humorous seventies poster of a topless woman being "examined" by a chimpanzee in a doctor's coat and stethoscope. He had time to talk, in short, and was surprised that I should have even thought of doubting the old woman's account. To his mind, the only uncertain aspect to her story was the red shark's very rarity: he claimed red sharks were constantly making the migration lakeward, and added that it was they, not the bull sharks, that were the man-eaters. The only reason no fisherman had yet hooked a red shark was that they were wily survivors, quick to learn. Sightings, once infrequent, were now very rare indeed.

So it existed, this mythical beast, or at least people believed it to exist, which amounted to much the same thing. Man creates his own monsters: if none exists, he imagines them into being. He is a sceptic, for sure, but his desire for belief always wins through. This river, with its unique beast, was a conduit for such fantasy, a channel not only of mud and silt and plantation runoff but of imagination born of necessity. The existence of the bull shark in these waters had spawned a whole subspecies of myth, all equally real, all cleaved to fiercely.

In the graveyard above the old woman's house, I walked through sticky-seeded grasses, the ground underfoot rough-tilled, uncertain. In the center was a giant tree, wide as a house; its roots spidered through the headstones, forcing a couple of them clean out of the earth. I kept returning here in the hope of discovering graves from Nelson's expedition, but the only headstones that were visible were of concrete, the names scratched roughly, and none dated back much further than the 1980s. There was a radio tower too, built from crosshatched steel like a mini-Eiffel, a technology that would have been more impressive had it been effective: for the last week all telephone links had been down and the navy-boilersuited Telcor workers, clearly in no rush to return to work, strolled the waterfront, greeting each other with cheery shouts of "*Sandino vive!*"

Toward evening, when the heat was more bearable, I would climb the fortress itself. From its battlements, standing atop the innermost keep with the wind beating warm from the forests to the north, I could trace the river through three long sweeps, almost to Bartola. From this height, with a view through 360 degrees, the whole town fell into place: red iron roofs lining the waterfront; fishermen spinning throw nets from dugouts tethered just below the rapids; a sloosh of dishwater, slapping into the shallows from a back window; men hauling lumber carts along the broken lanes. Below me, halfway down the fortress slopes, was a grass-cutter with a machete, one toe dug in against gravity. The fortress itself was compact, well tended, the only other visitors being teenage lovers whom I surprised mid-smooch, stumbling from a darkened alcove, wiping their mouths.

It was hard to imagine a more perfect defensible position: the height; the unbroken view down a good three-mile fetch of water; the near impassable rapids. A place to inspire confidence, in short, where a garrison could quickly imagine itself impregnable, and slip, inevitably, into complacency. Certainly this appeared to be the case in April 1780—a seventy-strong garrison, well stocked with provisions and cannon shot, ambushed with surprising ease by Nelson's forces.

The reason for the speed of the Spanish capitulation dawned only gradually. The complex, Nelson's physician discovered, was "worse than any prison . . . calculated only for the purpose of breeding infection," and it soon began to exact its revenge on the usurpers. Nelson, atremble with malaria, was evacuated downriver; the Miskito Indians, with no sign of their promised booty, deserted; the victorious soldiers, growing quickly bored, fell into endless sessions of rum drinking; the promised reinforcements, scurvy-ridden and malarial, never made the journey.

The English dead—and this can hardly have been much of a morale-booster—were thrown to the sharks or laid out on the riverbank, where their flesh was torn from their bones by turkey buzzards. By the autumn, only eight out of the original two-hundred-strong expeditionary force remained standing, and those in a parlous state. "The negligence of the officers and the drunkenness of the seamen [was] remarkably shameful," wrote an officer dispatched from Jamaica. By Christmas the Spanish were able to stroll unhindered back into their abandoned citadel.

Now, where before there had been the "intolerable stench" of the dying, the pus and ooze from corpses in ragged uniforms lying in gutters, there were smooth walkways of grass; what, during the civil war, had been Sandinista prison cells for captured Contra guerrillas were now storerooms for paintbrushes and machetes and tubs of whitewash. In the central keep there were now even the bones of a museum, with pen-and-ink likenesses of "*los piratas ingleses*" and an eccentric collection of objects unearthed from gardens: old muskets, rusted bayonets, nails the size of kitchen knives, scales for weighing seized Indian gold, wine bottles as small and opaque as cough-mixture bottles, and a cannonball so heavy I felt my back spasm as I struggled it off the floor. It felt like a repository for El Castillo's colonial past, and as I walked around, Arturo's scrawled "Spaniards" kept coming back to me. He'd intended it as an insult, but here, in the heart of the old fortress, it felt more than anything like a simple statement of fact.

Later that evening, under streetlights that pulsed and faded with the erratic supply, I ran into the old fisherman I'd first met on the coconut boat. He was part of a larger group—men in undershirts and sawed-off rubber boots, grilling river shrimp over a wildly spitting brazier. He greeted me with a shrimp tail in one hand, mouth half-full.

"Where you been, *amigo*?" They were all drinking rum, quaffing from ready-mixed quart bottles. He beckoned me to sit. "I thought you wanted to go shark fishing."

"I'm still keen," I said. "When do you want to go?"

"Oh, not me." He coughed a breathy laugh. He smelled of stewed fruit left too long in the sun. "I'm a bit old for all that, don't you think?"

I looked at him. His misshapen face was roughly shaved, his gut looked like it might shear loose at any moment. Since arriving here a few days ago he'd developed a shake, too, like the first stages of Parkinson's. "Okay," I said. "Who, then?"

"The best in town." He took two more shrimp, handed one to me. "César." He pointed his shrimp across the flames. "César!"

A man on the far side looked up, got to his feet. As he walked around to where we sat, I could hear the squelch of water in his rubber boots. He had a big face, and a nose the texture of bark. He shoved out his hand. "César. *Encantado*."

"Shark fishing," I said. "Francisco here says you'll take me."

"*Como no,* of course. Tomorrow morning?"

"Fine."

"Four o'clock? Best to start early." He paused, then looked at his watch, tapped the face. "On second thought let's make that five. You'll never be up by four."

Shortly before five, I found myself groping along blind, moonless lanes, the whole scene uncomfortably reminiscent of my first, fruitless, pre-dawn visit to Arturo. By now I was less curious about the practice of shark fishing itself than about whether, this far upriver, fishermen depended much on shark at all anymore. I suspected not: easier money was to be made in *guapote* and *mojarra*, sold dried and salted to Costa Rica and El Salvador and Mexico. In contrast to the Atlantic coast fishermen, who were still bullish about the living to be made from shark, those on the river seemed more generally depressed in spirit, certainly financially poorer, unsure where their shark, on which they'd depended for so long, had gone. To a man, they were convinced of one thing: that its absence was but temporary, and unrelated to their own feverish hunting of it over the past three decades. It was bigger than all of this, they believed, and answered to its own rhythms. It would return.

In a three-minute flush of electric orange I managed to locate César's house. I'd been heading in the right direction—uphill, away from the river—but without that surge of light, courtesy of a flaky electric grid, would never have found it. A cartoon

shark, I noticed, was charcoaled on the gatepost, but the gate
itself was bolted. I climbed over the fence, walked up the path,
and, with the street lamps sputtering once more into darkness, rapped harder than I'd intended on César's front door.
Silence, then, a moment later, a gravelly, early-morning cough,
followed by whispered cursing. I stepped back. When César
opened the door he was hitching up his pants, jawing at a white-
bread roll.

"You want some?" He rubbed his eyes. "No, you'll have
already eaten, right? Okay, let's get to the river. You're on
time—that's good. Never thought you'd make it. Thought I'd
be out there on my own. But what the hell, eh?" He upended his
boots, sprayed water across the darkness. "That's normal. That's
the way it goes."

All the way to the water he made excuses, as if an empty-
handed outcome was already a certainty. "It's not the new moon,
you know," he murmured, his voice still quaky with sleep.
"Sharks like the new moon."

We hit the quay. "And last new moon?" I said. "What happened then?"

"Good fishing. Of course." He stepped off the concrete edge,
onto the slick-clay mud at the water's edge, and leaned forward,
as if searching for something. "Good fishing all up the river."

Across the water there was a faint hum of light, the rapids
like breakwater, jeweled and glittering, rushing with noise.
César stood up, brandishing a paddle. He waved me over and
together we pushed out into the current. I groped forward,
stumbled blind over his netting and buckets and spindles of
line, barked my shins against the anchor—a rusted section of
cylinder casing that proved too heavy to move without tipping
the canoe clean over—and slumped down in the slimy hull.

For the first hour or more till dawn, it was just us, alone on the river. César lowered the anchor and paid out rope till we balanced in the still water just above the first rack of rapids. We were after bait fish, and he showed me how to cast with a full-arm swing, arcing the heavy shuttlecock-feathered hook with a lasso action, high across the top of the rapids, spooling back fast. We worked in silence—César at the stern, me in the bow—till, after a good twenty casts, with still no sign of a bite, he lowered heavily to his knees and sat back on his haunches.

"Careful you don't fall in," he said, yawning.

"Fine. Okay."

"You're with me," he said, picking at his teeth. "You're my responsibility. Three people drowned in these rapids last year." Of these, two had been grown men—a fisherman who'd lost his footing and cracked himself unconscious on a rock, and another out on a dare—as well as a child, who'd slipped from the far bank when the waters were in flood and had been unable to climb back in. "And that's before we even start worrying about the sharks."

By first light we'd caught just one fish—an olive-green *mojarra* with stickleback fins and startled eyes—which gulped at the air even after César had hammered it repeatedly across the cranium.

When he was reeling in, and in the quiet moments as he rested before casting out again, he talked politics with the everyday ease that had long since ceased to surprise me: politics in Nicaragua were not some abstract theorizing: they affected everyone, and no one held back on opinion. César himself was a refugee; he'd been a Sandinista captain during the civil war, fighting along the Honduran border. Before the revolution he'd run a fishing boat out of Cape Gracias, but when peace finally

came he was unable to settle to it again—those northern
stretches carried too much memory of war, and so he'd moved as
far as he could, all the way south, to the Costa Rican border.
That was three years ago, and though he'd split himself off from
the place of his childhood, he was, it seemed, generally at peace.
"It rains here, I can eat from my garden, I can fish in the river.
I'm tired of war. Here, if it starts again, I can be in Costa Rica in
three hours."

These were an immigrant's views: determinedly hopeful,
committed at all costs to the new life. From those who'd spent
their lives in El Castillo, a less certain picture emerged. From
Oscar Iván Abaunzo, an FSLN *consejero*, came a more familiar story,
of a town almost entirely without employment. During the war,
he said, the Sandinistas had built a palm-oil factory across the
river and had taken on five hundred workers, a quarter of those
from El Castillo. Three years ago, with the Sandinistas ousted
from government, the factory was privatized and the workforce
cut to sixty, of whom only twelve were El Castillo residents.

Oscar, a skilled engineer who supervised the conveyors and
the pulping machinery, still worked there, earning, like the others, a daily wage of just two dollars. For those without jobs, life
was a rickety improvisation. Fishing could be lucrative—twelve
salted *robalos* fetched twenty dollars—but even the most wake-
ful, intuitive fisherman was unlikely to land more than two of
these a day.

But then again, Oscar sighed, gazing out from his broken
balcony across the river at sunset, at least this was peace-
time. During the war there had been raucous gun battles right
in the center of town. A hundred El Castillo men—all of them
Sandinista—had been killed. Some nights, even now, Oscar

would wake hearing the rattle of automatic gunfire and find himself sitting upright in bed, his breath rabbit-quick, blinking around him in the absolute small-hours quiet, wondering where he'd put his gun, before realizing that the night was black and silent, and the only noises were the murmur of insects and the *snipsnip* of palm leaves in the breeze at the water's edge.

At nine, César hauled up the anchor and we moored at the quayside under a row of small boys teasing nylon lines into the oily shallows. César wanted a coffee before continuing, and so we heaved ourselves onto land and he strode off, promising to be back in an hour.

When César returned, two hours later, he was accompanied by another—his son, he said, though the gangling youth looked nothing like him, had yellow skin and pale-horse hair. The young man took the stern, motioned me to the middle.

"American?" he said.

I shook my head. César, still standing, turned to face us. "You think he'd be sitting here if he was American?" His son stopped paddling, let the dugout twist slowly downriver, nose toward the rapids.

"*Exactamente,*" César went on. "I will have nothing to do with the America of sick capitalism, where rich people buy and sell babies." He hooked his hands on his hips, set his jaw. "Give me Russia any day."

Through the hottest part of the day we moored again, covered the bait fish we'd caught with palm leaves, slooshed them with water. César and his son lay back on the bank, pulled their baseball caps over their faces, and fell asleep. I wandered the back lanes, spent long stretches of time sitting in doorways, feeling the heat in my chest as the town siesta'd all around me. With less forest cover, El Castillo was hotter than even San Juan del Norte, and certainly more so than the lower San Juan River, where the jungle gave shade and quiet.

By three they were awake and ready to go. César was abuzz after his siesta and shouted at me to grip tight. Hollering like a rodeo jock, he tillered hard for the center of the rapids. In seconds we were through, soaked and up to our backsides in water. We'd hit rocks, too, but the boat seemed unharmed. César's son bailed. César, diamond-eyed and breathless, shouted up ahead. "See there?" We were spinning toward the next set of rapids, but he was pointing toward the bend, where the river ran slow and deeper. "That black water. That's where the shark lie."

But we were not the first. Another fisherman, tethered close to the bank, was eyeing us as we approached. He was paying out line, his back to us.

"Hey, Carlos!" César shouted. "Any luck? Big ones? Little ones? Anything?"

The current was sweeping us toward the other man's boat—a deep-water whorl that, at the bank, appeared actually to be heading upriver, against the flow. The other fisherman angled a glance over his shoulder, sniffed the air, and began to take in line. Inside his canoe, I now saw, were two big tarpon, sleek as prize salmon.

César reached out his paddle and knocked it against the other man's canoe. "Not bad."

"I was here first," the other man muttered.

César rolled his eyes, withdrew his paddle. "No shark? *Ha visto nada?* You've seen nothing?"

"Here?" The fisherman swung his hook wide and cast upriver, close to the bank. "I don't think so."

César turned to face me. "This is the place. *El lugar favorito de los tiburones.*" And he pushed off, not throwing the anchor until we were some way onward, well into the deepwater bend, a good fifty yards downriver from the other man.

"The truth is," he said, passing each of us a line, "there are less shark than there were. They're clever: they know we're here; they know what a hook looks like; they remember these things."

"You sound like you've already given up."

"Hey!" He snapped round, let his line fall slack. "Did I say that?"

"It's just a feeling I get," I said, watching the sun splinter across the river like a million shoaling minnows. "Everyone I meet, every fisherman I spend time with, believes in the shark more than ever, yet sees it increasingly seldom."

Cesar raised his forearm to shade his eyes. "It's true." He nodded. "There are factors." The river was more polluted than it had ever been, and for this he blamed Costa Rican plantation owners, whose pesticides and chemical fertilizers leached into the river, reducing spawn yields. These farmers were driving out other species too.

Such as jaguar. Days earlier, I had gone to the prison in the hope of meeting the fisherman from downriver who'd been arrested and brought here for killing one of these great protected cats. The American missionary who'd told me the story had said the fisherman had killed in self-defense, with the beast about to leap him, and that the police, disbelieving his story, had jailed him here, in El Castillo, far from his home. For as many caught in possession, I guessed there must have been several hundred others who escaped detection. This man, facing a possible decade behind bars, was one of the unlucky ones. I wanted to hear his story.

I went expecting the worst. Long before, I had spent a morning in the Bluefields jail—twenty-five men to a cubicle, no separate space for the toilet drop, prisoners hunched like tense, underexercised bulldogs—and pictured the El Castillo lockup as much the same. I was wrong.

It was smaller, filthier, more cramped, with barred windows that gave out not onto their own concealed courtyard, as in Bluefields, but onto the street. Arms flailed from between the bars; all around the window was sweat and dirt ground black as pitch. As I neared, faces pressed up to the bars, silently mouthing. I kept expecting an explosion of noise, but none came. I moved closer, but they clawed for my clothing, and I drew back. I said I was there to meet the jaguar man, and the faces retreated into darkness. Suddenly, a policeman appeared at my shoulder, and began steering me away. No, he said, it was not possible to visit. These were dangerous men—couldn't I see that? When I asked again for the jaguar man, he pointed me down the street, back toward the river. "You don't want to be talking to these men. It's a beautiful day. Go enjoy yourself."

Before long, their hooks baited with *mojarra* fillets, both César and his son had snagged tarpon. They braced themselves crossways in the canoe and yelped and whooped and the other fisherman turned and stared, his face betraying no emotion, his line slack and sinking. In the rougher water his canoe started rocking and he put out his hands to steady himself, looking away, shaking his head.

I was watching César and his son testing the pull of their lines, getting the weight of their fish, when my line suddenly twitched, then pulled away from me. It jerked erratically on the way up, alternately atremble, then weightless, until I saw, to my surprise, that I'd snagged a crab, which was still clawed to the bait, trailing petticoats of seaweed. Hardly thinking, I lifted it over the side and the crab, sensing air, loosened its grip and hit the boat scuttling. César's son, jumping to a squat, piled fish in its way and the crab turned and made for César, who leaned sideways, lifted it by its one steroid-pumped claw, and without once losing sight of his own line lofted it high over his shoulder. It spiraled slowly in the late-afternoon sun, belly-flopped claws out, and sank slowly into the black water.

We fished until darkness came and an unexpected wind began to stir and it was clear that today's sharks, if there were any, would not be roused. César had his own theories—the moon was waxing, the water was too dark, too warm, the shark had grown wily. We paid in one last time, watching the lights of the town spill drunkenly across the rapids, the castle a blocky silhouette against the last embers of the day. César was muttering politics again, grumbling about the right-wing policies of the newly installed Alemán government. "But hey," he announced, to no one in particular, "that's democracy."

We hugged the shore on the way back upriver, cutting inside the other fisherman, making slow progress. "Just tell me one thing, Carlos," César called out as we passed. "Why didn't you vote Frente at the last election? Sandino needed your help."

The other man smiled, the first time that afternoon. "I was fishing."

It took half an hour to reach the town's bottommost jetty, and at that point, rather than fight on against the current, we bagged the catch and lifted the dugout clear of the water. César and his son hoisted it onto their shoulders, pointed me toward the fish and the netting and paddles, and up the shore lanes we stumbled, under sputtering streetlamps, confused by our own long shadows.

"César," I said, as the light died on us and, unable to see the way, we put down our loads and rested on a doorstep. "There's one thing you haven't mentioned, one thing that everyone here talks about all the time—the red shark. Have you seen it?"

He nudged my knee with his. "Who have you been talking to?" He laughed, gently. "No, I've not seen it. You talk to the old people in this place, you'll hear anything you want to hear." He paused. Above us, a half-moon sliced clear of the clouds. "Now if you'd asked me about the San Carlos shark, well that's a different matter."

"The giant shark? You've seen that one, then?"

"No. But I have a friend who has."

"Could I contact him?"

"He died."

"The shark got him?"

César sighed, looked up and down the street, then lowered his voice. "No, his wife. Every time he went fishing his wife thought he was visiting his girlfriend. Then one day, when he came back late, she was waiting for him behind the door. She put an ax in his head."

I felt a laugh rise in my throat. "And that," I said, just managing to choke it back, "that's typical?"

"No." He stood up to go. "That's San Carlos for you."

11

We rode upriver to the sea, all expectations reversed, the river widening and deepening where it should have been growing ever more shallow, the swell building as the banks receded to distant charcoal smudges, bending with the curvature of the broad-sky earth. It felt like the delta of a great waterway, yet we were riding to the source. Before us, horizonless, stretched El Mar, Cocibolca, Lake Nicaragua. People on the *colectivo* barge began to wake, adjusting their vision to a world without edges, squinting bleakly out through the rain at the approaching sea-gray desert, at the cut of spindrift far ahead that marked the border between the two waters, the end of human-sized vistas, the end of the river.

We'd started at four, well before dawn, piling onto the *colectivo* on the El Castillo quay. Even without electric light, this had not been hard to find: one simply followed the drift of diesel as if it were a bread-crumb trail, zeroing in through the alleyways on the commotion of the deckhands and the hammer of the engine.

Stars crowded the sky; the day-old moon lay still on the water. For the next hour, till dawn brought wind and cloud, we moved through the black water as if we were not moving at all: perfectly balanced, untroubled by pitch or yaw or any unexpected upswell, easing ever westward, soothed by the engine thrum and the cool night air. People slept. I sat at the edge and watched, mesmerized, as the creeping dawn revealed the slow beginnings of another riverbank day: horses being led to water, blue smoke from breakfast fires, the knife-quick jumping of the first fish. Dawn saw us traveling through curtains of mist.

We made stops to pick up freight and passengers for San Carlos and bought oversweet coffee and rubberized white-bread rolls from a seven-year-old urchin who pocketed all change despite repeated requests, entreaties, threats. The man next to me finished his coffee and set to his early-morning reading, a pamphlet entitled "What Does God Demand of Us?" He read aloud, grunting and nodding, and didn't look up when a family of dark-skinned Indians climbed aboard beside him.

They looked quite distinct from the others, like some newly poor aristocrats with their dark clear eyes, curled-lip sneer, high-boned faces, heads held high. The rest of the passengers— doughier, plainer, more obviously of European descent—stared till they grew noisily bored and began to shout to each other about San Carlos and the market day to come. The Indians stole snatched glances, and when one caught my eye it was as if he instinctively comprehended our enmeshed histories, his and my place in all this. I detected a sad wisdom in him, the knowledge that what had passed between us was blood.

I looked again at Arturo's few words of scrawled advice. He'd certainly done his best to unsettle me, to make each further step of the journey one to be feared. Of San Carlos, he'd written just that one word—"*peligroso*," dangerous—a sentiment echoed by César's final warning. Now, as we inched upriver, fear of the unknown, like the first pangs of homesickness, fluttered in my gut.

In between the rain there was sun, and the cabin, under the beat-iron roof, grew hotter and hotter. A little girl stroked her mother's hair. Trees with orange flowers reached down toward the water and behind them great plains stretched away into the distance. Far northward were rugged, mange-backed hills. Farmers loading lumber stopped to watch us pass, and on one landing stage, with the lake almost in sight, I glimpsed a pickup truck, the first vehicle I'd seen in nearly six weeks.

We docked at a concrete-slab quay to the hollerings of money changers looking for Costa Rican border customs and hawkers offering trayfuls of cheap digital watches. When I fought my way ashore and looked back one last time, the diesel was silent and the captain was already asleep over the wheel.

San Carlos. The one-time shark-fishing capital of Nicaragua, now as ground-down and anonymous as its name suggested. It was a border town, bridgehead to Costa Rica, and edgy and transient as any Tijuana. The day was close and windless, hotter than anyplace downriver. Russian-made jeeps, pressed into taxi service, their bodywork lesioned with rust, trailed dust cumuli

along the dirt lanes in a cacophony of horns and fat-driver exple-
tives. In places there was no sidewalk and I leapt to the wall, one
hand over my mouth, as the jeeps clattered past.

In my fist was my only San Carlos lead: the address of
Candida Aragon, from that night on the roof of the coconut
barge. *"Frente a Casa Sandinista,"* she'd written, this woman
who'd promised to introduce me to the shark-fishing under-
world, whose marriage to a shark fisherman had long since collapsed, but her directions were too scant to be of much use.
"Next to the red building," I'd be told, only to be pointed
toward the street up which I'd just struggled. And then midday
came, and the streets emptied; people retreated inside, away from
the heat, and half a mile away, down by the lakeshore, I could
hear the shouts of fishermen, heaving their skiffs onto land.

It was not only Arturo and César who spoke ill of San Carlos.
Even those I'd traveled with this morning would be returning
to El Castillo on the afternoon *colectivo*: once darkness fell, it
seemed, almost anywhere else was preferable. Arturo, long
before his final *"peligroso,"* had given vague warnings, but they'd
been too cryptic to make much sense of. He'd worked here in the
early 1970s, which had been boom time for bull sharks, when
the dictator Somoza's shark-processing plant at Granada had
fifty San Carlos men under full-time contract. These had been
the best years, with several thousand taken annually for their
fins, flesh, hide, and liver, and Arturo had become rich. Yet he'd
also fled, never to return. He'd gestured toward an explanation—
"There was blood in the water; too much money, and men get
greedy"—but had offered no more.

The town had never inspired much confidence. Built as a
defensive battery in 1667, the year after the completion of the El
Castillo fortress, it had been overpowered in both 1685 and

1690 by pirates on their way to what had by now become the ritual sacking of Granada. It grew only slowly: by 1849, to the supercilious eye of U.S. envoy Ephraim Squier, it consisted of "a few rusty guns" and "some twenty cane or board houses, occupied chiefly by the officers of the customs and the soldiers with their families."

It was not until a century later, according to one account, that San Carlos began to assume its present shape—by the 1950s, it was a cowboy town, where gold pieces were bartered for whores and gambling chips, and where the first commercial shark-fishing venture had just been established by, of all unlikely chancers, a Belgian businessman. He built his factory on the lakeshore, sold his fins to Chinese merchants in Bluefields, kept his Indian fishermen compliant with an endless supply of free marijuana. Before the Russian jeeps, before fire destroyed the town and saw slab concrete replace the wooden saloons, photographs showed hollow-eyed men with Stetsons teetering down the main street on skeletal ponies, the animals' necks down, muzzles to the ground, as if expecting each step to be their last.

As to the mythic giant shark, all I'd gleaned was this: that, some way off the San Carlos foreshore, there was said to be an emerald mine, visible from the surface as a patch of grayer water against the greeny shelf, and deep inside this the shark stood sentry. In the 1930s, so the story went, fifteen Indian divers had pushed off from San Carlos to investigate; not one of them reached the bottom, and although they all returned safely to shore, within a month each man was dead. A subsequent party of investigators from Managua found no shark, just a natural borehole through the lake floor where the mine was supposed to be, thirty times as deep as anyone had previously dared guess. And so the myth survived: no one doubted anymore that that icy blackness was the monster's lair. Proof was unnecessary: the abyss was evidence enough.

I knocked, waited, knocked again. I'd eventually found the house earlier but had left it till three-thirty before returning. The sun was a little less aggressive now, and down one side of the street there fell a wedge of shade. Under the knocker the tag read, "AtAGON"—capital letters, small *r* scratched in blotchy ballpoint. I stood under the lintel, out of the sun, and tried once more. This time I heard movement inside: shuffled footsteps, then silence. I knocked again, more gently, and took a step back.

The door opened very slowly. Out of the darkness peered a woman's face, hair tangled, cheek creased from sleep.

"*Sí?*"

"Candida?" I guessed this was she, but it had been nighttime when we'd last met, and she'd been flush with drinker's bravado. The woman before me looked slighter, less certain, dressed only in a robe and rubber beach thongs.

"*Sí?*" She pushed her hair back from her forehead, looked into my face, then at my pack, bleached with dust. She yawned.

"We met," I said. "You don't remember? On the boat."

"The boat . . ." She turned inside, her attention wavering.

"And you gave me your address." I uncrumpled the scrap of paper, held it out.

"Ah, yes." She nodded. "You're the Englishman. We talked about shark fishing—"

A man's voice came from the back room, calling her name.

She looked away, cursing. "Perhaps later?" she said, to me, her hand on the catch. "You could come back later?"

Behind her a light went on, *marimba* echoed from a transistor radio. Through the crack in the door I caught sight of a hefty-bellied man tightening his belt buckle, smoothing down his shirt. An instant later he was at the door, muscling through, avoiding my eye.

He beetled down the road, through the dredge of newspapers and banana skins and horseshit in the gutter, checked once more over his shoulder, sidestepped to avoid the corpse of a dog, and disappeared down a side alley.

Candida put a hand to her brow, sighed, pushed the door open. "Well, come in, I guess."

The house was three rooms, all on the ground floor, giving onto a small, sunless courtyard. There was no sign of a second bedroom, and I'd begun to explain that I didn't need a place to sleep, that I could easily find a hotel, when she pointed to my pack and led through a screen door into the courtyard beyond. There were three stories above us: small windows, a solitary air-conditioning unit dripping liquid. At the far side of the courtyard was a low door, which she opened. Inside was a storeroom—heaps of old books, pamphlets, chairs stacked to the ceiling.

She waved a hand across the chaos. "We'll clear a space. You can sleep here."

"No, no." It smelled sour and musty, like cases of limes gone bad. And I'd heard a scratching, too, the unmistakable noise of foraging rodents. "It's all right. It's not necessary, and I'd hate to impose. I'm just keen to talk, to hear your stories about San Carlos."

She reached down, wrestled my pack from me, laid it beside the storeroom door. "I will not hear of it. That is not the Nicaraguan way."

She made two cups of instant coffee and disappeared into the other room to pull on jeans and a T-shirt. We sat on wooden classroom chairs under a bare bulb in her tiny kitchen: a two-ring hotplate; a solitary, hip-height cupboard; no fridge; no oven; a single barred window that gave onto pavement, providing flashes of shopping bags and jangles of keys. When a jeep passed, a soft billowing of road dust settled weightlessly on everything in the room, spotting the surface of my coffee like fungus spores.

When Candida spoke of shark fishing her voice changed in tone, dropping low and soft till she sounded almost drugged. Her previously mobile features became expressionless; she stared at her hands, then gazed sightlessly beyond me, out the window, toward the street beyond.

In the mid-1970s, when shark fishing in San Carlos was reaching its peak, Candida had been in her late teens. Her father, Félix, had been something of a neighborhood hero: the most successful shark fisherman, married to the most beautiful woman, universally recognized and respected. Candida, an only child, who would wait all afternoon at the shore for her father's boat to come in, was soon adopted by the claque of younger fishermen. She watched them work, listened to their talk. The way she told it, she'd spent hours transfixed by their stories, sitting on the edge of their boats at sundown while they stowed their lines and cut up their catch. She liked to watch the boats arrive, to guess from the way the craft sat in the water how many shark they carried. And it was to one of these fishermen—Francisco—that, aged just twenty, she got married.

Over a period of months, one long dry winter, the fishermen began meeting for the evenings in Candida and Francisco's house. She'd extended no invitation, but now, with nightly crowds of ten or fifteen, was expected to play hostess. The men drank. They were earning good money and spent freely. Each night they'd stagger in, smelling of sweat and shark innards, with rum and fruit and Coca-Cola and American cigarettes, and drink raucously till the small hours.

They were skilled hunters and, though armed with just line and gaff and club, were rarely even hide-grazed. Candida could remember only one man in all those years who had been taken by his own catch, but he had been an older fisherman, with failing sight and reflexes dulled from too many years spent gazing out over the same stretch of water. The young men, rather than take his death as a warning, received it with relish, as a further challenge to their manhood.

It was also, as it turned out, a welcome distraction. As the seventies moved toward their close, and the scent of revolution grew ever stronger, the shark catches began to drop off alarmingly. Fishermen who'd previously averaged at least one sizable shark a day now went days or weeks without a bite. They sold their outboards, dug out sails that had not been used in a decade, and still returned home empty-handed. A handful of fishermen remained successful, but overall, inexorably, the trend was downward. When the Sandinistas seized power in 1979, one of their first acts was to close the shark plant at Granada, an establishment they viewed as emblematic of a profounder exploitation. Shark fishing in Lake Nicaragua was outlawed and Francisco disappeared, taking what remained of his savings, as well as all his shark gear, every last spool of line and a whole hundred yards of netting.

"And you haven't heard from him since?" I asked.

"No." She set aside her cup, still half full.

"Do you know where he is? Have you any idea?"

"Bluefields, I guess, someplace on the Atlantic coast."

Arturo, I thought, suddenly: Arturo and Francisco were one and the same. Arturo was the right age, certainly, and was, to my mind, sufficiently cagey about his past to have been Francisco in an earlier life. But as I let the possibility turn over in my mind, I realized that the other pieces did not fit. Arturo had two sons; Candida had no children. He had Miskito blood; Francisco, from what Candida had told me, had never before left the lake. It was tempting, the idea that Arturo might be able to reenter my story, to provide a human link between the coast and the lake, but the truth was that, except for a page of scrap paper listing his prejudices, he was gone for me, just as Francisco was gone for Candida.

In essence, however, I pictured the two men as much the same: silent, archetypal figures against an unchanging landscape, wedded to the water and their nemesis fish more than to any woman they'd ever known. And if this was true of them, how much more was it of Félix, Candida's father, who'd lived longer and seen more and caught more sharks than any other man. He, too, had drifted from Candida's life. He still lived in San Carlos, was now an old man, but these days she saw him rarely. He blamed her, she said, for the breakup of her marriage—she'd driven Francisco away.

"Would you mind," I suggested, "if I tried to find Félix?"

"Mind?" Candida laughed, raised her eyes to meet mine.

"Why should I mind?" She stood up, took my cup, began to rinse it under the tap.

"Where do I start?" A jeep had pulled up beside the window, its tailpipe coughing out black diesel. She swatted at the encroaching fumes.

"You could try the docks, for a start."

"But he's old. I thought you said he'd retired long ago."

She turned, her face set. "Sure, but he still goes down to the docks. In his mind he never retired. He never grew old. Those docks are his home."

I came back later that evening with a bottle of dark rum and some lemons and let myself in with the spare key. The rum was intended as a thank-you, and I was looking forward to cracking the seal and sharing a quart or so with her.

But her door was closed. From behind it came a man's laughter, then Candida's voice—softer, entreating. There was the whang of bedsprings, a papery scuffling noise, then a low moan. Clutching the bottle to my chest, I inched past the doorway on tiptoe, feeling like the snooper in some substandard 1960s sex farce. From the bedroom, the moans became grunts and whimpers, growing ever louder. I shouldered open the door to the courtyard and, as quietly as I could, let myself out.

I passed a broken night, stretched out on my mat in the courtyard itself, rather than the cramped storeroom, woken continually by the comings and goings of different men inside the house. I smeared myself with mosquito repellent, which worked well enough as deterrent but kept leaching into my eyes. From where I lay, pretending sleep, I could follow Candida's passage through the house as she waved off one and, a half hour later, welcomed the next. At around three she double-locked the front door and cut the lights and from then until dawn I slept.

When I left the house for the dockside, shortly after first light, Candida was fast asleep, her catarrhal snores audible throughout the house. Later on, I told myself as I set off for the quay, I would find a room elsewhere: I appreciated her generosity, but her house was also her place of business, and I wasn't sure how long I could remain invisible.

Dawn brought heat and flies. I walked downhill, past the yellow concrete church, the caretaker on her knees before a neon Christ, then followed the lanes toward the water. In the stillness the lake stretched unbordered to infinity, a shifting gauze of palest mauve, the earliest skiffs already setting out across the mist. I walked on, the lanes still in shadow, past two men barrowing a cartload of timber uphill, one donkey-harnessed in front, the other pushing from behind. On the main street, parallel to the water, stallholders were setting up the morning market—avocados, oranges, bananas, plastic shoes and cowboy boots, starchy nylon flesh-tone underthings. Another vendor was laying out ranks of cheaply pirated cassettes; American music pounded from defeated speakers. Through an alleyway between the stalls, past two men cradling bottles of Victoria, I glimpsed the water.

Fifteen or twenty fishermen were squatting on their haunches on a crook of muddy, rocky beach. Further on, where backs of houses rose straight up from the water, small boys were flinging themselves into the shallows. I sat on a rock between two men salting fish.

"We should have done this last night," one said, without

looking up. He was working with both hands, grinding clods of sodden crystal under the gills, deep between the leaves of flesh.

I looked at him. "Last night?"

"Mornings are for fishing; in the afternoons we do the salting."

"So what happened?"

"Oh, man." He turned; his gaze was unsteady, his eyeballs jittery. "What didn't happen?"

"I'm looking for Félix," I said. "You know him? The old fisherman?"

"Sure," he said, reaching for the bucket of salt. "Everyone knows Félix. But he's not here right now. He left this morning for the islands."

As we talked, and the sun rose higher, the dawn fishermen began returning. They hauled their boats up on the mud and covered their catch with netting and climbed past us through the market to the nearest bar. Women appeared at the back windows of houses, hurling pale green dishwater out across the shallows.

The fishermen went on salting as they spoke, laying the fish against the rocks to dry. If I was to catch Félix, they said, I'd have to get the next boat to the Solentiname Islands, but they weren't sure when that would be. Midweek, three days from now, was their best guess. Normally, they said, Félix seldom left San Carlos, but this occasion was special: the island fishermen had called a meeting to protest the poaching in their waters by boats from San Carlos, and Félix, who'd fished these waters all his life, had gone to listen in. It was, they said, a time of much tension: there were now three cooperatives, totaling 170 fishermen, working out of San Carlos, and each year the catches were falling. Too many people, not enough fish.

"And where do the fish come from, eh?" The first man held up a *gaspar*, gripped it round the gills, addressed himself straight at its tiny pouting mouth. "Eh? Where do you swim from? There's only the river, isn't there? There's only one way into the lake."

He drew the tip of his knife from throat to tail, looped out the innards with two fingers. "We never had this problem before. Once, we had enough for everyone." But Lake Nicaragua had fallen victim to its own success: sawfish and bull shark had been decimated, and now *machaca* and *gaspar*, *guapote* and *mojarra*—unlovely whitefish all of them, not much more interesting than cod—were going the same way. And the more they dwindled, the more clamorous the market grew. Export was mainly to Honduras, Guatemala, El Salvador, prices doubling en route from two to four dollars a kilo.

These two had started their working lives fishing shark. When they spoke of those times, something in their voices changed; they untensed a little, let their shoulders drop, salted with less desperate vigor.

"During Somoza time," the first said, "every day in San Carlos we caught perhaps two hundred shark. They were beautiful— big strong fish—and they made us rich."

"And now?"

"From time to time, yes, we get a shark, but most of the time we have to rely on these little fish." He brought the *guapote* close to his face, shook his head at it. "It is Somoza's fault."

"The dictator?"

"He is responsible. Of course you can say that sharks do not need protection, but what are they against all of us? Somoza didn't care. All he cared about was his fat wallet." He rubbed thumb against forefinger. *"Dinero, dinero, dinero."*

For the American zoologist Thomas Thorson, on the other hand, these fishermen, like those further downriver, retained a robust affection. Where Somoza had shown regard only for the present, and for his own immediate enrichment, Thorson, they recognized, had been working for the future. Not that this raised him above ridicule—they still snickered to recall the "peep peep peep" made by the *placas* with which he'd tagged the sharks—but he'd made them appreciate the uniqueness of their fish. Both these men had worked for him, happily accepting dollars in return for watching the sharks run free, and when Thorson returned the following year with news that a San Carlos shark had been netted off Sicily, they had experienced a quiet pride. "Of course, with our shark, anything is possible."

With the sun now high, we took seats at a food stall, in the shade. I bought beers, the only drink they were happy to accept. They sank theirs in unison, heads back, banging the bottles empty onto the table, squinting mournfully down the necks till I called for more.

"Different kind of place, Solentiname," the first one said, the beer having steadied his staccato eyeball. "Artists, artisans, hippies, men with many girlfriends." "Hippies," then, just as Arturo had written. But then, I guessed, to hardworking fishermen, perhaps anyone less than wholly conventional qualified as such.

The islands, the fisherman went on, weren't far from San Carlos—fifteen miles, he estimated—but had nourished quite different lives. They were also the cradle of the Sandinista revolution, where Ernesto Cardenal, priest and poet, had inspired his people to rise up against the dictatorship: thirteen Solentiname Islanders, artists and farmers, men and women, in a nighttime assault on the San Carlos garrison. The army crushed the uprising with brutal ease, looting and burning all across the islands, but the first fuse had been lit.

"We may be better fishermen than them," the fisherman sighed, "and our women may be sexier, but you can say, and it is the truth, that we owe them our freedom."

Two days later, in a rainstorm, I climbed aboard the ferry to Solentiname. It was a wooden longboat, with a puny outboard, and overcrowded—five people hip-to-hip across each bench seat. We pulled tarpaulins over our knees and up to our necks, and then the boat hauled head-on into the wind and the waves. Fruit and rice sacks and luggage were stowed underneath us, but already I could feel water rising in the hull. The skipper, a young man with a cheap straw Panama, took the rain against his bare chest, water coursing off his nose, the tips of his fingers. The worse it got, the harder he grinned.

I'd spent the last two nights in a hotel. At first Candida had protested, but when I stressed the reasons, that it had nothing to do with her hospitality, and was solely my wish not to intrude further into her privacy, she'd acquiesced easily enough. The hotel I found was empty, and the owner asleep on the ledger. When I woke him, explaining I wanted a room, he laughed out loud, but nonetheless insisted, still smirking, that I pay both nights in advance. He dug in the neck of his undershirt, drew out a key, and locked the cash I gave him in a wall safe.

Now, crouched in the longboat, plunging into the waves, I felt my spirits lighten: San Carlos, as Arturo had predicted, offered no pleasure greater than the leaving of it. Here was a frontier town, best viewed in fleeting transit, a place where barely teenaged girls shadowed late-night saloons in pencil heels and microskirts, preyed on by anyone—white, black, mestizo—with a few dollars to hand. A place where the radio station padded out its program with Stars-on-45 compilation records, and the DJ, on air, thought nothing of turning aside from his microphone and haranguing anyone—me, the janitor, his lone technician—who happened to be nearby; where, for one dollar, any passerby could have his or her personal message, however banal, broadcast to thirty thousand campesinos up the length of the San Juan. It was a place where the air smelled sour as old banknotes; where dead animals lay unremarked in the streets for days; where each day felt hotter than the last; where things of all kinds felt near their end.

And now, leaving, there was cool rain and wind and, after a while, what had been San Carlos on the horizon behind us became a grayish blurring with the sky and, after a further while, this too dissolved to a continuous pale pewter rainscape. Only when we were soaked and were about to give up the effort of covering ourselves did the rain draw back, drifting eastward to reveal a washed-blue afternoon and coveys of surprised cormorants. Ahead, the archipelago emerged like distant anthills.

A fat man, throwing off the tarpaulin, shouted across the boat at me. His tongue was algae-green. "You stay with me!"

The woman between us turned aside and I smelled his breath—fish guts.

"I'm waiting till we arrive," I yelled back, aware the whole boat was now listening.

He clapped his hands together. "Then you must stay with me! I know everyone! I have a boat! You will want for nothing!" He reached down inside his trousers, scratched at himself. His eyes rolled backward in his skull. "So, *hombre,* is decided?"

For the rest of the journey, with the weather closing in again,

I managed to avoid his eye. Twisting sideways, my back to the southern border, I rested one foot on the gasoline tank and attempted conversation with the skipper. Yes, he said, he knew of the upcoming fishermen's meeting. No, he didn't know when it was going to be, though guessed at Sunday, after Saturday's baseball.

"So where exactly *do* you think you're going to stay?" He eyed the squalling waters ahead as he spoke, one hand on the brim of his Panama. "You know I only go to San Carlos once a week?"

"I hadn't thought, to be honest. What do you suggest?"

"You could stay with me. I'm married." He winked. "You'll be safe."

The next three days, until the fishermen's summit, I tailed José—balsa-wood artist, part-time ferryman, my host. He lived in a two-room shack on a steep hillside, with a view across the water to Costa Rica, and he cleared one side of the house for me, leaving himself and his wife and baby with just one room between them.

Walking across the island in the evenings, in search of chilies or eggs or rice, it seemed everyone was family: José was the youngest of nine; his father, one of seventeen. Everywhere were cousins, siblings, uncles, nieces. José made his living carving balsa mobiles, which his wife painted in gaudy acrylics and his sister sold in Managua. Every night he'd fire up the battery-powered black-and-white television, and cousins from across the island would come and gawp till midnight at the poorly dubbed U.S. soaps from across the border, the endless commercial breaks—"Slimming belt! Lose three sizes in two weeks! Wait no longer!"

José himself had been drafted to the Honduran front as a seventeen-year-old and, like all Solentiname Islanders, still believed in the rightness of the Sandinista revolution. These days, though, life ran to easier rhythms. On afternoons of rain he took the longboat fishing; at dawn he bathed in the lake; on weekends he played baseball, in a team comprised of cousins and brothers, against another of the same.

He did not yet have a mistress, though, like most Nicaraguan men, guessed this was one day inevitable. His elder brother, a peasant farmer from the far side of the island, expressed astonishment that I, a married man, did not feel the same.

"When I see a pretty woman," he murmured, breaking off from husking maize, "I do my utmost to have *relaciones* with her."

José and his brothers were too young to have taken part in the attack on the San Carlos garrison that prefigured the 1979 revolution, but, like every other islander, referred to it constantly. The thirteenth of October, 1977, was day zero: weddings, birthdays, funerals were either *"antes del asalto"* or *"después del asalto"*—before the attack, or after. And politics here were as monochrome as on parts of the Atlantic coast, only with loyalties reversed. Where, on the coast, Creoles and Miskitos still claimed their babies had been kidnapped and rendered down to make soap for Sandinista cadres, here on the islands the most clearly remembered evil was that of Ronald Reagan, who in November 1980 had publicly stated his determination to crush the revolution. Where, on the coast, people still gave thanks for America's intervention—"We would have been slaves, like in Cuba, or Russia"—here in the Solentiname archipelago the bondage had been domestic, to a dictator who had grown fat as his peasants starved.

The survivors from 13 October 1977 had assumed, in the intervening twenty years, near mythic status. When José took me to meet Nubia, one of only three women to have taken up arms that night, he stood silent sentry at the door as we talked inside; afterward, as I thanked her, he stared straight ahead, straight-faced, the very butler.

Nubia encouraged such behavior: in conversation, she had the determined charm of the practiced politician and a weighted smile that she employed sparingly, and only then to reinforce a point. In the office of her *"hotel ecologico"*—freshly whitewashed, utterly empty of guests—she sat underneath a full-length oil of her late husband Alejandro, father to her four children. Alejandro, one of Ernesto Cardenal's original *comunidad*, had died four years earlier when his brakes failed on the San Carlos road, but for eternity would be preserved as I saw him now: the quintessential, khaki-clad revolutionary, red bandanna about his neck, eyes fixed on the heroic distance.

To other islanders, Nubia had become emblematic of a collective heroism—"La Nubia," never without her definite article. Her own speech consisted of long, articulated sentences, which scarcely required me as interlocutor. She moved seamlessly from *la lucha*, the struggle, to her *companeros'* battle for self-determination, to how violence, for this artistic, peaceable community, had been regrettable but necessary—"the price to pay."

As we talked, and afternoon turned to evening, mosquitoes

began to bite. She watched me as I slapped at my wounds and smiled benignly, as if immune to such trifling annoyances. After the attack on San Carlos, she continued, she and the other Solentiname guerrillas fled to Costa Rica; in revenge, Somoza's Guardia Civil wreaked a blanket destruction on the islands. Only the church, from which Padre Ernesto Cardenal had first preached revolution, survived.

Down the hill, past the church, I fell in with Bosco, another of the heroes of 1977 and a man whom the socialist revolution had treated generously indeed, providing him with a large avocado plantation on a neighboring island, a house in Managua, and another here, on Mancarrón Island. He had grown corpulent, and became breathless at the slightest exertion, snapping his fingers for coffee and biscuits, collapsing into his wicker armchair. From a photograph, taken before the revolution, which pictured members of the Comunidad de Nuestra Señora de Solentiname sitting down to dinner together, he was recognizably the same man, only bulky from muscle rather than fat, with a big jaw and a boxer's nose. Already, though, he was setting the pattern for the years to come, heaping his plate higher than any other. Beside him, the padre ate modestly, picking at his food with the tip of his fork.

Bosco showed me the community library, rebuilt from rubble. As I looked round, he leaned heavily against a bookcase, waving at objects of interest: portraits of the three who'd died in the attack, the rifles they'd used, a photographic record of the Guardia Civil destruction. There was less than half a shelf of books, all of which were new, since every one of the old volumes had been burned by the soldiers on their rampage.

Later, having passed through the padre's spartan rooms, noting the hammock in which this sprightly septuagenarian still, on his increasingly infrequent visits to Solentiname, passed his nights, we stood at the edge of the cliff and looked out across the lake. What troubled Bosco most these days was conflict of a different nature, between fishermen fighting each other for their future.

"Ten years ago," he wheezed, turning his chalky eye on me, "there were three fishermen with nets working from these islands. Today, there are thirty, with nets of two hundred meters. In San Carlos, there used to be forty fishermen; now there are four times that." The Solentiname archipelago, he claimed, held the lake's remaining fish stocks; increasingly, its waters were under siege from boats from every corner of the lake.

It started to rain. Bosco wiped his cuff across his brow. During his childhood, he said, no one had imagined the lake would ever cease to provide: at one point last century, shark had been so plentiful and rapacious that the Granada authorities had even placed a bounty on each one captured. And now? The last time he could recall a shark attack on the islands themselves was in the 1960s—a light aircraft that went down off Mancarrón: freak, wholesale carnage, never since repeated.

The rain grew heavier. Bosco, chest out, began to resemble the prow of a great warship, pitching into heavy seas. His voice rose, his gestures became more theatrical.

"And you know who I blame?"

I shook my head, though I had a feeling of what was to follow.

"Anastasio Somoza. Our blessed dictator—he and his associates. It was they who began the factory for shark meat in Granada, they who caused us to come to this."

"I've heard that said. I've—"

"It's true," he spat. "You are going to Granada? Go find the factory."

"You have been?"

"Many times." He shook the water from his face, and turned abruptly for cover. "But I have never found the men who became rich from it. I would like to find them. I would like very much to find them."

Crossing between islands, the Sunday of the meeting, José made slow progress, stopping at every landing stage and promontory to pick up fishermen. They traveled in silence, watching the skies. Into open water, out of the lee, the boat began to roll. Far off I could see rain. As soon as he could, José cut back toward land again, steering into the wind so that the front-riders, taking the brunt, covered their faces with their hands. On a sandbar between the last two islands we grounded and had to punt ourselves clear.

We were the last to arrive. In a small bay, pulled up onto rocks, were five fishing boats, nets heaped in their bows. On the hillside above, silhouetted in the pale morning light, stood twenty or thirty men, observing our arrival in silence, arms folded. Two of them climbed down to guide us in, heaving the bow up the beach, holding out hands for us to grip and jump to shore.

Standing apart, further uphill, was a markedly different cluster—two men and a woman, dressed in pale shirts and jeans, all with clipboards. These, José whispered, were the officials from San Carlos, and they were doing little to blend in. They stood aloof, waiting for the fishermen to gather, watching them as they began to settle on the ground. One of the men began to count heads, making notes on his clipboard, sucking the end of his pen.

I recognized some of the fishermen from the baseball game the day before. Then, drinking white rum and orangeade under a belting sun, foraging through the underbrush for lost balls, they'd veered between riotous support for whichever team was out on the square and a desperate gloom for the general state of things. On all sides they felt squeezed; never, they said, as another ball whanged past at head height, had so much pressure been placed on the fish stocks. "In San Carlos," said one, emerging from the bushes, "there are well-educated men—professors, teachers—who have turned to fishing because there is no other work." As for the freshwater shark, that once-plentiful harvest, only the foolhardiest fisherman would now attempt its hunting; since 1994 there had been fines for anyone found fishing them: five hundred córdobas for the first time, double that the next, with any further infringement punishable by confiscation of boat and nets.

And now the same fishermen were here, ghoul-eyed and watchful, greeting the men from our boat with silent, hungover nods. I waited at the shore while José made his boat fast to the bank. Great curtains of rain were sweeping across the horizon. I followed José up the path, chased by whirlwinds of leaves and dust, rain already spotting the ground.

"Is Félix here?"

"Félix? *Claro.* Of course." José indicated an old man, at the far side of the group, who sat apart, hat on his knees, hands rested on the brim. I put my hand up to wave to him.

José touched my shoulder. "Later, I think. Yes?"

▼ ▼ ▼

We were late, and when the last of us had reached the group, the three with clipboards walked down from where they stood and began ushering us into a circle. The ground was wet and the sky overhead threatened rain and the fishermen squatted on their haunches or found logs on which they spread leaves. When the officials began their introduction, the fishermen focused hard on the ground, or looked away across the water. The officials murmured soothing platitudes, repeating over and over words like "cooperation," "trust," "understanding." When they said these words they chose one face on which to settle, moving on again only when their speech continued. When the officials finished talking, the fishermen sat quiet for a minute. Above us, in the pine canopy, the wind was building to a howl.

Eventually one of the fishermen spoke up. *"Desarrollo,"* he said. "Development. Tourists. That's what we need. Nothing else is going to save us." A scurry of wind and leaves across the clearing splintered his voice to nothing.

An official stepped toward the center of the circle. He waited till the gale softened, then said, "If that's what you want, I ask myself why we are here. I thought we were here to talk about fishing—"

"It's all tied in," the fisherman said, starting to whittle at a knot of wood with his gutting knife. "Can't you see that? If we have no fish, then we have to sell ourselves to the tourists."

Another fisherman interrupted him. "Stop that talk. The man is right—this is no way to carry on. We have to think positive."

"Fine, okay," the other said, "but in that case we have to get these guys off our backs." He stabbed his knife in the officials' direction, at which point the woman—educated-looking, with good teeth, young enough to be daughter to most of the men that now stared her down—stepped forward.

"Let me explain," she said. "We are not on your backs, as you put it. We are from the government. We have listened to what the San Carlos fishermen have to say. Now we are here to listen to you. Now it's your turn. That's it. That's all."

The fisherman grunted, sheathed his blade, and the rain that had held off this long suddenly whipped through between us, flattening the leaves to mud, causing the old man to grab at his hat, the officials to hug their clipboards to their chests. "Okay," the woman shouted. "Into the pig shed."

From this point on, with people wedged in shoulder to shoulder, the smell of cooking grease and cheap hair oil rising from the fishermen's wet backs, the negotiations began to move forward a little. The woman, under instruction, began reluctantly to take notes. At moments, with the rain on the roof threatening to overwhelm, whoever was speaking would fall silent and we'd watch each other cautiously till the rattling ceased. A train of giant ants passed through our feet, portering triangles of green ten times their size. At the edge of the shelter they halted, appeared to sniff the air, then angled back along the perimeter, skirting the sheeting water.

The shortage of fish, agreed two of the older fishermen—brothers with identical sawed-off waders, the same fish-oily overalls—was caused by the predations of fishermen from San Carlos and the upper San Juan. The brothers spoke in unison, sometimes uttering the exact same phrases, working to a furious crescendo. "Time was we all used to work together. Now you"—as one, they pointed at the San Carlos officials—"you come and steal our fish."

Others, younger men, were more conciliatory. Fish, they argued, were free for all. Who could claim ownership? Where was that written? There were long pauses, the woman scratching away at her notepad, fishermen waiting for the next one to speak, big hands flat on their knees. They grew bellicose and entreating by turns, full of rage, then resignation. *"Es difícil."* "The government must come here and see." "Yes, and the *ejército*, the army." "And the police." They gazed at their boats through the rain, the hulls already filling with water, silvered as mercury.

Because of increased fishing along the San Juan, and the practice of gillnetting in the San Carlos headwaters, fewer and fewer fish were reaching Cocibolca, Lake Nicaragua. That much these fishermen understood all too clearly: that the lake possessed just this single outlet, and that fish could enter from nowhere else, certainly not the industry-diseased Lake Managua to the north. In which case, they went on to suggest, why not institute boundaries—a Solentiname cordon, a San Carlos cordon, all the way north to Granada—and thus force each community to care for its own. To protect their own livelihoods, they proposed a twelve-mile exclusion zone around the archipelago.

"Twelve miles? Twelve miles?" The woman looked up from her pad. "Which means that fishermen from San Carlos would be allowed just two miles out into the lake? A hundred and seventy fishermen in a two-mile strip? Interesting."

"How about a fish farm?" came a voice. Laughter. The smallest fisherman, bug-eyed as a lobster, held up his hand. "Okay, okay. Forget it."

From Félix—older than the rest, and anyway an outsider from San Carlos—there was no input, nothing to suggest which way he was thinking. Occasionally I saw his lips move, but his face betrayed nothing. He rested his head against the pillar and listened with his eyes closed. Once powerfully built, he was now beginning to look his age: wiry, tangled eyebrow hair, like so much forgotten vegetation, sprouted unchecked.

"In that case," said the first official, clipping his pen into his breast pocket, "we appear to have concluded our business. As I say, we're a new government, and we may not be able to do too much right away, but in time, be assured, we will be thinking of you."

A mumble was running through the shed. "*La carta*, the letter." They were looking one to the next, prodding each other in the chest. At the far end, where the roof gave scant cover, a fisherman was bending over, arm inside a plastic bag. There were shouts, and jeering, and when he stood straight again he was clutching something to his chest, crouching forward to protect it from the rain.

"The rain!" the man next to him shouted, grabbing the object. He passed it to the next, who passed it on again: an envelope, which the fishermen handled with extreme care, pinching just the corner, or laying it flat across their palms like an ancient family photo they feared smudging. At the end of the line the last fisherman handed it to one of the government officials, who pinned it to his clipboard.

"Go on!" someone shouted. "Open it!"

The official exhaled sharply, ran his finger under the seal. He unfolded it and scanned it through in silence. The fishermen waited, muttering low among themselves. The rain was easing off a little, and steam rose from the shoulders of those who stood at the outer edges of the shelter.

The official pushed back his shoulders, held the letter up in front of him. "Dear sir," he read aloud. "We, the cooperative of Solentiname fishermen, are writing to you because of the very serious situation that we find ourselves in." The tone was half-pleading, half-insistent. Lake Nicaragua was unique, with bull shark and sawfish and other species that existed nowhere else in the world. The Solentiname fishermen had lived here all their lives, but now, under pressure from predatory fishing, were find-ing themselves struggling to net even enough to eat. The letter demanded the imposition of a twelve-mile exclusion zone around the archipelago; it demanded, in conclusion, that the islanders' voice be heard.

The fishermen began to get to their feet. Two of them stepped close to the official and I could hear them saying, "You take that to your government." In seconds, all of them were standing and the official, touching his hair, was backing out of the shelter fast. Only Félix, watching silently, remained seated.

Down the hillside toward the beach all three officials broke into a trot. The fishermen, more perplexed than amused, stood at the rise in the lightening rain shaking their heads, big hands hooked in the pockets of their overalls.

The officials' boatman helped them up into their launch, pointing them to seats at the stern, then put his shoulder to the bow to heave it off the dry. With the boat afloat, the first official stood upright, brandishing the letter.

"Don't think we don't understand," he shouted, struggling for balance as his boatman pushed past him. "My father was a farmer. As he used to say, if you take the iguana's egg, then the iguana won't have babies." He shoved the letter into his shirt pocket.

On the seat beside him the woman tugged at his shirt. He shook her away, gesturing wildly at the island behind us. "The iguana lays only one egg each year. Same principle with fish." He grinned. "Only the numbers are different."

One of the fishermen cursed; another, turning away, laughed blackly. Down below, the outboard kicked into reverse, throwing the official, still gesticulating, flailing to his knees. He hauled himself back up, legs soaking, pearl-white shirt blotched with fish smear and whorls of oily water. He checked his pocket for the letter, raised an arm in farewell.

"Remember the iguana!" he called out, as his boatman shifted into gear. "Remember the iguana!"

But the fishermen were starting down the hillside toward the lakeshore and this time, heading for their boats, did not look up, nor even break pace.

To Félix the old shark fisherman, as to the ancients, Cocibolca, or Lake Nicaragua, was "*el mar*"—the ocean, nothing less. There was even, during the diurnal monsoon, a daily rise and fall of water that, unequivocally, seemed to elevate Cocibolca above the level of "*gran lago*." Before Columbus, Félix explained, Cocibolca was also home to some two million Indians, a pulsing population hub and a natural paradise: howler and spider monkeys, crocodiles, iguanas, macaws, teal, shovelers, baldpates, tree ducks, muscovies, spoonbill, and heron, as well as many species of remarkable fish. Within fifteen years of Gil González Dávila's discovery in 1522, disease, flight, and slaughter had reduced the Indians to a rump of less than a quarter of their original size.

The Spanish bound the remaining Indians into slavery, built warships, and from their base at Granada traded via the San Juan with Spain, Cuba, and Portugal. They built the city's finest mansions and houses of worship and broad-shaded public squares. They became rich, a state of affairs that could not remain a secret for long: from the Atlantic coast, in the mid–seventeenth century, forged pirates, who stole in by night in dugouts and razed Granada, plundering its altar gold and safe boxes. And throughout it all, twitching in the wake of all this troublesome humanity, came *Carcharhinus leucas*, the bull shark, a uniquely fitting object of terror for waters in which so much wrong had been committed.

By the middle of the twentieth century, with the conquistadores having made way, in an apparently seamless progression, for a U.S.–backed dictatorship, and with much of the country's forests sold down the San Juan, only the waters of the lake itself still gave any clue to the abundance of the past. Bull shark—"that genuinely ornery beast," according to one naturalist—were still plentiful, and many endemic species of fish survived. Here were seventeen different kinds of gold-red cichlid, sold in fish markets as *guapote*—unique specimens, found nowhere else.

Such, sighed Félix, warming to reminiscence, was the lake he remembered from childhood; back then, if you wanted shark, all you had to do was hang a meat hook from any promontory or jetty. In 1943, a *National Geographic* writer, fishing off San Carlos, claimed to feel a shark bite every five to ten minutes. His best specimens he packed in ice and despatched to the United States: Nicaragua's freshwater shark as trophy—one American's own brave stab at immortality.

Félix and I walked the clearing, through the forest to the far shore of the island, then back again. At first he had been suspicious of my interest, but once we edged from politics to his own memories of a fisherman's life, he grew more expansive and attentive.

"I was," he said, his gold-filled teeth sparking in the intermittent sunlight, "the best, *el mejor*. That's no secret." He'd fished for Thomas Thorson between 1972 and 1978, and Thorson, in recognition, had given him a farewell gift of a wall plaque that said just that—*"El mejor pescador en San Carlos— gracias."*

Until the 1970s, the fishermen of San Carlos had gone under sail, or paddled. Félix had worked alone, and routinely, he claimed, had landed shark of more than three meters. On one day he'd caught twelve—*"Pero eso,"* he said, giving one of his Gallic pouts, *"era normal."*

I wondered how much to believe. Félix was in his seventies now, and hadn't, I guessed, been shark fishing in at least a decade. To some extent it felt as if he were treating me like a biographer and, with one eye on his posthumous reputation, was exaggerating wildly.

Mid-decade, the fishermen had graduated from sail power to outboard engines, and it was the submarine disturbance from these—the grind of the propellers and general commotion, rather than the volume of bull shark caught—that had precipitated their disappearance. Any other suggestion, Félix snapped, in particular the notion that Somoza himself was somehow responsible, was *"absurdo."* To Félix, old believer, the shark lived on, and in as great a number as before; only, these days, it kept to the lake's deepest recesses, clustering in retreat from the whine of propellers. He passed an arm across the watery horizon.

"This shark," he said, "knows everything about what happens up here, on land. He is no fool, which is why he has kept out of sight these last few years. But he is still here. This is still his home."

Standing by the shore, one knee up on a boulder, Félix pushed his sleeve over his bicep and played out in mime the rolling fight of a big shark. His arms had grown puny with age, and his skin was loose as softest chamois, but down the underside of his arms flexed tendons thick as guy ropes, the remnant chassis of a once-powerful machine.

Alone in his dugout, frustrated at the number of times he'd played and lost the biggest sharks, he'd fallen to improvisation, and his innovation had been adopted, in no time, by the entire fleet. Rather than nylon line, he'd tried *"cuerda plástica,"* an all-purpose quayside rope that, until that moment, had been generally assumed too cumbersome for shark. He'd kept the meter-long steel trace, onto which the baited hook was clipped, but from trace to boat replaced the lightweight nylon filament with plastic hawser. He'd headed shoreward that night with revolutionary news: not only did the new line appear unbreakable, but sharks acted like it was invisible.

The other shark fishermen followed his lead, but already, by the mid-1970s, rope or no rope, catches were falling off. During these final years of the Somoza dictatorship, everything, it seemed, had begun to close inward. A once-buoyant industry, still in relative youth, was contracting before the fishermen's eyes, and there appeared nothing they could do about it. Félix, who'd set aside enough money to survive such lean years, decided to pull back a little, wait to see what happened. But with his daughter Candida married to one of the younger fishermen, this did not prove straightforward.

"The young men," Félix said, patting his trouser pocket for tobacco, "went *loco*, crazy." Of all the money they'd made in the good years they'd not thought to save one centavo and now, with whatever they could borrow or steal, they hit the bars. Mornings, when the stallholders were setting up their trestles, saw big men slumped in saloon doorways, barefoot, their pant legs marked with dark sugary stains, hardened drool at the corners of their mouths.

"In Bluefields," I said—sensing José suddenly at my side, guessing that pretty soon he'd be wanting to be off—"I met a fisherman called Arturo. He was in his fifties, I'd say. He fished out of San Carlos in the seventies, but then, abruptly, he left. He never said why."

"We had some Miskitos here then," Félix said, nodding. "It's true. Some men from the coast . . ." He tipped his hat at José, who was now climbing into the boat, settling himself at the stern, checking the gas. Félix, without finishing his sentence, followed José across the rocks and, with the agility of a much younger man, swung himself over the gunwale. I, the last, was left to unanchor the bow rope and shove out into the open water. The ride back, with the wind behind us, was gentler than our arrival. Cormorants followed us; a pair of turtles, basking on a rock ledge, slid into the shallows as we passed.

Further on, unprompted, Félix picked up the story again. With the drinking had come fighting, and the incomers, blamed increasingly for the fall in shark catches, had taken the brunt. Some nights saw uncontrolled brawls of thirty, forty men, with householders too scared to even unshutter their windows and shout for a little peace. The incomers had tried to carry on fishing, had even tried to reason, but were outnumbered and running short of funds themselves. Within the space of a few months, all had fled. None had ever returned.

"But Arturo?" I pressed. "You remember him? He was here some years. He's mixed race, with a nose you'd be unlikely to forget."

"The nose man, eh?"

"Yes! You knew him?"

Félix rolled his eyes. "No, of course I don't remember him. Big nose! They all had big noses, those men."

Back in San Carlos, toward midnight, drinking too-warm beer in a concrete-slab bar, the floor awash, every table thick with empties. Fishermen, still in their fish-ooze jeans, were drinking hard in a cluster at the counter. The barmaid wore clown-bright lipstick, and seemed under siege. The men kept grabbing at her across the beer-slick surface like some freakish outsize octopus; she parried them back with fresh bottles, her grin fixed and desperate. Two snot-encrusted teenagers crouched at the doorway, lunging for prematurely discarded beers, beaten back, with increasing ferocity, by the fishermen.

Four days had passed since the meeting on Solentiname and still the men could talk of little else. I'd encountered them on the quay, on the foreshore, each one determined that the status quo should remain as it was, that they be allowed to drop nets anywhere they chose. They laughed openly and mirthlessly at the islanders' plea for a twelve-mile exclusion zone. No one owned the lake, they argued, and each fisherman had equal rights to every stretch of water. The islanders, besides, were hippies, and lazy. They were better off carving their pretty birds.

They were fortunate that they were surrounded by rich fishing grounds, but that did not make those waters theirs. And on
and on.

In the bar there was more of the same, only at greater volume
and with the hatred ungilded by any attempt at reasonableness
or argument. I wasn't sure what I hoped to find here, and in
truth had dropped by solely because this was the bar nearest to
the bus station. I'd come in late, and needed a drink. Now I was
here, escape seemed unlikely. They knew who I was: I was not
leaving until I'd heard them out.

It had been a long two days since I'd ridden José's four A.M.
ferry back from Solentiname, two days spent hitching rides on
buses full of farmers, barreling up washboard roads north from
San Carlos. I'd followed the lakeshore where possible and finally
reached San Miguelito, a bleak *pueblito* facing straight into a
driving westerly, where boys grilled live iguana on braziers
down by the shore. I'd come to talk to fishermen, but stood and
watched awhile, mesmerized by the boys' gruesome dedication,
the way they turned the iguana in the flames like skilled barbe-
cue chefs, cooing when the claws frazzled to black, as the skin
shriveled and turned to charcoal, as the heads fell away, leaving
bloodied stumps and knuckles of bone.

Up here somewhere, by Félix's account, I'd find Playa de los
Muertos, the beach where Indians used to offer up sacrifices of
their own dead to the sharks. It was an extraordinary story—the
corpses draped in gold and emeralds in a ceremony that was
stumbled upon sometime last century by a traveling Dutchman
who, once the ceremonies were over, fished for the same sharks
and salvaged the gems. He became rich and built himself a mag-
nificent lakeside house. When the Indians discovered him, they
burned his new house to the ground and slit his throat.

I did not expect the beach to be labeled the same today—indeed, having sought out high-scale maps in San Carlos, could find nothing that even half-resembled it—but felt nonetheless that such a tale would surely have entered local folklore. Yet in San Miguelito, and in communities along the way, I met with only blank-eyed incomprehension.

From my questionings, however, emerged a new, altogether more compelling lead: Ometepe, a twin-cone volcanic island toward the northern end of the lake had, pre-Columbus, been home to a distinct, homogenous group of Indians. They were stonemasons and artists, but most of their statues and hieroglyphs had been looted by the Spanish and shipped to Granada. They had led religious, ordered, semimigratory lives, and had been massacred as savages by the crusading invaders. They had also, on their desolate beaches, in the shadow of the volcanoes, practiced systematic sacrifice to the sharks. If Playa de los Muertos existed, these fishermen told me, then it existed not here, on these dead and dying easternmost shores, but on Ometepe, where the land was still dark and rich and fishermen could still haul enough fish for a family to live on.

So I said good-bye to Candida, who at ten in the morning was tousled and confused and needed some reminding who I was, and then to Félix, the father she never mentioned. He lived further uphill, toward the fortress, in a cake-wedge house on an intersection permanently hazy with dust from the clatter-past of jeeps and motorcycles. There was a film of dust on everything and when I trod across his porch I left footprints. He was sitting in a folding classroom chair, the interior dark behind him, and gave a nod as I approached, as if he'd been expecting me.

"Here," he said, holding up an object. "I found it."

I blew dust off the top edge and held it up to the light. Below a fisherman's silhouette, cut from brass and riveted to the buffed-wood base, was a strip of steel with the words EL MEJOR PESCADOR EN SAN CARLOS—GRACIAS.

"Read it," Félix instructed. "Read out what it says." And so I did, and he closed his eyes, and his jaw—clumpily shaven, specked with crumbs and dirt—softened to a snag-toothed grin.

He led me downhill toward the quayside. He showed me the exact same spot he used to haul up his boat after a morning's fishing, where now a handful of boys were playing tag off rusted pilings. He threw an arm out across the lake in the direction of the deep blue of the emerald mine, and a dreaminess passed over his face.

Nearing midday, we found ourselves in the midpart of town, in a deserted concrete playground, the bones of an old truck sinking into the grass nearby. Above us, split with tree roots and clawed away by rockfalls, were the crumbling ramparts of the old fortress—walls that were two hundred years old, that had survived piracy and civil war, the empire-building ambitions of "Presidente" William Walker, even the Solentiname bombardment two decades before, but which now looked as if one hard night of rain might sluice them clean away.

"What's up there now?" I asked, as the bells of the church began to sound out their melancholy summons.

"The police, the prison. Come," he said, starting across the square. "I have friends."

In a small upstairs room in the police station, where cops in short-sleeved shirts jabbed at typewriters, Félix introduced me to the sergeant and then, to both of us, bade swift farewell. He looked old as he left, immeasurably ancient and worn down. He took the stairs hunched over, one hand against the wall, tracing the roughened tidemark of dirt left by many hundreds before.

It took a while for the sergeant to obtain the necessary permission. I sat and waited. A telephone rang on the wide desk at the head of the room. The policemen ceased typing, stared across their tables until the noise stopped, then one by one set to work again. On the floor above I could hear two men talking. From below, muffled through many walls of concrete, came a single, wildcat scream.

The sergeant came back. "Okay. I show you now." He strode ahead; I had to run to keep up.

We climbed past the police station, up the broken track between the slumped ramparts. Once inside the perimeter of the old fort, the ground leveled off. Ahead squatted three or four low concrete huts. A policeman was pissing noisily against a wall. He noticed us, turned away, leaving a dark stripe of urine against the whitewash. The sergeant drew to a halt.

"These," he said, taking my arm and swiveling in the other direction, "are the walls."

"So it's all part of the police station now, is it? Nothing to do with the army anymore?" A group of cops stood watching us, all smoking, hands half covering their faces.

Determinedly, the sergeant led me in the other direction. We stopped at an older building, sprouting horsehair from deep fissures in the adobe. "This is original."

"I see. And it's still in use?" There was a small barred window at the far end, set deep into the brickwork. I was sure I could hear voices from inside. There was an air of menace to the whole place; the other policemen, like bored mastiffs, were eyeing our progress. Here, I imagined, a jailer could run pretty much unchecked. I tried my guide once more. "I'm interested in the difference between before and after. What was it like then? Exactly what is it used for now?"

The sergeant about-turned smartly, snapped his heels together. "Those buildings over there," he said, cocking his head in the direction of the piss-streaked wall, "are new. And that's it. I'm busy. Now you go."

An hour later, heading downhill toward the ferry dock, I ran into Bosco, Solentiname veteran of the 1977 attack on the fortress. Today he looked like a man in a hurry, struggling to catch his breath as he paused to greet me, hefty dossier under his arm.

"So you came—" he gasped, sweat coursing down his neck. "You came to see the *cuartel*, the barracks." He managed a grin. "You couldn't resist."

"I wanted to see the place for myself."

"And?" He pulled into the shade and began swabbing himself with a washcloth.

"It's not much, is it? They've not done much to keep it up. Do you ever go? Just to reminisce?"

"Never." He narrowed his eyes. "I hope it rots into the ground."

And later, as I was fighting aboard the ferry with an hour to spare—time enough, I'd foolishly imagined, to guarantee a seat—a teenage money changer grabbed at my shirt. She gazed up at me, her wad of notes outstretched, eyes enormous. "Kiss me?" Her teeth were broken, her mouth full of blood.

On the last corner of floor space, on the top deck in a twisting wind, I tried to settle down for what I guessed would be a very long twelve hours until we reached the island of Ometepe. My neighbor, an elderly farmer who was trying to get comfortable on a rickety bed of maize sacks, focused hard on my shoes, my trousers, twisted his head round to check my watch face.

He nodded once, then thrust out his hand. "Sovietski?"

12

I stood at the rail as the ferry, hammering black smoke at the sky, pulled away from the quayside. The vendors and money changers lined the edge as our last rope was thrown aboard, shrinking to toy size as we grew more distant. Past the fishermen's docks, on our way toward open water, and the fishermen too looked up from their salting, like a line of startled shoeshine boys. We cut straight west, then began to arc northward: the same route the ship took every week, which would, so Félix had claimed, grant a good starboard glimpse of the entrance to the emerald mine. So I stood and scanned the surface, but could see no telltale darkening to indicate the mythic depth of water below.

Water as death, deep and unfathomable as eternity; the shark its perfect embodiment in flesh. In Spanish, shark was *tiburón*—a word unresonant, scarcely even memorable—but in French, the word was *requin*, from the obsolete but far more appropriately funereal *requiem*. And the bull shark—along with the tiger, whaler, blue, and gray reef sharks—belonged to just this line: *Carcharhinidae*, the requiem sharks. These fishes, characterized by a nictitating membrane and heterocercal tail fin, were found throughout tropical and temperate seas; they were voracious and nomadic, traveling long distances each day, migrating according to seasonal changes. Between them, they had the widest possible range of habitats of any group of sharks, but only the bull shark possessed the unique ability to thrive in both salt water and freshwater. The unique shark—and this, Lake Nicaragua, its crucible, its unglamorous, rough-shored, uniquely fitting home.

The ferry was of an age and decrepitude that, in a country with more money, would long ago have caused it to be retired. But its longevity, too, was appropriate: an American journeying from Granada to San Carlos in the 1940s noted that his vessel, the steamer *Victoria*, was stamped "Pusey and Jones, Wilmington, Delaware, 1882," making it already a good sixty years old.

Now, a half century on, any lingering romance attached to this crossing had long since evaporated; these days, the ferry was simply the sole means of passage and was, with no ticket limit, perilously overloaded. The bench seats inside, I learned, would have gone first thing that morning, children dispatched cat-fighting up the gangplank to stake their family's claim. And so, on to this blocky snub-nosed ferry, with single-file stairwells and safety plates that designated a maximum cargo of five hundred, were now shoehorned three times that number: people squatting atop their bags, clutching to their chests their precious vegetables and transistor radios; hard-eyed tamale sellers with lacy aprons and the most coveted, sheltered pitches; a brace of full-grown hogs, jostling like prizefighters in the ever-tightening space; a knot of young men throwing dice and slugging from a shared liter of rum that danced with flecks of phlegm.

When it rained, it blasted horizontally, hard as hail, forcing everyone flat to the metal. Above us, a lightbulb smashed; later, I found tiny splinters in my hair, caught in my clothing. With dusk, the wind quieted but the swell remained fierce. The horizon opened and the dipping sun and the distant rain made stripes of gray and gold.

A few attempted to sleep, but most, unable to find room to lie flat, sat slumped and staring. The gamblers grew louder and more raucous; a scant-toothed simpleton attached himself to their group, laughing and clapping at all the wrong moments, persevering even when they halted their cards and glared at him.

One of the tamale sellers began to shoot looks at me, angling her head downward in mock coyness so the light from the cabin behind threw her features into shadow. I caught her eye; she giggled, whispered something to her friend, and I, suddenly numbed by the inevitability of the interaction, shifted away.

From this new angle, poisoned by occasional blasts of bad-egg farmer's breath, I could see the moon on the water, shifting through clouds of gauze. When the simpleton laughed, a spider's thread of drool stretched from lip to floor, silver in the moonlight.

At the northernmost dock on Ometepe, early the next morning, cash was changing hands. Three trucks loaded with unripe bananas were pulled up in line, and men with baseball caps angled low over their faces were pressing up close to the door of a hut on the quayside. I watched from behind a high wire fence, saw each man peel off a wad of notes, then turn for his truck and the broken dirt road that led between the volcanoes to the far side of the island.

Later, passing by the harbormaster's hut, not daring to pose the question directly, I saw on the floor behind him what I'd guessed I'd see: a crate of ice-packed *sábalo real*, a fish now rare enough to serve as ideal bribery material, its flesh dark and blood-juicy as tuna steak. "You want some, huh?" he grinned. "I can see it in your eyes."

None of which, anymore, came as much of a surprise: in truth, it fitted perfectly with the history of the place, was yet another milestone on the road of exploitation and wanton disregard that distinguished the history of Nicaragua in general, and Ometepe in particular. Ometepe—literally, "two mountains," from the Nahuatl words *ome* and *tepec*—had, whatever Arturo's claim about its now being filled with "pirates," once been home to "pure Aztecs," according to one chronicler. They had not lasted long, their spears and arrows powerless against the muskets and shell-fire of the Spanish.

Their demise was paralleled nationwide: just two decades after Spanish occupation, recorded Bartolomé de las Casas, over half a million indigenous Nicaraguans had lost their lives to the invaders. A century on, the genocide was near-complete, with barely one twenty-fifth of the original population still standing.

Ometepe's story was typical. By the mid nineteenth century, it was being used as a field hospital, Vietnam-style, for the American wounded of "Presidente" William Walker's push for power. On this same island, Ephraim Squier, the U.S. envoy, stumbled on what remained of the "Aztec" art—gargoylish stone sculptures, with leering maws and gouged-out eye sockets—and had flunkies pack them in tea chests and ship them to Granada, where, to succeeding generations of tourists, they became known as the Squier Collection, nightmarish specters from a past now almost wholly forgotten.

At Moyogalpa, the island's westernmost port and link with the mainland, old Ometepe was fast disappearing. Fishermen and farmers now ran restaurants and guest houses, serving deep-fried *mojarra* and yellow-fat french fries to Mexican students and the occasional European tourist. The streets were still unpaved, but not much else remained the same. Even the old men seemed to have lost crucial memory, and struggled to recall even such recent milestones as the civil war, or the first democratic election. They could bring back the anti-Sandinista resistance that had lasted throughout most of the war—men who'd fled to caves on the slopes of the volcanoes—but little of any wider, less domestic import. Certainly there was little sense of the broader past, nothing that might have conjured alive their island's story, and not even a whisper about Playa de los Muertos.

By the time I ran into Simón Ajo that evening I'd as good as given up hope on this particular lead. He was sitting on the pavement outside his house and I'd pulled up solely to find the best way back across the island; light was getting short, I was footsore and in need of a little easy entertainment: a beer, a meal, sleep. He was shaking his head at me as I approached.

"I was wondering when you'd find me."

I stopped, squinted through the gloom. Had we met? I struggled to place him. He was elderly, but sat nonetheless upright and alert, hands fixed motionless on his knees. A home-painted sign behind his head read, CAFETIN AJO, though it was dark inside the house and the door was padlocked.

"You want to know Indian history. That is so?" He ran his fingertips over his mustache. "I have only one chair, but if you don't mind sitting on that crate . . ." He waited till I'd turned it over, drawn it close. "Then I'll begin."

News of my inquiries, as in any small town, had run well ahead of me: the priest, walking home from church, had dropped in on Simón and told him of my visit to him. And now Simón, the town's self-appointed historian, was waiting, sure in the knowledge that, sooner or later, and because there was no one else, I'd find him.

He'd grown up on an orange farm—fertile bottomland, on the broad skirts of the Madera volcano—but had been forced into finding other work when his father bequeathed the land, in its entirety, to his elder brother. He moved away, trained as an archaeologist, then returned to Ometepe to spend his thirties and forties grubbing through farmers' backyards in search of Indian ax heads and stone carvings—fitting together his own picture of how life here was lived before the Europeans came. In later middle age, his back threatening to seize up from so many years of genuflection, he returned to the fields of his birth, only this time as an advocate for organic farming methods. With earth as rich as this, he argued, chemicals were not only damaging to health and the land, but also an unnecessary extravagance. Most times, gauging perfectly the peasant mentality, he stressed the latter first and hardest, and was having some success: of Ometepe's six thousand producers, three hundred had successfully converted; more were doing so each year.

Today, organic or not, most farmland was given over to tobacco, which was shipped through wholesalers in Managua to America and Spain. It was an unlovely crop, with its stolid rows of bristle-backed leaves and its overbright, scentless flowers, but it paid well: to merchants, Ometepe, Nicaragua's biggest producer, was now "tobacco island."

Any peasant with any land to speak of grew tobacco; where, before, it had been fishermen whose grand hauls had commanded most respect, now it was the newly rich weed producers. The Indians, Simón said, had planted mixed, rotation crops—maize, frijoles, wheat—but the only people who grew those staples these days were those with insufficient land to try tobacco. Everything, Simón sighed, came down to tobacco, and it was clear that he, a man whose relations with the land had been thought out and respectful, was deeply saddened by the emergence of such an unchecked, brutal monoculture.

As we were speaking, the last bus eastward trundled past, dust souping in its wake. I jumped to my feet, threw up a hand, but the vehicle lacked side mirrors and was blacked out with dust and just carried on accelerating.

Simón tapped my knee, smiled. "It's okay. You go back tomorrow." He leaned round, shouted something, and at one of the windows of the house a child's face appeared.

"Two beers!" Simón called out, and the face disappeared. From inside there came shufflings and clinkings, the noise of chairs being moved, and before long the door was creaking open and a small boy was tottering toward us with a Victoria in each fist.

"My great-grandson." Simón grinned, knocking his bottle against mine. "He minds the shop when I'm in the fields."

He talked on as darkness fell, periodically calling for more beer, each time insisting the boy collect the bottle tops as well as the empties.

He became truly animated only when holding forth on

Indian culture. He spoke of these vanished people with a reverence that bordered on worship—for their pared-down lives, their aesthetic sensitivity, their freewheeling nomadism. Ometepe had had seven different Indian tribes, and each had knelt before a different god—the sun, the water, the shark, and so on. The tribes lived far apart from one another, and they had grown distinct in their art and agriculture as much as in their worship. They were pacific and seemed content to live within their territories. They were monogamous, and respectful of order and the hierarchy of priest and chieftain. *"Muy metódico,"* said Simón, with a wink. "One wife! Imagine that these days!"

The families were large—ten children was considered unremarkable—and each winter, when the ground had turned dry as biscuit, a mass migration took place, hundreds of canoes beetling south for the lake's remotest shore, toward what is now Costa Rica, where the rain fell heavy into unbroken rain forest. Here they traded—tobacco for gold—and returned home for spring.

They lived simply, in grass-roofed settlements by the water's edge or beside sheltered creek bottoms. Their only art was religious: effigies of their deities, many-limbed and gargoyle-eyed, chiseled from lava rock. As to human sacrifice, Simón was unsure, but this had been so widespread throughout central Nicaragua as to have been a virtual certainty here. In the absence of prisoners of war, the person sacrificed would have been a young male, especially raised, whose place in heaven was consequently guaranteed. His heart was eaten by the priest, his hands and feet by the *cacique*, or leader, and his innards and flesh by the ordinary Indians. His head was impaled on a tree, and prayers were uttered as the idol was slicked with his blood. It was practices such as these that provided easy justification for the later massacres by the conquistadores, and massacres they surely were: the Indians of Ometepe did not even last long enough to be sold into slavery.

It was now night. Simón's head was lowered, and I could see his expression only when he looked up and the street lamp lit his features. He appeared to be staring down the neck of his beer bottle, breathing very slowly.

I said, "All this—it seems so important. Why does no one else have the same knowledge?"

He lifted his head slowly. "Perhaps they do," he said. "But I have never met them."

"You should write it all down."

He pursed a half smile and looked down at his hands, a gesture that seemed to say, With these? After all these years?

He pointed to my beer, raised an eyebrow, and without waiting for my response, shouted for refills. The alcohol seemed to be calming him, but I could feel my senses blurring, lagged by tiredness and the heat of the day. How about books, I managed to ask. Had nothing been recorded?

"Yes," he said. "We did have a book on the island once. But the man who owned it died and his children, who could not read, burned his bookcases."

Simón's great-grandson pushed through the door, held out two fresh beers, and gathered the empties. Simón tipped his head back, sank three long draughts, then leaned toward me again.

"Anything else? Anything else I can help you with?"

I thought for a moment. "Playa de los Muertos? That mean anything to you?" I threw in everything I'd learned—the Indians who'd stuffed jewels in the mouths of their dead and fed the corpses to the sharks; the white man whose greed had precipitated a fittingly lurid death; my own suspicions that the whole yarn might be little more than legend, able to pass as fact only by virtue of having been around so long.

"Playa de los Muertos?" He shook his head, blew a spume of air upward into the cooling night air. "Let me tell you a story. Some way from here, on deserted land that is hard to reach, between the volcanoes, there is a freshwater lagoon near the water's edge—Laguna Verde."

There'd always been stories about the place and one day the team of archaeologists to whom Simón was assigned began quartering up the ground in preparation for a dig intended to determine, once and for all, the truth of all those decades of rumor.

"Very quickly," Simón said, "we began to find things." First shards of earthenware, then clusters of fruit kernels: clear evidence of burial, since these were goods considered indispensable for the afterlife. Then, nearby, as they'd guessed, the bones. From here on, expectations counted for nothing.

Simón clasped his hands together, almost in supplication. "The bones," he whispered, making parallel chopping motions, "were not laid out like a dead person's bones, not flat out like that, one after the other. They were packed tight together, like sticks of dynamite."

"And that was unusual?"

"Of course it was unusual!" He let out a little yelp; a couple of streets away a dog started howling.

"For all of us," he added, attempting to calm himself, "this was a mystery. Why had they been buried like that? What had happened to the bodies beforehand? Were they all sacrifice victims? Who had sliced them into such small pieces?" He paused, drew his chair closer still; I could feel the warmth of his breath on my face.

The breakthrough, when it came, was not his. One of the foreign archaeologists, fine-dusting a femur, had noticed a pattern of crushing and splintering that seemed too ordered to have been caused by the settling of rocks or the skewering of tree roots. But it was not until a tooth chip was discovered some days later that he'd felt confident enough to propose a theory: these were bull-shark victims, which had somehow—and against the fish's normal feeding habits—not been swallowed whole.

"Still puzzled?" Simón's eyes were enormous. "Let me tell you what we figured."

The bodies—both sexes, all ranks—had been fed to the sharks after death, rather than before. The corpses were shrouded in heavy-woven, broad-meshed nets and lowered off the beach near the lagoon. It would have taken little time for the sharks to fillet the flesh off the bones; what returned to the surface shortly afterward was ivory-clean, ready for an immaculate, boxed burial. Ceremonies took place at the new moon, when the shark gods were said to be hungriest.

Simón stood, set his chair against the wall of the house. "Now," he said, "you need somewhere to sleep. I've been talking too long. Yes?"

"True," I agreed. "A bed would be good."

As he made to open the door he turned to face me one last time, his features ghoulish in the plastic orange of the street-lamp. He was nakedly gleeful, broken teeth on full display.

"That, I'd wager," he muttered, "is your Playa de los Muertos."

The next morning, after a night spent on the pallet in Simón's front room, my brain soggy from beer, my stomach empty, I was not at my best. Simón suggested breakfast, but his larder, upon inspection, contained nothing but one shriveled onion. Shrugging, he made coffee and, while his great-grandson slept on, sketched a map of the island. According to this, if Ometepe was a loosely configured 8, the Madera and Concepción volcanoes rising flawless and symmetrical from each loop, then Laguna Verde lay on the wind-battered land spit between the two. The nearest hamlet was San José, served by intermittent buses. It was a fair distance, Simón intimated, along unmetaled roads, with little guarantee of a return ride.

Knowing by now Simón's predilection for understatement, I set off an hour later in an old Suzuki jeep, one of only two rental vehicles, as far as I could establish, in the whole town. The hotel owner breezed through a casual transaction—"Driving license? *No hay? No importa*"—and I took the road he'd described, heading roughly south into a building head of wind, making slow progress through outskirts unused to motorized traffic, waiting in the whirling sand while dogs and pigs and cows limped to the shoulder. Even when the way was clear, building up any speed was impossible: rain and wind and the passage of many million hooves had grooved the road into hard, transverse ridges, like militant speed bumps.

Some way on, the instrument panel rendered invisible by the same dust that I could feel clogging my ears and the corners of my eyes, working its way down the back of my trousers, I pulled over to pick up a hitchhiker. From what I could see through the windshield, he looked respectable enough, dressed in shoes and a crumpled tan suit. He also looked exhausted, leaning against a fence post, with barely enough energy to wave.

I stopped the jeep. In the space between us, the dust began to settle. He pushed himself upright, unsteady on his feet. He squinted through the sunshine at me and, from his pocket, pulled a handkerchief smeared with what looked like oil and blood; he held it to his mouth and hawked loudly.

"*Adónde?*" he croaked. "Where to?"

"Toward San José, Laguna Verde. You know it?"

He took a step, transferring his weight tentatively, as if negotiating a minefield. He watched his feet as he walked, stopping short of the passenger door, wiping his handkerchief round the back of his neck. "I come too?"

His breath, even at three yards, smelled powerfully of toilet bleach. For a moment, a nightmare vision ahead, I considered doing the sensible thing and leaving him there, but his hand was already on the door, his look beseeching. He yanked it open, missed his footing and slumped forward across the seat. When he slid back to try the maneuver again I noticed he'd deposited a slug of curdled drool on the gearshift.

I drove away slowly, wondering how soon I'd be able to find an excuse to abandon him. In the small cockpit we were almost shoulder to shoulder, and my hand bumped against something hard in his jacket pocket as I changed gear. He flinched, pulled away from me. Cowering, as if I afraid I might strike out, he extracted from his pocket a quart of white rum, which he began to siphon at noisily.

"How far are you going?" I said, raising my voice above the rattle of the body panels. Ahead of us was a bridge, and a dry-fissured riverbed that cut under the road. A man leading a cow was waiting for us to pass.

"No further than you, boss. Anywhere you wanna take me." He attempted a wink of solidarity, but coordination deserted him and both eyes closed at once. He sucked the last from his rum bottle and tossed it backward over his head.

Ahead, the man with the cow was laughing. He shouted up at us, pointing at me, then at the jeep.

"Not bad," he yelled as we passed. "Not at all bad."

"You better believe it," my passenger hollered back. "I got me a chauffeur now."

His name was Alberto, he said, attempting a handshake on a particularly tight corner. "Alberto," he repeated, and there was much he wanted to tell me: of his impoverished infancy in Panama, his children at university in Managua, his current hard-won status on Ometepe as a *"cultivador de tabaco muy fortunado."* He talked very fast and paused at unexpected moments, as if responding to questions echoing in his own head. When I finally gained his attention, he admitted that he'd never heard of Laguna Verde and in fact made it his business to stay well clear of water in general, since he could not swim.

"But I tell you what," he shouted, throwing an arm in the direction of an approaching side road. "I have a friend who does."

The gradient was steep, and I took it as slow as I could, but the brakes were poor and we kept slewing toward the bank. Tree roots scraped the undercarriage. Alberto slumped back, gripping the sides of the seat with both hands, his feet up against the dash. "Not far now," he breathed, eyes closed. "Not far."

The ruts were deep, heat-fired hard as clay, and even at low revs we struggled to remain seated. My foot kept being jolted from the gas pedal and then, with equal force, jammed back again. Vehicles, it was obvious, didn't often come this way: at points we were forced to snowplow through overhanging boughs and tangled creepers.

With Alberto's eyes still squeezed shut, we overshot the entrance to his friend's house and had to abandon the jeep in the track and tramp back up the slope on foot. Alberto, without a bottle handy, was fading visibly, his lips dry and bloodless, his breathing increasingly raspy. Every few yards he pulled up to rest, and I was beginning to wonder whether he wasn't about to lie down in the dirt right there and expire when there was a shout from further uphill. A tiny figure cut through the trees at the side of the track. He was carrying a pitchfork, and his bare feet detonated little mushrooms of dust as he trotted down the bank toward us.

With his help I levered Alberto to his feet and propped him against the hood of the jeep. This man—Jaime, a farmer—knew of Laguna Verde, but hadn't been there in years. Rarely, he said, did he find much cause to venture even as far as the main road, but, yes, he'd take me. It wasn't far. And besides, he added, running respectful fingers up the coachwork, we had transport.

He climbed in the back and began inspecting the window catches and seat-adjustment levers with a small boy's fascination. I threw Alberto's arm around my shoulder and heaved him into the passenger seat. He kept slumping forward and jerking upright, like a salesman who'd been on the road too long; when I started the engine again, he folded his forearms against the dash and rested his head as if asleep.

The final section of track, down to the shore, was the roughest yet, and Alberto's head bounced hard against the dash till, after much groaning, he was forced to give up and revert to upright. He glowered, spitting out curses. In the rearview, Jaime's eyes were on me—unblinking, expressionless as a driving-test inspector's. Thirty yards from the water, the track petered out to sand and I pulled up under a tree.

"This'll do fine," Jaime said, reaching for his pitchfork. "We'll walk from here."

We followed the shore a little way, past a clinker fishing boat big as a whale, which had been levered onto blocks on the beach. Two men were lying in hammocks in the shade, and I could sense their eyes slowly turning on us as we passed. Below them, on the sand, were a heap of tools, a chain saw, oily rags. They offered no greeting. A few yards on, one of them said something to the other and there was cold laughter; much later, when we'd taken the path away from the shore to climb the long incline toward the lagoon, I heard the hyena whine of the chain saw starting up again.

Coming out over the crest, the full force of the gale hit again—a hot wind, opaque with dust and the shed carapaces of locust-hard insects. Away from the lake, the volcano rose steeply into cloud. These lower slopes, which we skirted now, had been sunburned hard as brick, and two knife-hipped horses were attempting to find grazing, their incisors scratching at the dust.

Jaime went ahead, scything with his pitchfork through a field of maize, the ears withered and blackened through lack of moisture. We walked for half an hour into a rising bank of woodland, Alberto falling further and further behind, his shouts of "I'm thirsty" receding to distant echoes.

It was a landscape of archetypal barrenness, as if cursed; aside from the horses, I saw only two animals: a shriveled leather-backed cow, whose bones clicked as it walked, and above it a lone vulture, circling slowly in the heat.

Jaime kept throwing out miscellaneous pieces of information—the name of this shrub, that tree; his own distrust of any farmland that lay between the volcanoes—but showed no interest in my response. "Not far now, not far," he'd repeat, and before long the trees began to thin and we came out on a ridge. Before us lay a lake the color of oil, with orange tidemarks etched like the age rings of a tree down the rocks at its edge. At the far side, some three hundred yards from where we stood, egrets flurried from the water, trailing guano like so many city pigeons.

"You see the sea?" Jaime said, nodding ahead, where the birds were spiraling upward. A rock-shale hillside rose up behind the lake, but to either side there was nothing—the edge of the *laguna*, then opacity, haze, possibly water. "In the wet season," he said, "the sea comes in, fills the lake, and makes the water good again."

"And this is where the Indians lived?" It seemed hard to imagine a spot less inclined to the devotional life, even if that devotion had centered on the shark. Land giving onto the *laguna* was at a pitch poorly suited for building; the only level ground was where we stood, and that was no more than twenty yards wide.

"Oh, sure," he said, pulling a breathless Alberto up to the level. "All around this edge." The cemetery, he said, had been dug from the hillside opposite.

"And the shark beach?"

He clapped his hands together, gave Alberto a nudge in the spine with the handle of his pitchfork. "Not far now."

We kept to the edge of the *laguna*, then climbed over the perimeter bank one last time. The wind, from which we'd been sheltered till now, buffeted unfettered from the lake, making conversation impossible. We shouted at each other on the scramble down, but only snatches reached me.

The beach was black sand, studded with petrified horse

turds. The waves were whitecapped, and windblown spray had dampened the ground some way back from the water's edge and was now, as we approached, darkening our shirt fronts and matting our hair. A short way across the water was a small island; on the beach a canoe was on its side, half full of sand. There were just two trees at the edge: a nutless coconut palm and, closer, what looked like a gnarled oak, its bark flayed to prayer flags.

"And this is it?" I shouted. "This is where they took their dead?" It was a bleak wilderness place, but I'd hardly been expecting anything more glamorous. The important thing was to be here—finally, after all the stories and the false leads, to have arrived.

Jaime was bent over the canoe, testing his knuckles against the wood. He did not look up. Alberto, standing closer, shook his head, pointed at his ears. I cupped my hands to form a bullhorn and shouted again. The wind was black and howling, hungrily devouring every other sound.

He took a step toward me. *"Qué?"*

"Sharks," I yelled, almost in his ear. "Worship? Here?"

"Gracias!" There was froth at the corners of his mouth; his tongue was candy-pink, specked with sand.

"What?"

"Cerveza!"

"Beer?" He wanted beer? By some distance, this man was not the companion I needed right now. At this crucial moment, I wanted to be with someone of knowledge and authority, someone who could share my thrill at having reached this historic beach. Instead, I was burdened with a guide focused solely on his next alcoholic fix.

"Sí!" Alberto was against my ear now; I could feel spittle on my neck. "You're a good man!" he shouted. "I am very thirsty!"

▼ ▼ ▼

Though it was getting late, and by the time we got back to the jeep we'd been walking too long in the heat, Jaime, to my relief and gratitude, suggested we make one detour before dropping him back home. Not far from here, he said, lived an old man, an oracle who knew everything, who would be able to answer all the questions he'd failed to. He was embarrassed, he implied, at his own lack of knowledge: this man, he promised, would not disappoint.

I started the engine, once again charged with excitement. Finally, after so many charlatans and so much half information, I really was going to meet a man who could fully explain all that I'd seen. The "oracle," no less. I relished the mythic sound of the word—the repository of all knowledge, the holy grail. Once I'd heard this man out, I'd understand fully, and for the first time, the shark's true place in the history of these waters.

We drove north beside the beach—Alberto, from choice, squeezed in the back, Jaime directing from the front. Alberto had long since given up pleading for alcohol and seemed content with the arrangement we'd agreed on: that, after taking Jaime home, I'd drive him wherever he needed to go. He'd groaned when Jaime had proposed visiting the oracle, and now was doing his best to stretch out flat across the backseat, his jacket draped across his face even though the sun, falling low across the lake's western reaches, was hardly dazzling.

When we pulled up, finally, and I killed the engine, he was snoring loudly and Jaime and I climbed out gingerly, leaving the doors open so as not to wake him. We'd arrived at a concrete bungalow a hundred yards from the shore. The wind had dropped and from inside the house I could hear the rattle of a transistor radio, clearly audible even though all doors and windows appeared to be closed. Halfway across the yard was a well, but the winch carried no rope and the drop, when I craned over, echoed drily.

At the door, with the radio cranked to a building-site pitch, Jaime knocked. When there was no response, he rapped again, much harder, and the radio cut abruptly. There was a metallic shuffling, then the door eased back inch by inch to reveal, squinting up at us, a man with a caliper on one leg. He was fat—the fattest person I'd yet seen—and had baby-dimpled knuckles and knees that seemed to buckle backward under his weight. He was five feet two, if that. Not quite the suave-tailored, all-seeing savant I'd pictured, but it was, I told myself, his mind we'd come to pay homage to, not his external appearance. Breathless, I waited for him to speak.

"*Sí?*" he snapped.

Jaime explained.

"Well," the oracle murmured, coming outside, pulling the door shut behind him. "I know everything, as anyone on the island will tell you. So go right ahead—ask anything you like." He heaved himself into a rocking chair, feet off the ground, and blinked at us from behind spectacles of such high magnification that his eyeballs almost filled the lenses.

"How long do you have?" he asked.

"An hour or so," I answered, unsure how to begin, how to properly mine the riches that stood before me. "I'm driving Alberto and Jaime home afterward."

"An hour!" His dewlaps quivered. "To hear what I have to say you need five or six hours at the very minimum. How serious can you be? A scholar, indeed!"

"Perhaps we could just start, in that case," I hedged. "Wherever you like." How much, for instance, did he know about the Indians who'd peopled Laguna Verde?

He clasped his hands in front of him, a priest before his people. "Once upon a time," he began, "at the beginning of time, God created man and woman." This was *Genesis*, I realized with a shock: he really was aiming for the long version. I glanced at Jaime, but he was nodding studiously. "Heaven and earth," the oracle was murmuring, "the tree of life—"

"Very interesting," I broke in, hoping to nudge him forward a few millennia. "But how about you? Tell me something about yourself. How long have you lived here?"

He retracted his neck—an oddly tortoiselike, defensive gesture—and snapped out a short burst of answers, the end of each punctuated by a snort. He was eighty-seven, born in Granada; he'd bought the farm where we now sat in 1945; in recent years he'd turned historian, and had even written a book about the island's Indian past.

"A book?" I said, spotting my cue. "I'd be interested to read it."

"You can't." The barest hint of a smile.

"Oh—"

"Only one copy remains. I have it here." He brought a finger to his lips, and whispered low. "But it is hidden, and no one but me knows where."

"I see. Then perhaps you could tell me, in your own words, a little of what it contains—"

"Of course." He smiled again, then lapsed into silence.

"The Indians on Ometepe?" I prompted. "Before the Spaniards came?"

"Hmmm." He began toying with a mole on his cheek, rolling it between his fingers, tweaking and releasing it with an elastic snap. "They were similar to the Indians in Mexico but— how do you say?—a little more *civilizado*."

"Really?"

"Absolutely, and you know why? They learned Spanish faster." He was sniffing his fingers now, gazing upward dreamily into the dusk sky.

This was getting nowhere. After the adrenaline rush of expectation, I felt deflated. I needed neither his musings on the creation story nor his own personalized interpretation of the impact of colonialization. I was, however, keen to glean anything he knew about Indian life on Ometepe, and in particular the shark cult of Laguna Verde. I tried again.

He swiveled toward me, eyes aglow. "You have written nothing down. Ten minutes we sit here and you have not written one word."

I removed my pen top. "That's because I want to know about Laguna Verde. We haven't got on to that yet." I let the pen rest against the page.

"Devil worshipers," he muttered, and shot a glance at Jaime.

"True," Jaime nodded. "They had a pact with the devil."

"They worshiped the shark," I broke in. "Hardly the same thing."

The oracle mimed the snap-shut of a shark jaw, then bared his own, tiny-rodent teeth. "I think so, oh yes. Very much the same thing. They were profane, those Indians at Laguna Verde. Everywhere else on Ometepe the Indians were artistic and godly. Only at Laguna Verde did they worship the shark."

He paused, poked his glasses back up his nose. "And you saw the island, just off the beach? Isla de Amor, where young men and women would go . . . and . . ." He paused. "You know. . . ." He studied the ground between us. "It was a society of the flesh."

"I see." My disappointment was fast turning to hilarity at the bathos of this situation. I'd expected too much, too quickly, for the whole story to land, ready-wrapped, in my open hands. As I should by now have learned, this was not how it worked: truth, here, was a matter of scrabbling around for scraps, assembling them like so much detective work.

I felt laughter bubble up within me, and the more indignant and moralistic he became, the less able I felt to control myself. I scratched a couple of words in my notebook, took a deep breath.

"Two words?" The oracle was shaking his head. "That's all you can think to write down? I spend my time explaining the history of the island—history no one else knows—and you write down two words?"

"They will help me remember," I said, seizing the opportunity to stand up and make my excuses. Out of the corner of my eye I noticed Alberto sitting upright in the back of the jeep, gesturing to go. "You have been," I added, giving the oracle my hand, "most kind. Very generous of you to give me a little of your valuable time."

"You are going?" He grabbed my hand, pulled himself upright. He seemed suddenly flustered, unsure where to look.

"I'm afraid so," I said. "We have to get on."

"Could you not wait just five minutes more? You seem like a man of culture and taste. I have something in the house, something very rare, that you might be interested in."

I looked at Jaime, hoping for a lead, but his face betrayed nothing.

The oracle held up his thumb and forefinger, two inches apart. "An Indian ax head. Genuine. In New York or Managua, it would fetch many hundreds of dollars, but for you . . ." He touched my elbow. "I ask only twenty." He paused. "American."

"No," I laughed, turning for the jeep. "I don't think so. Not today."

He scuttled after us, his caliper clanking. "Fifteen, then. Ten?"

13

I'd been walking all morning when the limousine pulled up just ahead, an electric window eased open, and a hand motioned me forward. I'd trudged five or six miles in all, from the center of Granada to the last surviving lakeside fortification, and, with no taxi in prospect, had resigned myself to returning on foot as well. My own poor planning was at fault: I'd started late, and so had been forced to walk through a scorching midday, into a heat-bleached, upper-nineties afternoon, and now I was fading badly, each step more leaden and effortful than the last. Down by the lake I'd expected a cooling breeze, but the air had been lifeless; even insects lay immobile against the melted earth; no birds called from the flayed-bark eucalypts.

The fortress was a quarter mile offshore, and I'd hired a young entrepreneur with an outboard to take me there. Together we clambered over the ruin and gazed out across the hot-glass lake. Reinforced thick as a World War II air-raid shelter, this sentry post, built in 1523, the year before Granada was founded, had been as good as useless: scores of pirates had slipped by unnoticed, each time to plunder and sack and burn. My guide claimed an underwater tunnel ran from here to the distant city, but the entrance was not under the rock slab where he'd been told it was, and he quickly gave up, retreating back inside, away from the heat. The rocks on which the fortress was built had seen some of the nation's best shark fishing—the biggest, most sporting fish—and this was not hard to believe. A century and a half ago, Ephraim Squier visited this outlook and saw sharks "dashing about, with their fins projecting above the water."

An hour later, when the long Mercedes purred past, I'd not bothered to stick out my thumb, figuring that a car that reeked of this much ostentatious wealth would be the last in the world to stop for a hitchhiker as bedraggled as myself. And yet it did, and because I'd not flagged it down, I assumed it must have pulled over for some other reason and so did not hurry to catch it. Only when I saw the hand motioning from the open window, and heard opera murmuring from the interior, did I quicken my pace.

The passenger window opened as I approached, and I leaned forward into a rush of blessedly cool air.

"Jump in." A middle-aged man was turned my way, one finger balanced on the bottom rim of the steering wheel. I glanced into the car: in the middle of the backseat, on upholstery of pale ruched leather, lay a flaxen-haired sheepdog, its sleeping head drooling onto a velvet pillow.

"There's no one else," he said. "You appear in need of a ride. I say again—jump in."

With the windows up and the air-conditioning on full, I grew quickly chilled and had to sit with my arms folded tight, legs crossed for warmth. He drove very slowly, braking to a crawl as we passed a peasant cart, shouting boisterous greetings through his window before sealing us once again in smoked glass. He wore clip-on shades, and deck shoes, and insisted on conversing in English, which he spoke with a thick Latino-American lilt, peppering each phrase with incongruous business argot. "I'm a Nicaraguan, born in Granada," he'd explain. "And now I am rich, the richest man in the city. And you know my secret. Everything I sell, every business I own—satisfaction guaranteed."

Again Arturo's words suddenly seemed uncannily prophetic. On that scrap of paper, now badly foxed, that I carried with me everywhere, he'd written, "Granada—where all the money went." And now, in this Mercedes, it seemed I'd stumbled upon Granada's wealth made flesh—a man whose appearance in my own journey had somehow, I couldn't help feeling, been foreseen by a peasant shark fisherman from the far side of the country.

The rich man—"Call me Emanuel Garcia"—was talking; I struggled to bring myself back. He was boasting of his commercial interests—five businesses in Granada alone, including a textile factory, two farms, a coffee plantation, and a hotel—and stock in innumerable others elsewhere. His conversation was punctuated with stuck-animal grunts, as if he were in pain; even in the icy air-conditioning his skin was shiny with sweat. Whenever he reached a point he wished to stress, he up-angled his clip-ons so that I could see his eyes—bloodshot, jaundiced.

"During the Sandinista years," he said, flicking his clip-ons to horizontal, "I was in Miami. Why would I have wanted to stay here, under the buttocks of communists?"

In 1979, his businesses were seized; his house was appropriated as a billet for soldiers. "Anarchy! Everyone wanted a piece of your automobile, your factory. Everyone became thieves, trying to break into everywhere and steal everything. The Sandinistas grabbed everything I had—silverware, liquor, furniture, clothes, automobiles, all the equipment from the factory." And so, like a quarter of the four-million-strong population—the richest quarter—he'd fled.

In Miami, surrounded by many thousand other former Somoza stooges, he'd prospered; he had returned home for good just three months ago. With the election of a new right-wing government—an administration whose personnel and policies bore more than a passing resemblance to those of Somoza— Nicaragua was now, to his mind, finally free of the scourge of Sandinism and was, once more, a fit place to make his home.

We had turned away from the lake now and were cruising at a regal slowness up Calle La Calzada into town. In the shade of the Iglesia de Guadalupe a group of road workers turned to stare. They were silent, immobile, their shovels and picks hanging limply from their sides, as stunned as if a spaceship had just landed on the hot tarmac in front of them. Emanuel Garcia, glancing in their direction, grunted, allowed himself a brief smile.

"And you have to tell me something now," he said, still grinning. "How is my friend Mick Jagger?"

"Mick Jagger?" I coughed. "Can't say that I'd know. He's a friend of yours?"

He took both hands from the steering wheel, waved them

airily in front of him. "Oh, you know, you meet people. He was
married to a Nicaraguan girl, a very pretty Nicaraguan girl as a
matter of fact."

"Bianca. You knew her?"

"Of course! At one time I knew everybody. But she lives outside Nicaragua now." He traced an imaginary tear-track down
his cheek. "Very lamentable."

"So you don't see her anymore?"

He shook his head. "But I have photographs. We will drive
to my house and we will drink French champagne and I will
show you. You like French champagne?"

At the approach to the Parque Central the road ended and he
took a side alley, swinging the big car along a succession of narrow back streets, past darkened doorways set into heat-cracked
whitewash, covering with dust a wide-eyed street vendor just
emerging from his siesta. The only two cars we encountered
pulled up on to the curb to let us pass, their drivers squinting
hard at the impenetrable windows, seeing only their own gawp-
ing reflections and those of their rust-holed, broken-backed
jalopies.

Only belatedly, as we were finally coming onto the main
square, did he ask me what my interest was in Granada. When I
explained, he gave a little exhalation of amazement, cuffed himself across the forehead with the back of his hand.

"*Tiburones,*" he said, as we skirted the steps of the cathedral,
scattering small children like so many chickens. "Why didn't
you say?"

"Well, I—"

"I am the man to talk to. This shark factory you mention—I
was one of the major investors. For many years it made much
money."

"It also," I said, feeling a sudden fury that Arturo, had he been in my place, would no doubt have expressed far more violently, "came close to killing off the shark."

"Look," he said, with a grunt so loud the dog, behind us, spluttered awake. "It was a business, like any other. Get the product in, package it and sell it on. Profit and loss, supply and demand, satisfaction guaranteed. We give the customer what he wants. And if it wasn't for the Sandinistas, we'd still be doing it today. It was making us rich, that factory, but oh how much more we'd have made if those idiot communists hadn't closed it down."

Granada, more than anywhere else in Nicaragua, was the shark's home town. Its baseball players were "Tiburones"; its bakeries and bookshops, "Panadería el Tiburón" or "Librería el Tiburón"; the skiffs at its lakeside dock, *Tiburón I*, *Tiburón II*, *Tiburón III*. And, like the bull shark that once held sway in its waters, so the city, too, had once been all-powerful, unassailable.

Founded in 1524 by Francisco Fernández de Córdoba, it was, by midway through the last century, the archetypal exquisite colonial city, home to fifteen thousand inhabitants, rich in trading houses dealing direct, via the San Juan, with New York, London, Paris, Rome—"better known," according to one account, "than any other city in all Central America."

Its rise to prominence, however, had not been straightforward: throughout the late seventeenth century it was repeatedly ransacked by French and English pirates—small ruthless bands on hit-and-run raids that left churches ablaze and treasures looted. Typical was the English buccaneer John Davis, who according to a contemporary Dutch account, after sneaking his canoes up the San Juan under cover of darkness, posed as a fisherman crossing the lake, and, charging into Granada, "robbed all the money and plate [he] could find; neither did [he] spare the churches and most sacred things, all of which were pillaged and profaned without any respect or veneration." Yet Granada, like the *tiburón*, survived it all, to emerge, by the nineteenth century, Central America's preeminent city-state.

Crucial to its ascendancy was the San Juan River, its unique maritime link, and by the nineteenth century, with the piracy threat long since disappeared, and the prospect of a San Juan corridor canal looking increasingly likely, it seemed for a while that Granada was destined for a further, stratospheric rise. That it did not happen did not dim Granada's star; rather the reverse, for it left the river undammed, let the shark continue its centuries-old migrations, allowed the fishermen to continue working the waters undisturbed. It preserved the river in its elemental state (long since splintered by ever-worsening rapids); preserved, too, the possibility of this archetypal odyssey: ocean to source, backward in time, toward the heart and the beginning of things. Along these dream tracks, as much as up the actual river, had come first the fish, then the sharks, and finally the shark hunters. All roads led here, to Granada, and it was here, I sensed, that the story of the shark and those that had hunted it would finally come full circle.

It was a city in flux, with roofless derelict shacks, standing alongside freshly mortared "colonial-style residences" hopefully awaiting a surge of bold investors. Arriving direct at the central square, somehow having managed to avoid glimpsing the bleak outskirts, one might have imagined that Granada indeed was, as the new tourist bureau liked to put it, "Nicaragua's colonial jewel." But within just two blocks of this cool-shaded *zócalo* of live oaks and sprinklered gravel, just out of earshot of the tinkling of the bells on the ice-cream carts, the city began visibly to crumble. Overhead were birds' nests of phone wires, the cupolas of old churches fissured with cracks and discolored by decades of bird droppings.

For as much evidence as there was of eager redevelopment, there were mid-city stretches of wasteland. The arterial roads were narrow and crowded, choked with buses on which juice sellers and hawkers of strength pills fought for custom. In the Parque Central, shoeshine boys yelled after a solitary group of dazed European tourists and, at night, because they had come here from villages outside and had nowhere else to go, they covered themselves with threadbare blankets and slept right there.

The city's most expensive hotel sat plumb on the Parque Central, straight across from the cathedral, and on its terrace, from breakfast until night, tourists were propositioned by girls barely out of puberty. Sitting here alone one evening, during a brief lull in the endless sexual transactions, I overheard a group at the next table, loud with American and British accents, talking of the city's bright prosperous future, "if only these Nicaraguans could get it together." In five years, the businessmen toasted each other, Nicaragua would be "the new Guatemala," and Granada "the new Antigua." And they were probably right, if only because tourism, always questing for the next "best-kept secret," was fast becoming insatiable. And Granada, given a few more years' titivation, would, as these businessmen recognized, be perfect: it had "heritage," it had elegant colonial courtyards, its taxis were horse-drawn traps, it had cloistered convents and churches, it had the lake, and, for the hardier visitor, it had the sharks.

But for now, still impoverished and mangy, the city belonged to no one but itself. Two weeks I'd been here, and every afternoon, with Easter approaching, the city's craftsmen and hoboes and street hawkers had laid down their chisels and begging bowls and trays of matches and joined step with a procession headed by a full-size carving of Christ, bent double under the weight of his cross. Through the backstreets the procession crept, building in volume, stopping at each corner for prayers and hollered *Amen*s before the drums and trumpets and French horns struck up again and, like a funky New Orleans funeral, the shuffle onward began once more. Women waved handkerchiefs from balconies as the mass of worshipers passed below, their faces mournful, feet tapping, asway to the rhythm. It reminded me of some mafioso wake from the movies, and I half expected three black Cadillacs to block the road ahead and gunmen to burst out firing.

By nightfall, with the marchers footsore and the musicians sounding like a wound-down gramophone, the crowd snaked slowly across the Parque Central and filled the cathedral with candlelight and heat and noise and singing that lasted well into the night.

A block from the center, Emanuel Garcia drew the big Mercedes to a stop outside a broad, single-story mansion. Unlike the cracked roofless dwellings we'd passed on our way in, this was freshly painted—soft peach, with doors and window frames a dark olive green—and seemed more like a film star's Provençal retreat than the likely dwelling of any Nicaraguan. Even the pavement was swept clean, and appeared to be streaked with wet, as if freshly scrubbed.

Emanuel Garcia sounded the horn and a pair of double doors parted soundlessly. He swung the car off the street, up onto the pavement, and into the darkened interior. Behind us, the doors closed again. Ahead, a smaller door opened and a man appeared, dressed in black, a napkin over one arm, holding a silver tray.

"Home sweet home," Emanuel Garcia sighed. "Now I feel happy."

He stayed sitting as I climbed out, then gestured me to cross to the driver's door. Opening it, he reached for my arm and, pulling against me, began to inch himself sideways off the seat. Little beads of sweat pricked out across his forehead; twisting to lift his legs out, he emitted a low groan of pain. Getting him to his feet required me to brace myself against the car as he held on to my arm and levered his considerable bulk upright.

"Are you okay?" I said, recovering my balance. "Would you like to sit down?"

"I'm fine," he grunted. "It's an old wound. Fifteen years old. I broke my back in Florida. Don't you worry about me." He let go of my arm, steadied himself against the side of the car. He glanced up ahead, snapped his fingers.

"Drinks!" he shouted, and the butler, giving a small bow, reversed out of sight.

We came out from the garage into a verdant, sun-filled courtyard. Three maids in white pinafores were standing in a row, hands clasped in front of them; they smiled, heads lowered, as we approached. "Lunch!" Emanuel Garcia announced, with a further snap of his fingers, and they too scuttled off, leaving us alone with the shrubbery and the paintings and, in each corner, clusters of dark polished furniture.

The house was built to generous proportions, designed for the heat. The courtyard was broad, and, apart from the profusion

of plant life in the very center, shaded from direct sunlight. Off
it were dark rooms, slatted windows, velvet chaises longues.

"This house has been visited by many presidents of
Nicaragua, by the president of Germany," he said, waving an
arm across the courtyard. "Take a photograph."

"I don't have a camera."

He rolled his eyes heavenward. "No camera!" He exhaled
loudly, patted his hands against his hips, shoved them in and out
of his pockets. At the far edge of the courtyard I saw the butler
emerge from a back room, gliding with the tray held out ahead
of him. "The drinks arrive!" Emanuel Garcia shouted, gripping
my elbow. "Come, we will sit in the Presidents' Room!"

The butler brought cold beer in iced tankards and laid them
on ivory coasters on a low mahogany table. Emanuel Garcia dismissed him with instructions to walk the dog, then feed it, then
make up its bed with soft blankets. The butler reversed from the
room, as it we were medieval royalty, tyrants to be feared. He
paused just once, to switch on the ceiling fan, then continued his
reverse shuffle across the terra-cotta tiles and out of sight.

Emanuel Garcia took a long draft, wiped the foam from his
mouth. "You think I should feel sorry for these peasants?"

"Sorry?"

"You know how much they earn?"

"Your butler?"

"Any peasant you care to think of. Take those cigarette
sellers by the cathedral. You know how rich they are? They can
make two hundred and fifty cordobas a day, thirty dollars
American. Easy."

I nodded, said nothing. This seemed an extraordinary claim:
from vendors themselves I'd heard that one dollar was consid-

ered average, three or four, exceptional. Nationwide, at least half
the population survived on one dollar a day.

Emanuel Garcia called for another beer, then turned toward
me. "We are overrun," he said. "Ignorant campesinos—no wonder the country's in such a mess. They're no better than little
children. The ones who were given land by the Sandinistas have
no idea how to look after it—they eat the cows they are supposed to sell, then wonder why they are still poor. And what of
the future? Half our population is under sixteen years of age.
What do they know about anything?"

"Why so young?" This, by contrast, was an accurate figure,
or at least widely agreed on. "Because of the war?"

"Oh no." He lowered his voice, bent closer. "Because during
the war there was no electric light during the night. What else
were the peasants to do in the evenings but make whoopee?"

On the cherry-velvet walls of the "Presidents' Room" were
twenty or thirty black-and-white photographs, in identical
frames, ranked three deep. All featured one or more members of
Emanuel Garcia's family alongside assorted foreign royalty such
as King Juan Carlos of Spain, American film stars, and presidents and presidential aides from Nicaragua and abroad. Promi-
nent were shots of Arnoldo Alemán, the new president and a
highly popular figure among the rich for his policy of returning
Sandinista-seized properties, as well as snaps of numerous
Somozas. My attention was drawn to one in particular.

"That's Anastasio Somoza in that one, right? The last dictator? Who's that with him?" Both men looked similarly malevo-
lent: dark-suited, toadlike.

"My brother."

"They were close, then, the two families?"

He shrugged. "He was a good man, Somoza. He deserved better than he got, certainly. If I could bring him back to life? Yes, why not?"

At the end of the line of dignitaries were three or four less formal photographs, snapped at eccentric angles, as if by passersby, hurriedly. These were the shark-fishing trophy shots of archetype: the great fish gaffed up from gantries, dwarfing the men that stood beside them. Emanuel Garcia was in two; the other grinning bloodied faces belonged to his brothers, his father.

We ate lunch and drank chilled French mineral water, sitting at opposite ends of a long walnut-veneer dining table. More than once he apologized for the absence of champagne—it was in storage, he said, and would have been unpalatably warm. We ate salad, then fish with potato chips and rice, then slices of papaya. Whenever my plate was empty he'd press me to take more, and the maid, standing in the shadows, would step forward and pass the bowls between us.

He hadn't fished for shark, he said, since before the revolution. As a young man, he and his friends had gone out onto the lake most weekends with their "Hemingway rods" and fiberglass dories. They had fished for sport, and to impress their girl-friends, and had dressed in sawed-off jeans and raggedy work-men's shirts, baseball caps pulled low over their Ray-Bans.

"And then you sold them?" I said, guessing there were few business opportunities that passed him by.

"Sold them?" He laughed, motioning for the maid to clear his half-eaten plate. "Are you saying we were that desperate for money?"

"I, er, no—"

"I am from one of Granada's oldest families," he interrupted. "We have lived here for one hundred years."

"So what did you do with them? The sharks? Once you'd caught them?"

"We killed them and we threw them back."

"But you're a businessman," I went on, feeling my dislike of him suddenly start to harden. "You must have known you could have made money from selling the sharks."

"Oh, you are right." He grinned, swaying his head from side to side as if unsure how to respond to such flattery. "Absolutely right. Which is why when the opportunity came of investing in the factory, you can imagine how I leapt at it. That way we would not be dealing with one or two sharks, or perhaps five in a weekend's fishing, but many, many thousand, every year. That, I could tell, was the way to get rich. And, *gracias a Dios,* how right I was."

For a beast of such overwhelming physical presence, it was amazing how delicate a shark's actual flesh was, decaying almost immediately on contact with the air—there could be no clearer message, it seemed to me, that this fish was never meant to be hunted. Man, however, as much as he needs his monsters, also feels driven to kill them, to assert superiority. And so, with the shark, a whole secondary culture had arisen: the shark was not just a totem of loathing and fear, not solely a specter against which a man's bravery could be judged, but in equal part a way of earning a straightforward fisherman's living. No other fish, after all, could be broken down into so many commercial elements.

It was also, if one could act fast enough to save the meat from the onset of ammoniac decay, mighty fine to eat. I'd tried it only a handful of times—on the coast, once on the San Juan, once on the Solentiname Islands—and had found it rich and dense, like a toughish side of tuna. It responded best to being marinated in generous quantities of spices and oils—unripe lemons, onion, garlic, salt, chili, olive oil—and then baked or fried. Embryo sharks were tenderest; old sharks, it was generally agreed, were good for nothing but dog chow or fertilizer.

Without its fins, however, the shark would have been a gastronomic irrelevance, consumed only out of necessity. Its fins—the dorsal, the pectorals, the lower lobe of the tail—were the reason it had become such profitable prey, and around them a whole cuisine of snobbery had evolved.

Shark-fin soup, its cornerstone, began in old China, with fins imported at enormous expense from Calcutta. Initial preparation of the fins, undertaken before they even reached the kitchen, lasted an age: trimmed of excess meat, they were washed and then soaked overnight in brine. Drying took two weeks, the fins laid out on wire racks—silver wire, it was said, for best results—and carried under cover each night. The dried fins were sold with their precious gelatinous cartilage intact, and from this, soaked and steamed and finally shredded into a rich chicken stock, was the elusive essence derived—infinitesimal, hardly discernible, like the memory of something lost.

The rest of the fish, a giant rudderless slug without its fins, was hacked apart for its hide, its flesh, its liver. During World War II, many thousand sharks were torn open for their vitamin

A–rich livers, since the vitamin was held to be indispensable for night vision. From the liver came lubricants and paint bases. The hides were stripped of their thorny denticles and fashioned into shoes, eyeglass cases, bookbindings, cowboy chaps, the handles of samurai sabers, and drumheads. Shark vertebrae were chlorine-bleached, slipped over a metal rod and glued hard, and sold as walking canes. Even the beast's eyes were put to use— boiled, cut open, the hardened ovaloid lenses fashioned by canny jewelers into "shark pearls," must-have curios for the tourist looking for something just a little bit different.

Skinning, conducted at the processing plant, was the second stage in the great fish's ultimate exploitation. The speed of this process depended on the sharpness of the knife blade in use, but the routine was always the same: an incision up the spine, a double-loop round the eyes and gills, then a long oval cut for the ventral fin. If the cut was well executed, the hide came off in one piece. Washed down and soaked in seawater for four hours, the hide could easily be stripped of excess flesh with the knife; then it would be salted and stretched out to dry.

The carcasses were heaped on flatbeds or long trolleys, machine-ground into thick-grade mincemeat, then fed into a hot-air dryer. Further pulverized, the meat was bagged as fertilizer—a plant food so nutritious it had to be diluted with lower-potency manures if it was not to frazzle everything it came into contact with. The livers, finally, were hacked into fist-size hunks and rendered down in great vats; the oil was skimmed off, cooled, canned, and shipped to U.S. dealers from "factories" all over the Gulf of Mexico and Central America.

It was, for much of the century, a flawless, effortlessly profitable venture of apparently bottomless resource. Oil was sold by fast-talking salesmen as "Sun Shark Liver Oil—Nature's Own

Tonic." From Ketchikan to Monterey, from Cojímar to Lake
Nicaragua, a crucial shift in perception had taken place: in fishing towns where, for centuries, the shark had been a feared and
hated adversary, it was now providing a whole new way of life,
the possibility of buying outboard motors, of progressing
beyond the level of penniless peasant.

Small wonder, then, that as the century progressed, the
massacre of sharks accelerated. Each time a man killed a shark—
clubbing the last life out of it or lancing it with a cartridge-
tipped "bang stick"—he experienced a blood rush of pure
euphoria unequaled anywhere else in his hunting of big fish.
Contained in that final snuffing-out of life, as the eyes of the big
fish went dead in its skull, were centuries, millennia, of pent-up
powerless rage, howling their final revenge.

I walked. Sitting in the Parque Central in the broad cool of one
of those great live oaks, it had been easy to imagine the four
miles to the shark plant as little more than a pleasant hike. It
was a warm day, certainly, but if I kept to the shady side of the
street and didn't hurry, then I'd reach it within an hour or two.
Besides which, I had little choice: with Easter now only two days
away, the thoroughfares to the center were packed solid with
worshipers. Buses and taxis had long since given up regular service and stood wheel-up on the sidewalks, their drivers asleep
across the seats or leaning against the fenders, cigarettes stuck to
their lips.

In the high sunshine the colors of the buildings were rich
matte, expensively ochred, evidence of a corporate munificence
entirely absent even one block further out. It was as if it was
hoped that the force of these colors, these terra-cottas and dark

bananas and sandy pinks, might somehow leach outward toward the poorer districts and affect some kind of joyous, spontaneous rebirth. Yet, if anything, it was happening the other way round—the bank and the hotel and the private residences on the park already beginning to fade, the upsplash of mud from the last rains left to go hard as clay; around the pillars were dark flowers of dog piss. As one moved north, the sidewalks quickly disintegrated to rubble. At one corner was a harrow, its tines embedded in the crushed sidewalk, and I wondered how a piece of agricultural machinery came to be here, this far from any fields, and why no one had bothered to claim it or tow it away.

Where there was no shade, men stood flat against the buildings, shirts pulled up to cool their bellies. They remained motionless as I passed, only their eyes swiveling as they traced my passage onward. The distance between blocks seemed interminable and, not for the first time, I'd brought too little water. I pulled my collar as high up my neck as it would go and prayed for the sun to drop a little, enough to throw the thinnest wedge of shade through which I might smuggle myself.

After a while, though, past the last of the lottery vendors and *panaderías*, past the residential quarter and into industrial wasteland, the streets grew wider, with even less chance of shade. Occasionally, off the road, there'd be a lone tree, and I'd stop and sit awhile at its foot, realizing that the temperature was as paralyzing here as in direct sunshine. My watch felt hot-welded to my wrist; the metal rivets in my trousers scalded my skin.

On these arterial roads, away from the congestion of Easter pilgrims in the center, the traffic was moving on again, and the diesel fumes seemed to hug the asphalt. It smelled sweet, like burned dessert. No one else was on foot, and truck drivers slowed up as they passed, leaning on their horns.

I was heading for the baseball stadium—the Tiburones' home ground—and could see the floodlight stands from far off, high over the rooftops, beckoning me onward. I was going on Emanuel Garcia's directions, and had, as well, a map drawn for me on Solentiname by Bosco; both placed the factory in the stadium's shadow, on the main sweep heading northwest from town. As I drew closer, posters flagging the next Tiburones game began to proliferate—all illustrated with a generic grinning cartoon shark, baseball bat raised above its head.

It had been this same image—minus bat—that had marked each of the previous two stages of the journey. Obregón, the Bluefields shark-fin dealer, had hawked for custom with a similarly oafish fish; on the fisherman César's gate in El Castillo there'd been the same Tom-and-Jerry image, the shark's normally downturned mouth cajoled to a puckish if jagged grin. In all three, the shark was belittled and reduced. This puzzled me, but then it struck home: How better to sanitize a monster than to do the Walt Disney on it? As with the long-gone bear of the forests of medieval Europe, we exterminate our monsters, and only then, when we feel safe, do we allow ourselves to grow fond of them. So we killed the bear, and then in its image we made cuddly toys, with which small children could soothe themselves to sleep. From this, surely, it was but a short step to Disney bull sharks.

The stadium, set some way back from the road across a sun-bleached strip of rough grass and rocks, appeared deserted. The gates were barred and padlocked; paper pennants and napkins eddied down the concrete walkways. I could see no sign of an office.

Further up the road ragged children were playing baseball in the ditch, one of them pitching with a small rock, another waiting with a knobbly branch as bat, unprotected by helmet. Behind them stretched shanty dwellings of corrugated steel, cobbled-on planking, torn rags as windows; dogs chased one another through the dust; women walked amid the desolation, scarcely seeming to move.

I crossed the ditch and scrambled down the bank on the other side, but when I asked one of the women for directions she looked straight through me, the whites of her eyes splintered with blood lines, as if heavily sedated. She was joined by more women, and together, their arms full of firewood and small children and bundles of clothes, they stared uncomprehendingly at me till I fled back up the bank. Standing there, wondering which way to turn, I could feel the heat of the road through the soles of my shoes.

At the crest of the hill, some quarter mile further on, I came to the gates of an army base. A sentry stood in the shade, behind him a huddle of low buildings, the blue and white of the Nicaraguan flag, an armored car shimmering in the heat haze. We spoke as a truck gunned by on the road behind, and ended up shouting. Why was I on foot? he demanded. Didn't I know the shark plant had closed down many years ago? When I persisted, he lifted his rifle to his hip and pointed it up the road.

"That way," he said. "You'll find it." As I hit the road again I heard him mutter, "What do you expect to find there anyway?"

To this, a question I'd long asked myself, I could only shrug, smile, keep walking. It felt inevitable, that much I understood— the logical end to the pilgrimage, cradle to grave. I didn't expect much in the way of event, just knew that, in some way, the journey must end here. The bales of cocaine on the Atlantic shore, the coastal people who feared and hated those from the interior, the sharks that patrolled the San Juan bar, the men who hunted jaguars in those lower jungles, the shark hunters from San Carlos whose days of glory were now long gone, the fast-fading Indian history from Lake Nicaragua's islands—all ended here, on this long hike in the burning sun out to a factory no one now remembered.

And so, much slower now, feeling my legs becoming shaky under me, I walked on. After fifty yards, a dog started barking—long rolling yelps, punctuated by the snapping of jaws, that grew louder with each step I took. Not far ahead I noticed a sprawling compound, half-obscured by gone-wild shrubbery and tangled underbrush. There was a high steel fence topped with razor wire, and against this a German shepherd, the size of a small horse, was howling and slobbering, its chain leash cutting deep into its neck. It stood on its hind legs, clawing at the mesh, its fur matted with drool.

I stopped where I was, trying to gauge the best approach. Aside from the crazed dog, the compound seemed abandoned. It stretched back two or three hundred yards, with low concrete sheds in ranks. Down the middle was a broad roadway that had cracked as if in an earthquake, and from the fissures great thistles had sprung. Hammered onto most walls were scarlet PELIGRO! signs, each stamped with a cautionary skull and crossbones. Standing close to the perimeter fence at the far side of the compound were four sizable machines, like stripped juggernaut engines or diesel generators, their bulk reflected in a pool of oil that seemed to be leaking from the door to one of the sheds.

A man emerged from the nearest building, rubbing his eyes. He screamed at the dog, grabbed the chain with both hands, then, mid-heave, looked up.

"Hey!" he shouted. "You!"

I took a few steps closer, struggling to make myself heard above the yelping.

"Yes?" he screamed. "What do you want?" He drew a black-jack from his belt and clubbed the dog about the skull, jabbing it in the chest till it backed off.

"This place," I said. "It's the shark plant, is that right? Can you tell me about it?"

"How should I know? I'm only the security guard."

"Is there anyone else here?"

He shook his head. "Just me. For eighteen years, since the day it closed down, I have been alone here."

"Who closed it down?"

He took off his cop's hat, passed a finger over the glossy plastic peak. "You know the story, everyone knows the story."

"Do you remember the sharks coming in? How many at a time? What happened to them all?"

"Again, you're asking me?" he said, throwing a hand in the air. "How should I know? All I have to do is make sure no one breaks in."

I looked over his head toward the deserted compound. The roofs of some of the sheds were beginning to splinter; doors swung open or sagged on rotten hinges.

"What's left?" I said. "Is there really anything worth guarding?"

"Okay, fine." He turned toward the door of the shed he'd come from, the dog on a tight chain. "You think that, that's your choice. I have my orders."

"Wait," I called after him. "Can't you show me around?"

He stopped at the open doorway. "Of course not."

"But there's no one else here. A quick look?"

"No." He unleashed the dog, kicked it into the darkness. "I have my orders. Okay?"

"I understand," I said. "Tomorrow, then? Another day?"

"For the last time," he shouted. "No! It's over. There's nothing to see. *Entiende?*" He pressed his index finger to his temple. "Understand?"

"Okay. Fine." I looked round for the track back up to the road. "Thank you."

"Good," he said. "And don't come back, you hear?" He gave a crooked smile. "Or I'll set the hound on you."

Turning back, able from this rise to see clear across the steeples of the old town to the lake beyond, I felt unnervingly light-headed, as if my blood was fast exiting my body. I began walking, and felt a breeze on my skin where none had been before. I wondered if the weather was changing, but what trees there were up here remained lifeless. In the ditches, the trash lay motionless. I walked slowly, uneasily.

My mind was empty. This was not the ending I'd had in mind on starting the journey, on first meeting Arturo, on my first glimpse and taste of the wild shore, but this was what had happened. I wasn't sure how much hope I could dredge from this final image of dereliction, but guessed that Arturo, at least, would have wanted me to follow the trail all the way to its conclusion.

I took his piece of paper from my pocket, unfolded it, read it through one more time. When I walked on I held it tight in my hand, unsure now what to do with it. Through that handful of words came the truest distillation of everything he'd ever done

and seen, everything he most lamented and despised, the sorry
way he'd seen things go.

Five minutes later I was passing the army base again when I
heard a car behind me. I stepped off the asphalt to let it pass, but
could sense it slowing too. I heard its tires bite gravel at the
road's edge. I turned. A silver Mercedes limousine had pulled to
a stop. Leaning from the driver's window was Emanuel Garcia.
He patted the coachwork, beckoned me over.

"You're walking," he said. "I can't believe it." Through the
open window I could feel the cool of the air-conditioning, smell
the leather. "Everywhere you go you walk."

"Yes," I nodded "I—"

"So you've been to see my shark factory," he went on, checking his watch. "Quite some place it used to be."

I rested a hand on the roof, suddenly faint. I could sense him
waiting for me to agree, but I was too weary from the heat, and
too tired of him, to fake enthusiasm. Right at that moment all I
could think was how badly I needed a lift back into town. I
opened my mouth to suggest it, but he wouldn't be interrupted.

"Yes." He revved the engine. "Good day for it, young man
like you. You're lucky to be here, fortunate to have seen a bit of
history." He pulled back the gearshift, buzzed his window up
till only an inch remained open.

"I . . ." I said. "I was—"

"What's that in your hand?" he broke in, shifting comfortably in his seat, preparing for the off.

"Nothing." I closed my hand. "Nothing."